Denis Florence MacCarthy

The Book of Irish Ballads

Denis Florence MacCarthy

The Book of Irish Ballads

ISBN/EAN: 9783744734783

Printed in Europe, USA, Canada, Australia, Japan

Cover: Foto ©Thomas Meinert / pixelio.de

More available books at **www.hansebooks.com**

THE BOOK

OF

IRISH BALLADS.

EDITED BY

DENIS FLORENCE MAC-CARTHY, M.R.I.A
AUTHOR OF DRAMAS AND AUTOS
FROM THE SPANISH OF CALDERON, ETC.

A NEW EDITION,
REVISED AND CORRECTED,
WITH ADDITIONAL POEMS AND A PREFACE.

Dublin:
JAMES DUFFY AND CO., LIMITED,
15 WELLINGTON QUAY.

TO

SAMUEL FERGUSON, ESQ., LL.D., Q.C., M.R.I.A.,

DEPUTY-KEEPER OF THE PUBLIC RECORDS
OF IRELAND,

TO WHOM "THE BOOK OF IRISH BALLADS" WAS
ORIGINALLY DEDICATED,

THIS LITTLE VOLUME,

IN A NEW AND REVISED EDITION, IS AGAIN

Inscribed,

WITH EVERY FEELING OF AFFECTION AND
ESTEEM,

BY HIS FRIEND

THE EDITOR.

CONTENTS.

	Page
DEDICATION,	3
INDEX OF AUTHORS,	8
ADVERTISEMENT,	10
PREFACE,	11
INTRODUCTION,	15

Names of Ballads.	Authors' Names.	
Thomas Davis, His Life: His Death: His Work:	Samuel Ferguson, LL.D.,	27
The Old Story,	O—— —.	29
The Fairy Well of Lagnanay,	Samuel Ferguson, LL.D.,	32
The Bay of Dublin,	D. F. Mac-Carthy,	35
Hy-Brasail,	Gerald Griffin,	37
The Mountain Sprite,	Thomas Moore,	38
The City of Gold,	Anonymous,	39
Thubber-na-Shie; or, the Fairy Well,	James Teeling,	40
Fairy Revels,	Anonymous,	43
The Enchanted Island,	Anonymous,	44
The Fairies' Passage,	Clarence Mangan,	45
The Phantom City,	Gerald Griffin,	48
Kate of Kenmare,	D. F. Mac-Carthy	49
Arranmore,	Thomas Moore,	51
The Island of Atlantis,	Rev. G. Croly,	52
The Haunted Spring,	Samuel Lover,	53
Alice and Una,	D. F. Mac-Carthy	55
The Fetch,	John Banim,	69
Cusheen Loo,	J. J. Callanan,	70
The Burial,	Rev. J. Wills,	71
The O'Neill,	Anonymous,	72
The Wake of the Absent,	Gerald Griffin,	76
Kathleen's Fetch,	Anonymous,	77
The Doom of the Mirror,	B. Simmons,	78
The Fairy Nurse,	Edward Walsh,	82
Earl Desmond and the Banshee,	Anonymous,	83
The Bridal Wake,	Gerald Griffin,	86
The Caoine.	Crofton Croker	97

Names of Ballads.	A.D.	Authors' Names.	Page
The Saga of King Olaf and his Dog,	1000	Thomas D'Arcy M'Gee,	88
Lamentation of Mac Liag for Kincora,	1015	Clarence Mangan,	93
The Death of King Magnus Barefoot,	1102	Thomas D'Arcy M'Gee,	95
The Battle of Knocktuagh,	1189	Anonymous (G.),	98
A Vision of Connaught in the 13th Century,	1224	Clarence Mangan,	104
The Battle of Credran,	1257	Edward Walsh,	106
The Battle of Ardnocher,	1328	Anonymous, (G.),	109
The Battle of Tyrrell's-Pass,	1597	Anonymous, (G.),	111
The Death of Schomberg,	1690	Digby Pilot Starkey, LL.D.,	118
The Battle of the Boyne,	1690	Colonel Blacker,	121
The River Boyne,		Thomas D'Arcy M'Gee,	124
The Pillar Towers of Ireland,		D. F. Mac-Carthy,	126
Timoleague,		Samuel Ferguson, LL.D.,	128
Avondhu,		J. J. Callanan,	131
The Rock of Cashel,		Rev. Dr. Murray,	132
Loch Ina,		Anonymous.	135
The Returned Exile,		B. Simmons,	136
Glenfinishk,		Joseph O'Leary,	138
The Mountain Fern,		Anonymous (G.),	139
To the Memory of Father Prout,		D. F. Mac-Carthy,	141
Those Shandon Bells,		D. F. Mac-Carthy,	143
Adare,		Gerald Griffin,	144
Deirdra's Farewell to Alba,		Samuel Ferguson,	145
A Sigh for Knockmany,		William Carleton,	146
Tipperary		Anonymous,	147
The Welshmen of Tirawley,		Samuel Ferguson, LL.D.,	148
The Outlaw of Loch Lene,		J. J. Callanan,	159
Aileen the Huntress,		Edward Walsh,	160
Shane Dymas' Daughter,		Anonymous,	163
O'Sullivan Beare.		Thomas D'Arcy M'Gee,	166
The Robber of Ferney,		Anonymous,	169
Waiting for the May,		D. F. Mac-Carthy,	171
The Virgin Mary's Bank,		J. J. Callanan,	172
Owen Bawn,		Samuel Ferguson, LL.D.,	174
Ailleen,		J. Banim,	176
Eman-ac-Knuck to Eva,		J. B. Clarke,	177
O'Donnell and the Fair Fitzgerald,		Hon. Gavan Duffy,	179
The Coolun,		Samuel Ferguson, LL.D.,	181
Brighidin Ban Mo Store,		Edward Walsh,	183
The Lamentation of Felix M'Carthy,		J. J. Callanan,	184

CONTENTS.

Names of Ballads.	Authors' Names.	Page.
Pastheen Fion,	Samuel Ferguson, LL.D.,	187
The Patriot's Bride,	Hon. Gavan Duffy,	189
The Coulin Forbidden,	Carroll Malone,	191
The Irish Emigrant's Mother,	D. F. Mac-Carthy,	193
The Muster of the North,	Hon. Gavan Duffy,	197
Dark Rosaleen,	Clarence Mangan,	201
Drimin Dhu,	Samuel Ferguson, LL.D.,	204
Shane Bwee,	Clarence Mangan,	205
The Voice of Labour,	Hon. Gavan Duffy,	207
The Wexford Insurgent,	Anonymous,	209
The Dream of John M'Donnell,	Clarence Mangan,	211
The Orangeman's Wife,	Carroll Malone,	213
The Irish Chiefs,	Hon. Gavan Duffy,	215
Darrynane,	D. F. Mac-Carthy,	217
Lament for the Sons of Usnach,	Samuel Ferguson, LL.D.,	220
The Penal Days,	O ——	222
Carolan and Bridget Cruise,	Samuel Lover,	227
The Streams,	Mrs. Downing,	228
Irish Mary,	J. Banim,	230
The Last Friends,	Frances Browne,	231
The Irish Exiles,	Martin MacDermott,	232
A Shamrock from the Irish Shore,	D. F. Mac-Carthy,	236
Spring Flowers from Ireland,	D. F. Mac-Carthy,	239
Wings for Home,	D. F. Mac-Carthy,	242
Italian Myrtles,	D. F. Mac-Carthy,	243
Not Known,	D. F. Mac-Carthy,	244
The Paschal Fire of St. Patrick,	D. F. Mac-Carthy,	247
Over the Sea,	D. F. Mac-Carthy,	248
The Convict and the Cross,	Anonymous (M.),	250
The Celtic Tongue,	Rev. Michael Mullin,	252

INDEX OF AUTHORS

A

ANONYMOUS:

	Page
The Old Story (O.),	29
The City of Gold,	39
Fairy Revels,	43
The Enchanted Island,	44
The O'Neill,	72
Kathleen's Fetch,	77
Earl Desmond and the Banshee,	83
Battle of Knocktuagh (G.),	98
Battle of Ardnocher (G.),	109
The Battle of Tyrrell's-Pass (G.),	111
Loch Ina,	135
The Mountain Fern (G.),	139
Tipperary,	147
Shane Dymas' Daughter,	163
The Robber of Ferney,	169
The Wexford Insurgent,	209
The Penal Days (O.),	222
The Convict and the Cross (M.),	250

B

ANIM, JOHN:

The Fetch,	69
Ailleen,	176
Irish Mary,	230

BLACKER, COLONEL:
The Battle of the Boyne, 121

BROWNE, FRANCES:
The Last Friends, — 231

C

CALLANAN, J. J.

Cusheen Loo,	70
Avondhu,	191

CALLANAN, J. J. (continued).

	Page
The Outlaw of Loch Lene,	159
The Virgin Mary's Bank,	172
The Lamentation of Felix M'Carthy,	184

CARLETON, WILLIAM:
A Sigh for Knockmany, 146

CLARKE, J. B.:
Eman-ac-Knnck to Eva, 177

CROKER, CROFTON:
The Keen, — 87

CROLY, REV. GEORGE:
The Island of Atlantis, — 53

D

DOWNING, MRS.:
The Streams, — 208

DUFFY, THE HON. GAVAN:

O'Donnell and the Fair Fitzgerald,	179
The Patriot's Bride,	189
The Muster of the North,	197
The Voice of Labour,	205
The Irish Chiefs,	216

F

FERGUSON, SAMUEL, LL.D.:

The Fairy Well of Lagnanay,	32
Thomas Davis, His Life: His Death: His Work:	27
Timoleague,	125

INDEX OF AUTHORS.

FERGUSON, SAMUEL, LL.D. *Page*
(continued).
 Deirdra's Farewell to Alba, — 145
 The Welshmen of Tirawley, — 149
 Owen Bawn, — 174
 The Coolun, — 181
 Pastheen Fion, — 187
 Drimin Dhu, — 204
 Deirdra's Lament for the Sons of Usnach, — 220

G

GRIFFIN, GERALD:
 Hy-Brasail, — 37
 The Phantom City, — 48
 The Wake of the Absent, — 76
 The Bridal Wake, — 86
 Adare, — 144

L

LOVER, SAMUEL:
 The Haunted Spring, — 53
 Carolan and Bridget Cruise, — 227

M

MACCARTHY, D. FLORENCE, M.R.I.A.
 The Bay of Dublin, — 35
 Kate of Kenmare, — 49
 Alice and Una, — 55
 The Pillar Towers of Ireland, — 126
 To the Memory of Father Prout, — 141
 Those Shandon Bells, — 143
 Waiting for the May, — 171
 The Irish Emigrant's Mother, — 193
 Darrynane, — 217
 A Shamrock from the Irish Shore, — 236
 Spring Flowers from Ireland, — 239
 Wings for Home, — 242
 Italian Myrtles, — 243
 "Not Known," — 244
 The Paschal Fire of St. Patrick. — 247
 Over the Sea. — 248

M *Page*

MACDERMOTT, MARTIN:
 The Irish Exiles, — 222
M'GEE, THOMAS D'ARCY:
 The Saga of King Olaf and his Dog, — 88
 The Death of King Magnus Barefoot, — 95
 The River Boyne, — 124
 O'Sullivan Beare, — 166
MALONE, CARROLL (M'BURNEY):
 The Coulin, Forbidden, — 191
 The Orangeman's Wife, — 213
MANGAN, CLARENCE:
 The Fairie's Passage, — 45
 Lamentation of Mac Liag for Kincora, — 93
 A Vision of Connaught in the 13th Century, — 104
 Dark Rosaleen, — 201
 Shane Bwee, — 205
 The Dream of John Mac Donnell, — 211
MOORE, THOMAS:
 The Mountain Sprite, — 33
 Arranmore, — 51
MULLIN, REV. M.:
 The Celtic Tongue, — 253
MURRAY, REV. DR.:
 The Rock of Cashel, — 132

O

O'LEARY, JOSEPH:
 Glenfinishk, — 138

S

SIMMONS, B.
 The Doom of the Mirror, 78
 The Returned Exile, — 136
STARKEY, DIGBY PILOT:
 The Death of Schomberg, 118

T

TEELING, JAMES:
 Thubber-no-Shie, or the Fairy Well, — 40

W

WALSH, EDWARD:
 The Fairy Nurse, — 82
 Battle of Credran, — 106
 Aileen the Huntress, — 160
 Brighdin Ban-mo-Store 183
WILLS, REV. J.
 The Burial, — 7

ADVERTISEMENT

TO THE FIRST EDITION, 1846.

"THE BOOK OF IRISH BALLADS," is intended as a sequel to "THE BALLAD POETRY OF IRELAND." I trust it will be found not unworthy of taking its place beside that volume. It has been my most anxious wish that this collection of native ballads should be altogether divested of a sectarian or party complexion, and that every class of which THE IRISH NATION is composed should be poetically represented therein. Should there be in those ballads which admit of the introduction of religious or political sentiment, a preponderance of one kind over another, the inequality is to be attributed to the abundance or scantiness of my materials, and not to any prejudice or bias of my own.

PREFACE.

[1869.]

"THE BOOK OF IRISH BALLADS" was first published in 1846 as a companion volume to "THE BALLAD POETRY OF IRELAND," then recently edited with so much taste and ability by Mr., now the Hon. Gavan Duffy. The near relationship of the two books naturally secured for the latter a portion of the unprecedented success which had been at once attained by the former. Like its elder brother, it was received with eager welcome in many successive editions at home, and with it eventually emigrated to the United States, where the original stereotype plates, though now much worn and defaced, are still in their way doing good service. The book, however, had some grave defects, which I have been long anxious to remove, and it was therefore with much pleasure that I acquiesced in the wish conveyed to me by the excellent and patriotic publisher, that I should revise and recast, if I thought proper, this the second collection of ballads in English, by native Irish writers, that had ever been attempted. Not to speak of minor inaccuracies, principally typographical, which might have been silently emended, "THE BOOK OF IRISH BALLADS" (as, for shortness sake, they must be called) laboured under the disadvantage of containing several poems which, however excellent as rythmical tales or emotional lyrics, were either absolutely un-Irish in expression, or, when the sentiment and language were local, the form and treatment were opposed to that rapidity of movement and of metre, without which no poem can be said to be a ballad. As an example of the first class, I may mention the poem with which the volume originally opened. It was the "Fairy Tale" of Parnell. This poem, which should, as it were, have struck the key-note of the whole book, was written, as the author himself says, ' in the ancient English style."—a style that has never had a local habitation in this country. Others that had not this obvious defect of language could not, in any sense of the word, be considered ballads. Of these, perhaps "The Saint's Tenant," by Thomas Furlong, was the most striking example. It is a painful story, and all the more painful that it is true. It is told, too, with a bitterness that may well be excused in one who had the misfortune of living at a time when such a system of intolerance and injustice was fostered and enforced by the so-called government of the country; but it is as little of a ballad as one of the tales of Crabbe. How the same subject could be thrown into a ballad form and vivified by a ballad spirit, was evidenced in the volume itself by the poem of "The Penal Days," written by the author of the exquisite Idyll, "The Old Story," which, for the first time correctly printed, I have the pleasure of introducing into the present edition. Why, or on what principle I acted in introducing these and a few other poems, to which a similar objection would apply, I cannot at this moment determine. It was not for want of materials, for most of the ballads by which they are now replaced were then written. Scanty as the supply was some twenty-five years ago, compared with the abundant harvests of Irish song that now await to be gathered into granaries and so preserved, neither Mr. Duffy nor I had any serious difficulty in making our collections. Our principal merit lay in beginning the work at all. In this way I have often found a pleasure in fancying that in our more limited sphere we acted something like Juan de Timoneda and others, who in Valencia, or Seville, during the sixteenth century, commenced those precious little *Romanceros* and *Cancioneros*, out of which eventually the *Romancero General* or great Ballad-book of Spain was compiled. The materials for such a complete collection in Ireland are every day accumulating, and I have no doubt, that when the fit time arrives, an Irish Duran will be found as competent and enthusiastic as the Spaniard, in arranging and elucidating the rich stories of Irish Ballad Poetry which will then be at his disposal.* To return to my own

* For the present "The Ballads of Ireland," so admirably edited by Edward Hayes, (James Duffy, Dublin and London) must be considered our "Romancero General." But Irish song has already overflown even the ample limits of that publication, and is ever seeking a still wider and a deeper channel.

little volume, having the opportunity of removing the defects I have alluded to, I thought I would be failing in my chief duty as an editor if I failed to do so. I have, therefore, rejected every poem that could not fairly be considered from its form or sentiment an Irish Ballad. Having thus referred to the class of poems which I have removed from the present edition, it remains for me only to allude to a few of those that take their place. I have already mentioned "The Old Story"—a sweet and tender Idyll, the very purity of which alone would make it Irish. Parnell's "Fairy Tale" gives way, though not exactly in the same position, to "The Fairies' Passage" of Mangan, which will be new to most of my readers, and which, though founded on a German original, is so characteristic of the writer, as well as "the good people" it describes in such a lively way, that I have no hesitation in claiming it as an Irish ballad, and have had no scruple in altering a few letters to adapt it to this country. As I have said, the first poem in such a collection as this should strike, as it were, the keynote of the volume. This note is now struck, and struck effectively, by the elegy on THOMAS DAVIS, which is not only a most pathetic lamentation on his death, but a powerful figurative picture of his life and of his work. In the title which I have given it (for in the long prose article where hitherto it has been lost, it has none), I have drawn attention to the three aspects of his career which the poem presents with such felicity and power. As to its literary merits, it seems to me as if the very spirit of the ancient Gaelic Bards breathes in this fine composition. As a specimen of Anglo-Irish versification, it is, I think, the most successful and vigorous effort of its author, for, though published anonymously, there can be no possible doubt as to who he is. The style is as marked and unmistakeable as a ballad by Browning. *The Battle of Tyrrell's-Pass*, by the author of "The Monks of Kilcrea," supplies the place of *Grana Uaile and Elizabeth*, a picturesque and pleasing poem, but written in the Spenserian stanza, a measure which Scott himself could not bend to the requirements of the ballad. I have retained the historical ballads from Scandinavian Sagas, by the gifted and ill-fated M'Gee, though ballads by him more directly Irish in language and subject could be found, principally because those I allude to are not in the selections from his poems given by

Mr. Hayes in "The Ballads of Ireland." I have, however added his melodious and thoughtful poem of *The River Boyne* as a sort of moral to the Orange Ballad on *The Battle of the Boyne*, by Colonel Blacker, which I have retained. With regard to my own pieces, I have withdrawn two of my most popular and best-known lyrics to make room for poems more in accordance with the strict rules I have prescribed to myself in preparing this new edition. Two or three smaller pieces are omitted, as possessing no particular Irish interest; their place being supplied by poems which, from their subjects, are sure of meeting with a wider and more general sympathy; and which are for the first time included in any of our ballad books. The original Introduction I have left pretty much as it was. Had I to write it now, "the years that bring the philosophic mind," would doubtless have moderated somewhat of its enthusiasm; but, as the book will principally be in the hands of the young, I think it better still to appeal to those feelings which they possess, and which I myself would be sorry to have outgrown. With these changes, and with these observations, I take my final leave of "The Book of Irish Ballads."

D. F. MAC-CARTHY.

74, *Upper Gardiner-st., Dublin,*
1st *June,* 1869.

INTRODUCTION.

It has been said, by a well-known authority, that the ballads of a people are more influential than their laws, and perhaps he might have added, more valuable than their annals. The most comprehensive survey that the eye of genius can take in—the most ponderous folio that ever owed its existence to the united efforts of industry and dulness, must fail in giving a perfect idea of the character of a people, unless it be based upon the revelations they themselves have made, or the confessions they have uttered. Without these, history is indeed but the "old almanack" that an illustrious countryman of ours* has called it; a mere dry dead catalogue of dates and facts, useless either as a picture of the past, or as a lesson for the future. A people of passionate impulses, of throbbing affections, of dauntless heroism, will invariably not only have done things worthy of being recorded, but will also have recorded them. Myriads of human beings cannot be moved about noiselessly, like an army of shadows. The sullen sound of their advancing will be heard afar off; and those wh see them not, will listen to the shrill music of their fifes and the merry echoes of their bugles. The great heavings of a people's heart, and, from time to time, the necessary purifying of the social atmosphere, will make themselves felt and heard and seen, so that all men may take cognizance thereof—as the waves of the ocean dash against each other with a war-cry, or as the electric spirit proclaimeth its salutary mission in a voice of thunder.

In almost all countries the BALLAD has been the instrument by which the triumphs, the joys, or the sorrows of a people have been proclaimed.

Its uses have been numerous; its capabilities are boundless.

* Lord Plunkett

Long ago, in the fresh youth and enthusiasm of the world, how harmonious were its modulations—its revelations how divine! Then it sang of gods and heroes, and the milk-expanded warm breasts of the beneficent mother; and the gift of Ceres, and the olive of Minerva, and the purple clusters of the son of Semele. Then it was, that "standing on a pleasant lea," men could

> "Have glimpses that would make them less forlorn,
> Have sight of Proteus rising from the sea,
> Or hear old Triton blow his wreathed horn."*

Then it was that the earth was truly peopled. Neither was the air void, nor were the waters desolate. Shapes of beauty—

> "Schöné Wesen aus dem Fabelland"†—

wandered familiarly with men; and nymphs and shepherds, and fauns and hamadryads, danced together beneath the eye of Jove himself in the shadow of blue Olympus, or beside the Venus-bearing foam of the sparkling isle-surrounding Hellespont. Had not poetry preserved this memory of the golden age—had not Hesiod and Homer built their beautiful and majestic structures on the original ballads that were probably floating among the people,—how dark, and gloomy, and indistinct would be our ideas of the old world: What visions that have been delighting the eye of man these three thousand years would have been lost: Of what examples of devotion, of heroism, of love of country, would the sincere and zealous of all nations have been deprived.

Poetry, after all, is the only indestructible gift that genius can bequeath to the world. The shield of Achilles, though the work of a god, has disappeared from the world, but the bounding words in which it has been described are immortal. This very shield itself, as Schiller remarks, is the type of the poet's mind, and of all true poetry.‡ On

---

* Wordsworth.
† "Lovely beings from the Fable land."—SCHILLER.
‡ "As the god and the genius, whose birth was of Jove,
   In one type all creation reveal'd,
When the ocean, the earth, and the star realm above,
   Lay compress'd in the orb of a shield,—
So the poet, a shape and a type of the All,
   From a sound, that is mute in a moment, can call!"
[From "The Four Ages of the World."—Bulwer's Translation.]

it, we are told, were figured, not only representations of cities, implements of husbandry, corn-fields and vineyards, sheep and oxen, and other things adapted to particular localities, and which may vary under different circumstances, — but the great fabricator had also introduced representations of the unchangeable wonders of creation, which are the same yesterday, to-day, and to-morrow, —

"For in it he represented earth—in it the sea and sky—
In it the never-wearied sun—the moon, exactly round;
And all those stars with which the brows of ample heaven are crown'd!" *

Thus a genuine poem must be true not only to the character of the age in which it is written, but in accordance with the principles of nature and of truth, which are unchangeable.

The Latins, a people very different from the Greeks, added but little to the beauty of the mythology they borrowed, or to the literature they imitated. With the exception of Egeria,—"a beautiful thought, and softly bodied forth,"—there are none of their native divinities that interest us much. Their early history, so full of stern, unbending justice, self-denial, and heroism, is considered either allegorical or wholly fabulous, and founded upon the memory of rude ballads, which had ceased to exist even at the time when their earliest annals were written.† In their latter years, the lyrics of Horace redeemed the character of their literature from the reproach of servile imitation; and some of these, and a few of the shorter tales of Ovid, are the only poems they have left us partaking, however remotely, of the character of Ballad Poetry, but much closer to the modern than to the ancient Homeric standard. After this there is no trace of the ballad spirit in Latin literature. Its writers became more servile and less vigorous in their imitation, until, in the reign of Theodosius, the race of old Roman poets became extinct in the person of Claudian.

While this lamentable but natural decline of intellectual vigour, consequent upon the effeminacy and excesses of Imperial Rome, was developing itself along the sunny shores of the Mediterranean, a new order of things was

* Iliad, Book xviii., Chapman's Translation.
† It is almost superfluous to remind the reader that Macaulay's "Lays and Legends of Ancient Rome" are founded on this supposition.

maturing amid the mountains and forests of northern and western Europe. The human mind—which, in these remote regions, like their wintry seas, had been perpetually frozen—now began to melt and dissolve into brilliancy and activity. Those who lived upon the stormy shores of the ocean followed the Sea Kings in their adventurous expeditions among the islands. Those who lived amid the dark forests of the interior, marched in search of brighter skies and more fruitful plains, towards the genial regions of the south. And it was in these expeditions, particularly the former, that the Bards of the Sea Kings gave the ballad its modern shape and character. The sagas composed by them, to commemorate the triumphs or to bewail the disasters of their chiefs in "Icy Ierne"—the Scottish islands and Iceland—strongly resemble, both in structure and design, the more vigorous of the modern ballads. A new race of divinities and a new race of heroes superseded the old classical models. Thor and Wodin succeeded Mars and the son of Priam, and like the songs in which they were commemorated, what they lost in interest and beauty was compensated for by vigor and durability. The black and chilly waters of the northern seas were not a fitting birthplace for the Aphrodisian Venus; instead of the queen of love and gladness, the mighty kraken and the winged dragon were their children, who in many a stormy ballad have played their fearful and important parts ever since.

Again, in the sunny South, but not in exhausted Italy did the harmony of song arise. Spain, that magnificent country, combining together the grandeur and the beauty of the North and South—the bold mountains and caverned shores of Norway, and the enchanting graces of Parthenope—had already, even in the most palmy days of Latin literature, contributed some of the most boasted names to the catalogue of Roman writers. Lucan, who sang of Pharsalia; the two Senecas, the younger of whom is the only Roman tragic writer who has come down to us; and Martial, whose wit and licentiousness at once enlivened and disgraced the reign of Domitian, were natives of Spain; the three former of Corduba, and the latter of Aragon. But it was in the eighth century that the splendour and interest of Spanish history commence. In that century the Saracens conquered Spain, and introduced into it, along with a knowledge of letters and the sciences superior to what was possessed by any other people then in Europe, all the splendour and imagination of Oriental poetry. About the end of the twelfth century the celebrated poem of "The Cid" was written, commemorating the valorous exploits and adventures of the hero, Rodrigo de Bivar. Since that period Spain has been pre-eminently rich in ballad poetry. Its grand, sonorous language, so musical as to have earned the epithet of "the poetry of speech," has been employed to good purpose; and nobler ballads than the Spanish, in praise of heroism, of virtue, of piety, and of love, the world has never seen. The capabilities of the ballad have there been put to the severest test. Those of the heroic class, which detail the struggles of the old Spaniards with the Goth or with the Saracen, like Chevy Chase, "stir the heart as if with a trumpet;" while the sighing of a summer breeze in Andalusia is not more soft and gentle than the harmony of the passionate ballads that to this day are sung beneath the curtained balconies of moonlit Sevilla. Gracilasso, Lopé, Calderon, Cervantes—great names are these, of which Spain and human nature may be proud.

The Ballad Poetry of England and Scotland has been very copious and very excellent for several centuries; and the ballads of each contrast not so much in merit as in character. In the song, which may be called the very essence and spirit of the ballad, or the musical utterance of feeling and passion in the very proxysm of their presence, Scotland has immeasurably the superiority. In that Pythian moment, when the mind is in its state of utmost activity, and the dominancy of passion is supreme, the concentrated expression of both is song; and its appearance and the frequency of its return depend principally upon the character and constitution of each people. The ballad, on the contrary, requires not the same degree of excitement—narrative, which is almost an essential portion of it, being incompatible with that mental and sensuous excitation which gives birth to the song, and which is but momentary in its abiding. And thus the different success of the two, in the different nations of Europe, is as marked and distinct as the races of which they are composed. In Italy and France, in Scotland and Ireland—all nations sprung from the one family—the song has been cultivated with the greatest success: whereas in the northern nations, in Germany and in England, the natural expression of the poetical instincts of the people has been through the calmer and more lengthened channel of the ballad. Spain has succeeded better in both, perhaps, than any other nation—the dominion of the Goths leaving after it much of the solemnity of thought and feeling of the Germanic races, while the lyric capabilities of the language are such as to render the expression of high-wrought sentiment easy and obvious. In England the ballads are generally of a quiet and pastoral beauty—quite in character with the rural and sylvan charms of its scenery. The Robin Hood ballads, which so delight us in boyhood, and which give us visions of "Merry Sherwood"—

> In summer time, when leaves grow green,
> And birds sing on every tree,

that we never forget, and which are only replaced by the still more exquisite glimpses that Shakspeare opens to us of The Forest of Ardennes—all partake of this character. In them there is many a merry trick played, and many a mad adventure—

> "Of brave little John,
> Of Friar Tuck and Will Scarlet,
> Loxley, and Maid Marion."

Bold Robin and Allin-a-Dale, or the "Jolly Tanner" Arthur-a-Bland, have many a good contest with stout quarter-staffs—right merry to read and well described; but the writers scarcely ever forget, even for a few stanzas, the beauty of the summer woods where their heroes dwell, and satisfy their own hearts, and will delight their readers for all time, by this frequent recurrence to the unchangeable and everlasting delights of nature. Indeed, this continued reference to the beauty of the external world, which we meet in the old English poets, particularly in Chaucer (whose pictures of many a "May Morn-ing" are still so fresh after many years), may be the reason that they are read even now, notwithstanding the difficulties of an antiquated and obsolete dialect.

The Scotch ballads are less numerous and less varied than the English; but in point of perfection—in the particular class, at least, of sentiment and the affections—they

are not only superior to these, but, as I humbly conceive, to
any ballads that have ever been written. Their simplicity
never degenerates into bald commonplace, nor their homeli-
ness into vulgarity; and they are as far removed from
maudlin sentimentality in their passionate heartiness, as
from frigid conceits and pettiness in their illustrations.
The very hearts of the Scottish people bound in their
ballads; we can listen to the ever-varying changes of its
pulsation; now heavy and slow as the tides of Loch Lomond,
now rapid and bounding as the billows of the Clyde. The
"bonny blue e'en" of the lassie glance through her
waving hair like a stream through the overhanging heather;
and her arch reply or her merry laugh rings on our ears like
the song of the mavis or the throstle. The ballads of a few of
her humblest children have rendered Scotland dear to the
hearts of all whose affections are worth possessing; they
have converted (to the mind at least) her desolate heaths and
barren mountains, into smiling gardens and olive-bearing
hills; and have constructed amongst mists and storms, and
the howling of the lashed Northern Ocean, an Arcadia
dearer than that of yore, where "the shepherd's boy piped
as though he should never be old."* Although my space
here is very limited, I cannot refrain from presenting to
some of my readers, perhaps for the first time, a specimen of
these ballads, taken almost at random, in support of what
I have asserted, and as a model (in connection with those
written in a kindred spirit by some of our own countrymen
—Griffin, Callanan, Davis, and Mr. Ferguson) of this most
exquisite department of Ballad Poetry:—

MARY OF CASTLE-CARY.†

Saw ye my wee thing, saw ye my ain thing,
  Saw ye my true-love down on yon lea—
Crossed she the meadow yestreen at the gloaming,
  Sought she the burnie where flowers the haw-tree?
Her hair it is lint-white, her skin it is milk-white,
  Dark is the blue of her soft rolling e'e;
Red, red are her ripe lips, and sweeter than roses,
  Where could my wee thing wander frae me?

I saw nae your wee thing, I saw nae your ain thing,
  Nor saw I your true-love down by yon lea;

---

* Sir Philip Sidney.
† Written by Hector MacNeill; born 1746, died 1818.

But I met my bonnie thing late in the gloaming,
   Down by the burnie where flowers the haw-tree;
Her hair it was lint-white, her skin it was milk-white,
   Dark was the blue of her soft rolling e'e;
Red, red were her ripe lips, and sweeter than roses,
   Sweet were the kisses that she gave to me.

It was nae my wee thing, it was nae my ain thing,
   It was nae my true-love ye met by the tree;
Proud is her leal heart, and modest her nature,
   She never loved ony till ance she loved me,
Her name it was Mary—she's frae Castle-Cary,
   Aft has she sat when a bairn on my knee;
Fair as your face is, were't fifty times fairer,
   Young bragger, she ne'er wad gie kisses to thee.

It was then your Mary; she's frae Castle-Cary,
   It was then your true-love I met by the tree;
Proud as her heart is, and modest her nature,
   Sweet were the kisses that she gave to me.
Sair gloomed his dark brow, blood-red his cheek grew,
   Wild flashed the fire frae his red rolling e'e;
Ye'se rue sair this morning your boasts and your scorning,
   Defend ye, fause traitor, fu' loudly ye lee.

Away wi' beguiling, cried the youth, smiling—
   Off went the bonnet, the lint-white locks flee,
The belted plaid fa'ing, her white bosom shawing,
   Fair stood the loved maid wi' the dark rolling e'e
Is it my wee thing, is it my ain thing,
   Is it my true-love here that I see?
O Jamie, forgi'e me, your heart's constant to me,
   I'll never mair wander, dear laddie, frae thee.*

    The most modern, and perhaps the most important class of ballads, remains to be alluded to—namely, the German. The sudden awakening, the rapid maturity, the enduring vitality, and the acknowledged supremacy of German literature, are facts as wonderful as they are consoling. Little better than a century ago, with the exception of a few theological and historical writers, the Germans were more destitute of a native literature, and were more dependant on other countries, particularly France, for intellectual supplies, than we have ever been; and now their works crowd the book markets of the world. Little more than a

---

[* Ballads turning on a similar deception are to be found in the Romaic Spanish, Portuguese, Breton, German, and Italian language. The Spanish Ballad, *Caballero de lejas tierras*, may be referred to. See Duran's *Romancero General*, 1, p. 175   Ed.]

century ago a German prince, Frederick the Great, a philosopher and a patron of philosophers, pronounced his native language but fit for horses,—little dreaming of the angels and angelic women—of the Katherines, the Tecklas, and the Undinês—from whose inspired lips that rough, nervous language would flow so harmoniously that all men would listen to the melody thereof. In no intellectual field have the Germans of the past and present centuries been defeated. Their drama is superior to any other that has appeared in Europe during the same period—for I presume there can be no comparison between the Shaksperian power of Schiller and the soft graces of Metastasio, or even the more maculine classicalities of Alfieri. Their histories are the mines in which even the most industrious writers search for the precious ore of truth. Their philosophy has been either a beacon or an *ignis fatuus* to the inquiring intellects of Europe; while some of their artists have come off victorious even in the Eternal Metropolis of art itself. In every department of literature, German intellect has been renewing the almost exhausted fountains of the world. Like the Egyptian river, the great German Rhine has been overflowing the earth, and fruits, and flowers, and waving corn are springing luxuriantly in all lands. In the ballad the Germans have pre-eminently succeeded. It is with them somewhat of a short epic, in which the romance and chivalry of the middle ages find a suitable vehicle for their illustration. They seldom treat of humble life and simple passion, like the Scotch; or individual heroism, like the Spanish. They are more historical and legendary than directly sentimental or heroic; but through all runs a vein of philosophical abstraction and thoughtful melancholy, which imparts to them a peculiar and enduring charm. There is scarcely an historical event of any importance—a legend possessing the slightest interest—a superstition not destitute of grace, sublimity, or terror—a river or a mountain that has anything to recommend it, that has not found an illustrator, an admirer, and a laureate among the German Balladists. And the consequence is, that not only is the German intellect honoured and respected, but the German land is also strengthened and enriched. The separate though confederated nations of Germany have been bound together as one people, by the universal language of their poetry;* and year after year pilgrims and students from strange lands wander thither, not attracted so much by the gloom of her woody mountains and the magic windings of her Rhine, as because (thanks to poetry) through the former the wild Jager still hunts and the witches dance on Walpurgist nights, and because the latter has been made the crystal barrier of a free people, and the emblem, in its depth, its strength, and its beauty, of the German character and intellect.

It only remains for me to advert to what has been done, and what I conceive may be done, in Ireland with the ballad. If we recollect the constant state of warfare—the revolution upon revolution—the political struggles, and the generally unsettled condition of the people ever since the invasion, it is matter of surprise that there could be found any persons with hearts or intellects sufficiently strong to escape from the realities around them into the abstractions and idealities of poetry; but that there were many who did so, and with a power and beauty for which they get little credit, must be evident from Mr. Duffy's "Ballad Poetry," and, I trust, also from this volume. I speak now, of course, of our native Gaelic writers. To us there can scarcely be anything more interesting or more valuable than these snatches and fragments of old songs and ballads, which are chapters of a nation's autobiography. Without these how difficult would it be for the best disposed and the most patriotic amongst us to free our minds from the false impressions which the study (superficial as it was) of the history of our country, as told by those who were not her children or her friends, had made upon us. Instead of the rude savage kerns that anti-Irish historians represent our forefathers to have been, for ever hovering with murderous intent round the fortresses of the Pale, we see them, in their own ballads, away in their green valleys and inaccessible mountains, as fathers, as brothers, as

---

* "Where'er resounds the German tongue—
Where German hymns to God are sung—
There, gallant brother, take thy stand!
That is the German's Fatherland;"
[Mangan's "Anthologia Germanica." vol II., p. 180.]

† Walpurgis is the name of a saint to whom the 1st of May is dedicated.

lovers, and as husbands, leading the old patriarchal life with their wives and children, while the air is musical with the melody of their harps and the lowing of their cattle we see them hunting the red deer over the brown mountains, or spearing the salmon in the pleasant rivers,—or, borne on their swift horses, descending in many a gallant foray on the startled intruders of the Pale. What is of more importance, we look into the hearts and minds of these people—we see what they love with such passion— what they hate with such intensity—what they revere with such sacred fidelity. We find they had love—they had loyalty—they had religion—they had constancy—they had an undying devotion for the "green hills of holy Ireland," and as such they are entitled to our respect, our affections, and our imitation. The best ballads they have left us are those of the affections, and they are, according to Mr. Ferguson, of the utmost possible intensity of passion compatible with the most perfect purity. Even in their political ballads, where a thin disguise was necessary, the allegory has been so perfect, and the wail of sorrow, or the yearning of affection, so exquisitely imitated (as in the instance of the *Roisin Dhu*, or "Dark Rosaleen"), as to make so excellent a critic and so true a poet as Mr. Ferguson doubt if they be in reality political ballads at all.

Upon the subject of our Anglo-Irish Ballads, I have nothing to add to what Mr. Duffy has so ably and so truly written in his Introduction to the "Ballad Poetry o. Ireland." That there is a distinct character and a peculiar charm in the best ballads of this class, which the highest genius, unaccompanied by thorough Irish feeling, and a thorough Irish education, would fail to impart to them must be evident to everyone who has read that volume To those among us, and to the generations who are yet to be among us, whose mother tongue is, and of necessity must be, the English and not the Irish, the establishing of this fact is of the utmost importance, and of the greatest consolation—that we can be thoroughly Irish in our feelings without ceasing to be English in our speech; that we can be faithful to the land of our birth, without being ungrateful to that literature which has been "the nursing mother of our minds;" that we can develop the intellectual resources of our country, and establish for ourselves a distinct and separate existence in the world of letters. without depriving ourselves of the advantages of the widely-diffused and genius-consecrated language of England, are facts that I conceive cannot be too widely disseminated. This peculiar character of our poetry is, however, not easily imparted. An Irish word or an Irish phrase, even appositely introduced, will not be sufficient; it must pervade the entire poem, and must be seen and felt in the construction, the sentiment, and the expression. Our writers would do well to consider the advantages, even in point of success and popularity, which would be likely to attend the working of this peculiar vein of Anglo-Irish literature. If they write, as they are too much in the habit of doing, in the weak, worn-out style of the majority of contemporary English authors, they will infallibly be lost in the crowd of easy writers and smooth versifiers, whose name is legion, on the other side of the channel; whereas, if they endeavour to be racy of their native soil, use their native idiom, illustrate the character of their country, treasure her legends, eternalize her traditions, people her scenery, and ennoble her superstitions, the very novelty will attract attention and secure success.

1845.

BOOK OF IRISH BALLADS.

THOMAS DAVIS.
HIS LIFE: HIS DEATH: HIS WORK.
BY SAMUEL FERGUSON, LL.D., Q.C., M.R.I.A.

I walked through Ballinderry in the Spring-time,
  When the bud was on the tree ;
And I said, in every fresh-ploughed field beholding
  The sowers striding free,
Scattering broad cast forth the corn in golden plenty
  On the quick seed-clasping soil,
Even such, this day, among the fresh-stirred hearts of Erin,
  Thomas Davis is thy toil !

I sat by Ballyshannon in the summer,
  And saw the salmon leap ;
And I said, as I beheld the gallant creatures
  Spring glittering from the deep,
Through the spray, and through the prone heaps striving onward
  To the calm clear streams above,
So seekest thou thy native founts of freedom, Thomas Davis,
  In thy brightness of strength and love !

I stood on Derrybawn in the Autumn,
  And I heard the eagle call,
With a clangorous cry of wrath and lamentation
  That filled the wide mountain hall,

O'er the bare deserted place of his plundered eyrie;
   And I said, as he screamed and soared,
So callest thou, thou wrathful-soaring Thomas Davis,
   For a nation's rights restored!

And, alas! to think but now, and thou art lying,
   Dear Davis, dead at thy mother's knee;
And I, no mother near, on my own sick-bed,
   That face on earth shall never see:
I may lie and try to feel that I am not dreaming,
   I may lie and try to say "Thy will be done"—
But a hundred such as I will never comfort Erin
   For the loss of the noble son!

Young husbandman of Erin's fruitful seed-time,
   In the fresh track of danger's plough!
Who will walk the heavy, toilsome, perilous furrow
   Girt with freedom's seed-sheets now?
Who will banish with the wholesome crop of knowledge
   The flaunting weed and the bitter thorn,
Now that thou thyself art but a seed for hopeful planting
   Against the resurrection morn?

Young salmon of the flood-tide of freedom
   That swells round Erin's shore!
Thou wilt leap against their loud oppressive torrent
   Of bigotry and hate no more:
Drawn downward by their prone material instinct,
   Let them thunder on their rocks and foam—
Thou hast leapt, aspiring soul, to founts beyond their raging,
   Where troubled waters never come!

But I grieve not, eagle of the empty eyrie,
   That thy wrathful cry is still;
And that the songs alone of peaceful mourners
   Are heard to-day on Erin's hill;

Better far, if brothers' war be destined for us
  (God avert that horrid day I pray !)
That ere our hands be stained with slaughter fratricidal
  Thy warm heart should be cold in clay.

But my trust is strong in God, who made us brothers,
  That He will not suffer those right hands
Which thou hast joined in holier rites than wedlock,
  To draw opposing brands.
Oh, many a tuneful tongue that thou mad'st vocal
  Would lie cold and silent then ;
And songless long once more, should often-widowed
    Erin
  Mourn the loss of her brave young men.

Oh, brave young men, my love, my pride, my promise,
  'Tis on you my hopes are set,
In manliness, in kindliness, in justice,
  To make Erin a nation yet :
Self-respecting, self-relying, self-advancing,
  In union or in severance, free and strong—
And if God grant this, then, under God, to Thomas
    Davis,
  Let the greater praise belong.

THE OLD STORY.

"Old as the universe, yet not outworn."—The Island.

He came across the meadow-pass,
  That summer-eve of eves,
The sunlight streamed along the grass,
  And glanced amid the leaves ;
And from the shrubbery below,
  And from the garden trees,
He heard the thrushes' music flow,
  And humming of the bees ;
The garden-gate was swung apart—
  The space was brief between ;
But there, for throbbing of his heart,
  He paused perforce to lean.

He leaned upon the garden-gate;
　　He looked, and scarce he breathed;
Within the little porch she sate,
　　With woodbine overwreathed;
Her eyes upon her work were bent,
　　Unconscious who was nigh;
But oft the needle slowly went,
　　And oft did idle lie;
And ever to her lips arose
　　Sweet fragments faintly sung,
But ever, ere the notes could close,
　　She hushed them on her tongue.

Her fancies as they come and go,
　　Her pure face speaks the while,
For now it is a flitting glow,
　　And now a breaking smile;
And now it is a graver shade
　　When holier thoughts are there—
An Angel's pinion might be stayed
　　To see a sight so fair;
But still they hid her looks of light,
　　Those downcast eyelids pale—
Two lovely clouds so silken white,
　　Two lovelier stars that veil.

The sun at length his burning edge
　　Had rested on the hill,
And save one thrush from out the hedge,
　　Both bower and grove were still.
The sun had almost bade farewell;
　　But one reluctant ray
Still loved within that porch to dwell,
　　As charméd there to stay—
It stole aslant the pear-tree bough,
　　And through the woodbine fringe,
And kissed the maiden's neck and brow,
　　And bathed her in its tinge.

Oh! beauty of my heart, he said,
　　Oh! darling, darling mine,

Was ever light of evening shed
    On loveliness like thine?
Why should I ever leave this spot,
    But gaze until I die?
A moment from that bursting thought
    She felt his footstep nigh.
One sudden, lifted glance—but one,
    A tremor and a start,
So gently was their greeting done
    That who would guess their heart.

Long, long the sun had sunken down,
    And all his golden trail
Had died away to lines of brown,
    In duskier hues that fail.
The grasshopper was chirping shrill—
    No other living sound
Accompanied the tiny rill
    That gurgled under ground—
No other living sound, unless
    Some spirit bent to hear
Low words of human tenderness,
    And mingling whispers near.

The stars, like pallid gems at first,
    Deep in the liquid sky,
Now forth upon the darkness burst,
    Sole kings and lights on high;
In splendour, myriad-fold, supreme—
    No rival moonlight strove,
Nor lovelier e'er was Hesper's beam,
    Nor more majestic Jove.
But what if hearts there beat that night
    That recked not of the skies,
Or only felt their imaged light
    In one another's eyes.

And if two worlds of hidden thought
    And fostered passion met,

Which, passing human language, sought
  And found an utterance yet;
And if they trembled like to flowers
  That droop across a stream,
The while the silent starry hours
  Glide o'er them like a dream;
And if, when came the parting time,
  They faltered still and clung;
What is it all?—an ancient rhyme
  Ten thousand times besung—
That part of Paradise which man
  Without the portal knows—
Which hath been since the world began,
  And shall be till its close.
                        O—.

1846

THE FAIRY WELL OF LAGNANAY.

BY SAMUEL FERGUSON, LL.D., M.R.I.A.

I.

MOURNFULLY, sing mournfully—
  "O listen, Ellen, sister dear:
Is there no help at all for me,
  But only ceaseless sigh and tear?
  Why did not he who left me here,
With stolen hope steal memory?
  O listen, Ellen, sister dear,
(Mounfully, sing mournfully)—
  I'll go away to Sleamish hill,
I'll pluck the fairy hawthorn-tree,
  And let the spirits work their will;
  I care not if for good or ill,
So they but lay the memory
  Which all my heart is haunting still!
(Mournfully, sing mournfully)—
  The Fairies are a silent race,
And pale as lily flowers to see:

I care not for a blanched face,
　Nor wandering in a dreaming place.
So I but banish memory :—
　I wish I were with Anna Grace !"
Mournfully, sing mournfully !

II.

Hearken to my tale of woe—
　'Twas thus to weeping Ellen Con,
Her sister said in accents low,
　Her only sister, Una bawn :
'Twas in their bed before the dawn,
And Ellen answered sad and slow,—
　" Oh Una, Una, be not drawn
(Hearken to my tale of woe)—
　To this unholy grief I pray,
Which makes me sick at heart to know,
　And I will help you if I may :
—The Fairy Well of Lagnanay—
Lie nearer me, I tremble so,—
　Una, I've heard wise women say
(Hearken to my tale of woe)—
　That if before the dews arise,
True maiden in its icy flow
　With pure hand bathe her bosom thrice
　Three lady-brackens pluck likewise,
And three times round the fountain go,
　She straight forgets her tears and sighs.
Hearken to my tale of woe !

III.

All, alas ! and well-away !
　"Oh, sister Ellen, sister sweet,
Come with me to the hill I pray,
　And I will prove that blessed freet !"
　They rose with soft and silent feet,
They left their mother where she lay,
　Their mother and her care discreet,
(All, alas ! and well-away !)

And soon they reached the Fairy Well,
The mountain's eye, clear, cold, and grey,
　　Wide open in the dreary fell:
How long they stood 'twere vain to tell,
At last upon the point of day,
　　Bawn Una bares her bosom's swell,
(All, alas! and well-away!)
　　Thrice o'er her shrinking breasts she laves
The gliding glance that will not stay
　　Of subtly-streaming fairy waves:—
And now the charm three brackens craves,
She plucks them in their fring'd array:—
　　Now round the well her fate she braves,
All, alas! and well-away!

IV.

Save us all from Fairy thrall!
　　Ellen sees her face the rim
Twice and thrice, and that is all—
　　Fount and hill and maiden swim
　　All together melting dim!
"Una! Una!" thou may'st call,
　　Sister sad! but lith or limb
(Save us all from Fairy thrall!)
　　Never again of Una bawn,
Where now she walks in dreamy hall,
　　Shall eye of mortal look upon!
Oh! can it be the guard was gone,
That better guard than shield or wall?
　　Who knows on earth save Jurlagh Daune!
(Save us all from Fairy thrall!)
　　Behold the banks are green and bare,
No pit is here wherein to fall:
　　Aye—at the fount you well may stare,
　　But nought save pebbles smooth is there,
And small straws twirling one and all.
　　Hie thee home, and be thy pray'r,
Save us all from Fairy thrall.

THE BAY OF DUBLIN.

BY DENIS FLORENCE MAC-CARTHY, M.R.I.A.

I.

My native Bay, for many a year
I've loved thee with a trembling fear,
Lest thou, though dear and very dear,
    And beauteous as a vision,
Shouldst have some rival far away—
Some matchless wonder of a bay—
Whose sparkling waters ever play
    'Neath azure skies elysian.

II.

'Tis Love, methought, blind Love that pours
The rippling magic round these shores—
For whatsoever Love adores
    Becomes what Love desireth:
'Tis ignorance of aught beside
That throws enchantment o'er the tide,
And makes my heart respond with pride
    To what mine eye admireth.

III.

And thus, unto our mutual loss,
Whene'er I paced the sloping moss
Of green Killiney, or across
    The intervening waters—
Up Howth's brown sides my feet would wend,
To see thy sinuous bosom bend,
Or view thine outstretch'd arms extend
    To clasp thine islet daughters;

IV.

Then would this spectre of my fear
Beside me stand—how calm and clear
Slept underneath, the green waves, near
    The tide-worn rocks' recesses;

Or when they woke, and leapt from land,
Like startled sea-nymphs, hand in hand,
Seeking the southern silver strand
    With floating emerald tresses;

V.

It lay o'er all, a moral mist,
Even on the hills, when evening kist
The granite peaks to amethyst,
    I felt its fatal shadow;—
It darkened o'er the brightest rills,
It lower'd upon the sunniest hills,
And hid the wingéd song that fills
    The moorland and the meadow

VI.

But now that I have been to view
All even Nature's self can do,
And from Gaëta's arch of blue
    Borne many a fond memento;
And from each fair and famous scene,
Where Beauty is, and Power hath been,
Along the golden shores between
    Misenum and Sorrento:

VII.

I can look proudly in thy face,
Fair daughter of a hardier race,
And feel thy winning well-known grace,
    Without my old misgiving;
And as I kneel upon thy strand,
And kiss thy once unvalued hand,
Proclaim earth holds no lovelier land.
    Where life is worth the living.

HY-BRASAIL—THE ISLE OF THE BLEST.

BY GERALD GRIFFIN.

[" The people of Arran fancy that at certain periods they see *Hy-Brasail* elevated far to the west in their watery horizon. This had been the universal tradition of the ancient Irish, who supposed that a great part of Ireland had been swallowed by the sea, and that the sunken part often rose, and was seen hanging in the horizon! Such was the popular notion. The *Hy-Brasail* of the Irish is evidently a part of the *Atlantis* of Plato,* who, in his 'Timæus,' says that that island was totally swallowed up by a prodigious earthquake. Of some such shocks the Isles of Arran, the promontories of Antrim, and some of the western islands of Scotland, bear evident marks.—*O'Flaherty's Sketch of the Island of Arran.*]

On the ocean that hollows the rocks where ye dwell,
A shadowy land has appeared, as they tell ;
Men thought it a region of sunshine and rest,
And they called it *Hy-Brasail* the isle of the blest.
From year unto year on the ocean's blue rim,
The beautiful spectre showed lovely and dim ;
The golden clouds curtained the deep where it lay,
And it looked like an Eden, away, far away !

A peasant who heard of the wonderful tale,
In the breeze of the Orient loosened his sail ;
From Ara, the holy, he turned to the west,
For though Ara was holy, *Hy-Brasail* was blest.
He heard not the voices that called from the shore—
He heard not the rising wind's menacing roar ;
Home, kindred, and safety, he left on that day,
And he sped to *Hy-Brasail*, away, far away !

Morn rose on the deep, and that shadowy isle,
O'er the faint rim of distance, reflected its smile ;
Noon burned on the wave, and that shadowy shore
Seemed lovelily distant, and faint as before ;
Lone evening came down on the wanderer's track,
And to Ara again he looked timidly back ;
Oh ! far on the verge of the ocean it lay,
Yet the isle of the blest was away, far away !

* For a ballad on this subject, by the Rev. G. Croly, see page 62.

Rash dreamer, return! O, ye winds of the main,
Bear him back to his own peaceful Ara again.
Rash fool! for a vision of fanciful bliss,
To barter thy calm life of labour and peace.
The warning of reason was spoken in vain;
He never re-visited Ara again!
Night fell on the deep, amidst tempest and spray,
And he died on the waters, away, far away!

[A curious 4to tract relating to this tradition is in the possession of the editor. It is called "The Western Wonder, or O Brazeel, an Inchanted Island discovered; with a relation of *Two Ship-wracks* in a dreadful *Sea-storm* in that discovery. London, printed for N. C., MDCLXXIV."—ED. 1869.]

THE MOUNTAIN SPRITE.

BY THOMAS MOORE.

In yonder valley there dwelt, alone,
A youth, whose moments had calmly flown,
'Till spells came o'er him, and, day and night,
He was haunted and watch'd by a Mountain Sprite.

As once, by moonlight, he wandered o'er
The golden sands of that island shore;
A foot-print sparkled before his sight—
'Twas the fairy foot of the Mountain Sprite!

Beside a fountain, one sunny day,
As bending over the stream he lay,
There peeped down o'er him two eyes of light,
And he saw in that mirror the Mountain Sprite.

He turn'd, but, lo! like a startled bird,
That spirit fled!—and the youth but heard
Sweet music, such as marks the flight
Of some bird of song, from the Mountain Sprite.

One night, still haunted by that bright look,
The boy, bewilder'd, his pencil took,
And, guided only by memory's light,
Drew the once-seen form of the Mountain Sprite.

"Oh, thou, who lovest the shadow," cried
A voice, low whispering by his side,
"Now turn and see"—here the youth's delight
Seal'd the rosy lips of the Mountain Sprite.

"Of all the Spirits of land and sea,"
Then wrapt he murmur'd, "there's none like thee ;
"And oft, oh oft, may thy foot thus light
"In this lonely bower, sweet Mountain Sprite !"

THE CITY OF GOLD.

[This is another ballad on the beautiful fable of a phantom island in the Atlantic.]

Years onward have swept,
   Aye ! long ages have rolled—
Since the billows first slept
   O'er the City of Gold !

'Neath its eddy of white
   Where the green wave is swelling,
In their halls of delight
   Are the fairy tribes dwelling.

And but seldom the eye
   Of a mortal may scan,
Where those palaces high
   Rise unaided by man.

Yet, at times the waves sever,
   And then you may view
The yellow walls ever
   'Neath the ocean's deep blue.

But I warn thee, O man !
   Never seek to behold,
Where the crystal streams ran
   In the City of Gold !

Like a beauty with guile,
  When some young knight has found her.
There is death in her smile,
  And dark ruin around her!

Like a Poet's first dream
  In his longings for glory;
A dagger whose gleam
  With the life-blood is gory.

Like wishes possessed,
  And for which we have panted,
When we find us unblest,
  Tho' our prayers have been granted.

Like ought that's forbidden
  Weak man to behold,
Death and sorrow are hid in
  The City of Gold.

Rash youth! dost thou view it,
  The ransom thou'lt pay,
Alas! thou must rue it,
  Death takes thee to-day!

Cobaṗ-na-Sia;*

OR,

THE FAIRY WELL.

BY JAMES TEELING.

[Amongst the many old and fanciful superstitions embodied in the traditions of our peasantry, some of the most poetical are those connected with spring wells, which in Ireland have been invested with something of a sacred character ever since the days of Druidical worship. It is in some parts of the country an article of popular belief, that the desecration of a spring by any unworthy use is invariably followed by some misfortune to the offender; and that the well itself, which is regarded as the source of fruitfulness and prosperity, moves altogether out of the field in which the violation had been committed.—*Dub. University Mag.*, vol. viii., p. 447.]

* Thubber-na-Shie.

Oh ! Peggy Bawn was innocent,
   And wild as any roe ;
Her cheek was like the summer rose,
   Her neck was like the snow :

And every eye was in her head
   So beautiful and bright,
You'd almost think they'd light her through
   Glencarrigy by night.

Among the hills and mountains,
   Above her mother's home,
The long and weary summer day
   Young Peggy Blake would roam ;

And not a girl in the town,
   From Dhua to Glenlur,
Could wander through the mountain's heath
   Or climb the rocks with her.

The Lammas sun was shinin' on
   The meadows all so brown ;
The neighbours gathered far and near
   To cut the ripe crops down ;

And pleasant was the mornin',
   And dewy was the dawn,
And gay and lightsome-hearted
   To the sunny fields they're gone.

The joke was passing lightly,
   And the laugh was loud and free ;
There was neither care nor trouble
   To disturb their hearty glee ;

When, says Peggy, resting in among
   The sweet and scented hay,
" I wonder is there one would brave
   The Fairy-well to-day !"

She looked up with her laughin' eyes
   So soft at Willy Rhu ;
Och murdher ! that she didn't need
   His warnin' kind and true !

But all the boys and girls laughed,
   And Willy Rhu looked shy ;
God help you, Willy ! sure they saw
   The throuble in your eye.

"Now, by my faith !" young Connell says
   I like your notion well—
There's a power more than gospel
   In what crazy gossips tell."

Oh, my heavy hatred fall upon
   Young Connell of Sliabh-Mast !
He took the cruel vengeance
   For his scorned love at last.

The jokin' and the jibin'
   And the banterin' went on,
One girl dared another,
   And they all dared Peggy Bawn.

Till leaping up, away she flew
   Down to the hollow green—
Her bright locks, floating in the wind,
   Like golden lights were seen.

They saw her at the Fairy well—
   Their laughin' died away,
They saw her stoop above its brink
   With heart as cold as clay.

Oh ! mother, mother, never stand
   Upon your cabin floor !
You heard the cry that through your heart
   Will ring for evermore ;

For when she came up from the well,
    No one could stand her look !
Her eye was wild—her cheek was pale—
    They saw her mind was shook :

And the gaze she cast around her
    Was so ghastly and so sad—
" O Christ preserve us !" shouted all,
    " Poor Peggy Blake's gone mad !"

The moon was up—the stars were out,
    And shining through the sky,
When young and old stood mourning round
    To see their darling die.

Poor Peggy from the death-bed rose—
    Her face was pale and cold,
And down about her shoulders hung
    The lovely locks of gold.

" All you that's here this night," she said,
    " Take warnin' by my fate,
Whoever braves the Fairies' wrath,
    Their sorrow comes too late."

The tear was startin' in her eye,
    She clasp'd her throbbin' head,
And when the sun next mornin' rose
    Poor Peggy Bawn lay dead.

FAIRY REVELS.

The fairies are dancing by brake and bower,
For this in their land is the merriest hour.

Their steps are soft, and their robes are light,
And they trip it at ease in the clear moonlight.

Their queen is in youth and in beauty there,
And the daughters of earth are not half so fair.

Her glance is quick, and her eyes are bright,
But they glitter with wild and unearthly light.

Her brow is all calm, and her looks are kind,
But the look that she gives leaves but pain behind.

Her voice is soft, and her smiles are sweet,
But woe to thee who such smiles shall meet.

She will meet thee at dusk like a lady fair,
But go not, for danger awaits thee there.

She will take thee to ramble by grove and by glen,
And the friends of thy youth shall not know thee again.

THE ENCHANTED ISLAND.

[The tradition in this beautiful little ballad is almost the same as that on which "The City of Gold," "Hy-Brasail," and other poems in this c*-*lection are founded, except in point of locality; the scene of the latt r ballads being placed in the Atlantic, to the west of the Isles of Arran, while "the Enchanted Island" is supposed to be in the neighbourhood of Rathlin Island, off the north coast of the county Antrim. The name of the island, which has been spelled a different way by almost every writer on the subject, is supposed to be derived from *Ragh-erin*, or "the Fort of Erin," as its situation, commanding the Irish coast, might make it, not unaptly, be styled "the fortress of Ireland."—See *Leonard's Topographia Hibernica.*]

To Rathlin's Isle I chanced to sail,
   When summer breezes softly blew,
And there I heard so sweet a tale,
   That oft I wished it could be true.

They said, at eve, when rude winds sleep,
   And hushed is ev'ry turbid swell,
A mermaid rises from the deep,
   And sweetly tunes her magic shell.

And while she plays, rock, dell, and cave,
   In dying falls the sound retain,
As if some choral spirits gave
   Their aid to swell her witching strain.

Then, summoned by that dulcet note,
   Uprising to th' admiring view,
A fairy island seems to float
   With tints of many a gorgeous hue.

And glittering fanes, and lofty towers,
   All on this fairy isle are seen ;
And waving trees, and shady bowers,
   With more than mortal verdure green.

And as it moves, the western sky
   Glows with a thousand varying rays ;
And the calm sea, tinged with each dye,
   Seems like a golden flood of blaze.

They also say, if earth or stone,
   From verdant Erin's hallowed land,
Were on this magic island thrown,
   For ever fixed, it then would stand.

But, when for this, some little boat
   In silence ventures from the shore—
The mermaid sinks—hushed is the note,
   The fairy isle is seen no more.

THE FAIRIES' PASSAGE.

BY CLARENCE MANGAN.

I.

Tapp, tapp ! Rapp, rapp ! "Get up, Gaffer Ferry-
   man."
"Eh ? who is there ?" The clock strikes Three.
"Get up—do, Gaffer ! you are the very man,
   We have been long—long, longing to see."
The ferryman rises, growling and grumbling,
And goes fum-fumbling, and stumbling, and tumbling,
   Over the wares in his way to the door.
        But he sees no more
        Than he saw before,

Till a voice is heard—" O Ferryman, dear !
Here we are waiting, all of us here !
We are a wee, wee colony, we ;
Some two hundred in all, or three.
Ferry us over the river Lee
  Ere dawn of day,
  And we will pay
  The most we may,
  In our own wee way !"

II.

" Who are you ? Whence came you ? What place are
 you going to ? "
" O, we have dwelt over long in this land.
The people get cross, and are growing so knowing, too ;
 Nothing at all but they now understand ;
  We are daily vanishing under the thunder
  Of some huge engine or iron wonder ;
  That iron—O, it has entered our souls !"
  —— " Your souls ? O, Goles !
  You queer little drolls !
Do you mean —— ?" " Good Gaffer, do aid us with
 speed,
For our time, like our stature, is short indeed !
 And a very long way we have to go,
 Eight or ten thousand miles or so,
 Hither and thither, and to and fro.
  With our pots and pans,
  And little gold cans ;
  But our light caravans
  Run swifter than Man's !"

III.

" Well, well, you may come !" said the Ferryman,
 affably ;
" Patrick ! turn out, and get ready the barge !"
Then again to the little folk : " Though you seem
 laughably
Small, I don't mind, if your coppers be large."

O, dear! what a rushing, what pushing, what
   crushing
(The waterman making vain efforts at hushing
   The hubbub the while) there followed these
    words!
          What clapping of boards!
          What strapping of cords!
What stowing away of children and wives,
And platters, and mugs, and spoons, and knives!
Till all had safely got into the boat,
And the Ferryman clad in his tip-top coat,
And his wee little farers were fairly afloat!
          Then ding! ding! ding!
          And kling! kling! kling!
          How the coppers did ring
          In the tin pitcherling?

IV.

Off then went the boat, at first very pleasantly,
   Smoothly, and soforth, but after a while
It swayed and it swagged this way and that way, and
    presently
   Chest after chest, and pile after pile,
   Of the little folk's goods began tossing and rolling,
   And pitching like fun, beyond fairy controlling!
O, Mab! if the hubbub was great before,
It was now some two or three million times more:
Crash went the wee crocks, and the clocks, and
   the locks
Of each little wee box were stove in by hard
   knocks:
   And then there were oaths, and prayers, and
     cries—
    "Take care!"—"see there!"—"oh, dear! my
     eyes!"
   "I am killed"—"I am drowned"—with groans
    and sighs;
        Till to land they drew;
        "Yeo heo! Pull to!
        Tiller-rope, thro' and thro'!"
        And all's right anew.

V.

"Now, jump upon shore, ye queer little oddities!
... Eh! what is this? Where are they at all?
Where are they, and where are their tiny commodities?
  Well! as I live!" He looks blank as a wall,
    The poor Ferryman! Round him, and round him
      he gazes,
    But only gets deeplier lost in the mazes
    Of utter bewilderment! All, all are gone—
      And he stands alone,
      Like a statue of stone,
In a doldrum of wonder. He turns to steer,
And a tinkling laugh salutes his ear
With other odd sounds: "Ha! ha! ha! ha!
Tol, lol; zid, ziddle—quee, quee—bah! bah!
Fizzigigiggidy! psha! sha! sha!"
"O, ye thieves! ye thieves, ye rascally thieves!"
  The good man cries. He turns to his pitcher,
  And there, alas! to his horror perceives,
    That the little folk's mode of making him
      richer,
  Has been to pay him with—withered leaves!

THE PHANTOM CITY.

BY GERALD GRIFFIN.

A STORY I heard on the cliffs of the west,
  That oft, through the breakers dividing,
A city is seen on the ocean's wild breast
  In turreted majesty riding.
But brief is the glimpse of that phantom so bright,
  Soon close the white waters to screen it;
And the bodement, they say, of the wonderful sight,
  Is death to the eyes that have seen it.

I said, when they told me the wonderful tale,
  My country, is this not thy story?
Thus oft through the breakers of discord we hail
  A promise of peace and of glory.

Soon gulphed in those waters of hatred again
  No longer our fancy can find it,
And woe to our hearts for the vision so vain,
  For ruin and death come behind it.

KATE OF KENMARE.

BY DENIS FLORENCE MAC-CARTHY, M.R.I.A.

Oh! many bright eyes full of goodness and gladness,
  Where the pure soul looks out, and the heart loves to shine,
And many cheeks pale with the soft hue of sadness,
  Have I worshipped in silence and felt them divine!
But hope in its gleamings, or love in its dreamings,
  Ne'er fashioned a being so faultless and fair,
As the lily-cheeked beauty, the rose of the Roughty,*
  The fawn of the valley, sweet Kate of Kenmare!

It was all but a moment, her radiant existence,
  Her presence, her absence, all crowded on me;
But time has not ages, and earth has not distance
  To sever, sweet vision, my spirit from thee!
Again am I straying where children are playing—
  Bright is the sunshine and balmy the air,
Mountains are heathy, and there do I see thee,
  Sweet fawn of the valley, young Kate of Kenmare!

Thine arbutus beareth full many a cluster
  Of white waxen blossoms, like lilies in air;
But, oh! thy pale cheek hath a delicate lustre,
  No blossoms can rival, no lily doth wear;
To that cheek softly flushing, to thy lip brightly blushing,
  Oh! what are the berries that bright tree doth bear?
Peerless in beauty, that rose of the Roughty,
  That fawn of the valley, sweet Kate of Kenmare!

* The river Roughty discharges itself at the head of the great river or bay of Kenmare.

Oh! beauty, some spell from kind Nature thou bearest,
   Some magic of tone or enchantment of eye,
That hearts that are hardest, from forms that are fairest,
   Receive such impressions as never can die!
The foot of the fairy, though lightsome and airy,
   Can stamp on the hard rock* the shape it doth wear,
Art cannot trace it nor ages efface it—
   And such are thy glances, sweet Kate of Kenmare!

To him who far-travels how sad is the feeling—
   How the light of his mind is o'ershadowed and dim,
When the scenes he most loves, like the river's soft stealing,
   All fade as a vision and vanish from him!
Yet he bears from each far land a flower for that garland,
   That memory weaves of the bright and the fair;
While this sigh I am breathing my garland is wreathing,
   And the rose of that garland is Kate of Kenmare!

In lonely Lough Quinlan in summer's soft hours,
   Fair islands are floating that move with the tide,
Which, sterile at first, are soon covered with flowers,
   And thus o'er the bright waters fairy-like glide! †
Thus the mind the most vacant is quickly awakened,
   And the heart bears a harvest that late was so bare,
Of him who in roving finds objects in loving,
   Like the fawn of the valley, sweet Kate of Kenmare!

---

* In the vicinity of Kenmare is a rock called *The Fairy Rock*, on which the marks of several feet are deeply impressed; they are, of course, supposed to have been the work of fairies.

† Dr. Smith in his *History of Kerry*, says—"Near this place is a considerable fresh-water lake, called Lough Quinlan, in which are some small floating islands much admired by the country people. These islands swim from side to side of the lake, and are usually composed at first of a long kind of grass, which, being blown off the adjacent grounds about the middle of September, and floating about, collect slime and other stuff, and so yearly increase till they have come to have grass and other vegetables grown upon them."

Sweet Kate of Kenmare, though I ne'er may behold
    thee—
  Though the pride and the joy of another you be—
Though strange lips may praise thee and strange arms
    enfold thee,
  A blessing, dear Kate, be on them and on thee !
One feeling I cherish that never can perish—
  One talisman proof to the dark wizard care—
The fervent and dutiful love of the Beautiful,
  Of which thou art a type, gentle Kate of Kenmare !

ARRANMORE.

BY THOMAS MOORE.

["The inhabitants of Arranmore are still persuaded that in a clear day they can see from this coast Hy-Brasail, or the Inchanted Island, the Paradise of the Pagan Irish, and concerning which they relate a number of romantic stories."—*Beaufort's Ancient Topography of Ireland.*]

Oh ! Arranmore, loved Arranmore,
  How oft I dream of thee ;
And of those days when, by thy shore,
  I wander'd young and free.
Full many a path I've tried, since then,
  Through pleasure's flow'ry maze,
But ne'er could find that bliss again
  I felt in those sweet days.

How blithe upon the breezy cliffs
  At sunny morn I've stood,
With heart as bounding as the skiffs
  That danced along thy flood ;
Or when the western wave grew bright
  With daylight's parting wing,
Have sought that Eden in its light,
  Which dreaming poets sing.

That Eden, where th' immortal brave
  Dwell in a land serene—
Whose bowers beyond the shing wave,
  At sunset oft are seen ;

Ah, dream, too full of saddening truth!
  Those mansions o'er the main
Are like the hopes I built in youth,
  As sunny and as vain!

THE ISLAND OF ATLANTIS.

BY THE REV. GEORGE CROLY,

Author of Salathiel, &c.

["For at that time the Atlantic Sea was navigable, and had an island before that mouth which is called by you the pillars of Hercules. But this island was greater than both Libya and all Asia together, and afforded an easy passage to other neighbouring islands, as it was easy to pass from those islands to all the continent which borders on this Atlantic Sea. * * * But, in succeeding times, prodigious earthquakes and deluges taking place, and bringing with them desolation in the space of one day and night, all that warlike race of Athenians was at once merged under the earth; and the Atlantic island itself, being absorbed in the sea, entirely disappeared."—*Plato's Timæus.*]

Oh! thou Atlantic, dark and deep,
  Thou wilderness of waves,
Where all the tribes of earth might sleep
  In their uncrowded graves!

The sunbeams on thy bosom wake,
  Yet never light thy gloom:
The tempests burst, yet never shake
  Thy depths, thou mighty tomb!

Thou thing of mystery, stern and drear,
  Thy secrets who hath told?
The warrior and his sword are there,
  The merchant and his gold.

There lie their myriads in thy pall,
  Secure from steel and storm ·
And he, the feaster on them all,
  The canker-worm.

Yet on this wave the mountain's brow
  Once glow'd in morning's beam ;
And, like an arrow from the bow,
  Out sprang the stream ;

And on its bank the olive grove,
  And the peach's luxury,
And the damask rose—the nightbird's lo
  Perfumed the sky.

Where art thou, proud Atlantis, now ?
  Where are thy bright and brave—
Priest, people, warriors' living flow ?
  Look on that wave.

Crime deepen'd on the recreant land,
  Long guilty, long forgiven;
There, power uprear'd the bloody hand,
  There scoff'd at Heaven.

The word went forth—the word of woe—
  The judgment thunders pealed ;
The fiery earthquake blazed below ;
  Its doom was seal'd.

Now on its halls of ivory
  Lie giant weed and ocean slime,
Burying from man's and angel's eye
  The land of crime.

THE HAUNTED SPRING.

BY SAMUEL LOVER.

[It is said, Fays have the power to assume various shapes for the purpose of luring mortals into Fairyland; hunters seem to have been particularly the objects of the lady fairies' fancies.]

GAILY through the mountain glen
  The hunter's horn did ring,
    As the milk-white doe
    Escaped his bow,
  Down by the haunted spring.

In vain his silver horn he wound,—
　'Twas echo answered back ;
For neither groom nor baying hound
　Were on the hunter's track ;
In vain he sought the milk-white doe
That made him stray, and 'scaped his bow ;
For, save himself, no living thing
Was by the silent haunted spring.

The purple heath-bells, blooming fair,
Their fragrance round did fling,
　　As the hunter lay
　　At close of day,
Down by the haunted spring.
A lady fair, in robe of white,
　To greet the hunter came ;
She kiss'd a cup with jewels bright,
　And pledged him by his name ;
" Oh, lady fair," the hunter cried,
" Be thou my love, my blooming bride,
" A bride that well might grace a king
" Fair lady of the haunted spring."

In the fountain clear she stoop'd,
　And forth she drew a ring ;
　　And that loved Knight
　　His faith did plight
Down by the haunted spring.
But since that day his chase did stray,
　The hunter ne'er was seen,
And legends tell, he now doth dwell
　Within the hills so green ;*
But still the milk-white doe appears,
And wakes the peasants' evening fears,
While distant bugles faintly ring
Around the lonely haunted spring.

---

* Fays and fairies are supposed to have their dwelling-places within old green hills.

ALICE AND UNA.

A TALE OF "Ceim-an-eiċ."†

BY DENIS FLORENCE MAC-CARTHY, M.R.IA.

[The pass of Céim-an-eich (the path of the deer) lies to the south-west of Inchageela, in the direction of Bantry Bay. The tourist will commit a grievous error if he omit to visit it. Perhaps in no part of the kingdom is there to be found a place so utterly desolate and gloomy. A mountain has been divided by some convulsion of nature; and the narrow pass, about two miles in length, is overhung on either side by perpendicular masses clothed in wild ivy and underwood, with, occasionally, a stunted yew-tree or arbutus growing among them. At every step advance seems impossible—some huge rock jutting out into the path; and, on sweeping round it, seeming to conduct only to some barrier still more insurmountable; while from all sides rush down the "wild fountains," and, forming for themselves a rugged channel, make their way onward—the first tributary offering to the gentle and fruitful Lee:
"Here, amidst heaps
Of mountain wrecks, on either sides thrown high,
The wide-spread traces of its watery might,
The tortuous channel wound."
Nowhere has nature assumed a more appalling aspect, or manifested a more stern resolve to dwell in her own loneliness and grandeur undisturbed by any living thing; for even the birds seem to shun a solitude so awful, and the hum of bee or chirp of grasshopper is never heard within its precincts.—*Hall's Ireland*, vol. i, p. 117.]

AH! the pleasant time hath vanished, ere our wretched
    doubtings banished.
All the graceful spirit people, children of the earth and
    sea—
Whom in days now dim and olden, when the world
    was fresh and golden,
Every mortal could behold in haunted rath, and tower,
    and tree—
They have vanished, they are banished—ah! how sad
    the loss for thee,
        Lonely Céim-an-eich!
Still some scenes are yet enchanted by the charms that
    Nature granted,
Still are peopled, still are haunted, by a graceful spirit
    band.

† Céim-an-eich (the path of the deer), pronounced, Keim-an-ec.

Peace and Beauty have their dwelling where the infant
  streams are welling—
Where the mournful waves are knelling on Glengariff's
  coral strand ; *
Or where, on Killarney's mountains, Grace and Terror
  smiling stand,
    Like sisters, hand in hand !

Still we have a new romance in fire-ships, through the
  tamed seas glancing,
And the snorting and the prancing of the mighty engine steed ;
Still, Astolpho-like, we wander through the boundless
  azure yonder,
Realizing what seemed fonder than the magic tales we
  read—
Tales of wild Arabian wonder, where the fancy all is
  freed—
    Wilder far, indeed !

Now that Earth once more hath woken, and the trance
  of Time is broken !
And the sweet word—Hope—is spoken, soft and sure,
  though none know how,—
Could we—could we only see all these, the glories of
  the Real,
Blended with the lost Ideal, happy were the old world
  now—
Woman in its fond believing—man with iron arm and
  brow—
    Faith and Work its vow !

Yes ? the past shines clear and pleasant, and there's
  glory in the present ;
And the future, like a crescent, lights the deepening
  sky of Time ;

---

* In the bay of Glengariff, and towards the N.W. parts of Bantry Ba·
they dredge up large quantities of coral sand.—*Smith's Coast*, vol.
p. 286.

And that sky will yet grow brighter, if the Worker
    and the Writer,
If the Sceptre and the Mitre join in sacred bonds
    sublime,
With two glories shining o'er them, up the coming
    years they'll climb
        Earth's great evening as its prime!

With a sigh for what is fading, but, oh! earth, with
    no upbraiding;
For we feel that time is braiding newer, fresher flowers
    for thee—
We will speak, despite our grieving, words of Loving
    and Believing,
Tales we vowed when we were leaving awful Céim-an-eich—
Where the sever'd rocks resemble fragments of a frozen
    sea,
        And the wild deer flee!

   *   *   *   *   *

'Tis the hour when flowers are shrinking, when the
    weary sun is sinking,
And his thirsty steeds are drinking in the cooling
    western sea;
When young Maurice lightly goeth, where the tiny
    streamlet floweth,
And the struggling moonlight showeth where his path
    must be—
Path whereon the wild goats wander fearlessly and free
        Through dark Céim-an-eich.

As a hunter, danger daring, with his dogs the brown
    moss sharing,
Little thinking, little caring, long a wayward youth
    lived he;
But his bounding heart was regal, and he looked as
    looks the eagle.

And he flew as flies the beagle, who the panting stag
    doth see—
Love, who spares a fellow-archer, long had let him
    wander free
        Through wild Céim-an-eich !

But at length the hour drew nigher when his heart
    should feel that fire ;
Up the mountain high and higher had he hunted from
    the dawn ;
Till the weeping fawn descended, where the earth and
    ocean blended,
And with hope its slow way wended to a little grassy
    lawn—
It is safe, for gentle Alice to her saving breast hath
    drawn
        Her almost sister fawn.

Alice was a chieftain's daughter, and, though many
    suitors sought her,
She so loved Glengariff's water that she let her lovers
    pine ;
Her eye was beauty's palace, and her cheek an ivory
    chalice,
Through which the blood of Alice gleamed soft as
    rosiest wine,
And her lips like lusmore blossoms which the fairies
    intertwine, †
        And her heart a golden mine.

She was gentler, she was shyer than the sweet fawn
    that stood by her,
And her eyes emit a fire soft and tender as her soul ;
Love's dewy light doth drown her, and the braided
    locks that crown her
Than Autumn's trees are browner, when the golden
    shadows roll,
Through the forests in the evening, when cathedral
    turrets toll,
        And the purple sun advanceth to its goal.

† The lusmore (or fairy-cap)— literally, the great herb. *Digitalis Purpurea*

Her cottage was a dwelling all regal homes excelling,
But, ah! beyond the telling was the beauty round it
    spread—
The wave and sunshine playing, like sisters each
    arraying—
Far down the sea-plants swaying upon their coral bed,
As languid as the tresses on a sleeping maiden's head,
    When the summer breeze is dead.

Need we say that Maurice loved her, and that no
    blush reproved her
When her throbbing bosom moved her to give the
    heart she gave;
That by dawn-light and by twilight, and oh! blessed
    moon, by thy light—
When the twinkling stars on high light the wanderer
    o'er the wave—
His steps unconscious led him where Glengariff's
    waters lave
        Each mossy bank and cave.

He thitherward is wending—o'er the vale is night
    descending—
Quick his step, but quicker sending his herald thoughts
    before;
By rocks and streams before him, proud and hopeful
    on he bore him;
One star was shining o'er him—in his heart of hearts
    two more—
And two other eyes, far brighter than a human head
    e'er wore,
        Unseen were shining o'er.

These eyes are not of woman—no brightness merely
    human
Could, planet-like, illumine the place in which they
    shone;
But nature's bright works vary—there are beings, light
    and airy,

Whom mortal lips call fairy, and Una she is one—
Sweet sisters of the moonbeams and daughters of the sun,
  Who along the curling cool waves run.

As summer lightning dances amid the heavens' expanses,
Thus shone the burning glances, of those flashing fairy eyes;
Three splendours there were shining—three passions intertwining—
Despair and hope combining their deep contrasted dyes
With jealousy's green lustre, as troubled ocean vies
  With the blue of summer skies!

She was a fairy creature, of heavenly form and feature—
Not Venus' self could teach her a newer, sweeter grace—
Not Venus' self could lend her an eye so dark and tender,
Half softness and half splendour, as lit her lily face;
And, as the stars' sweet motion maketh music throughout space,
  There was music in her pace.

But when at times she started, and her blushing lips were parted,
And a pearly lustre darted from her teeth so ivory white,
You'd think you saw the gliding of two rosy clouds dividing,
And the crescent they were hiding gleam forth upon your sight—
Through these lips, as through the portals of a heaven pure and bright,
  Came a breathing of delight!

Though many an elf-king loved her, and elf-dames grave reproved her,

The hunter's daring moved her, more wildly every
    hour ;
Unseen she roamed beside him, to guard him and to
    guide him,
But now she must divide him from her human rival's
    power.
Ah ! Alice—gentle Alice ! the storm begins to lower
       That may crush Glengariff's flower !

The moon that late was gleaming, as calm as child-
    hood's dreaming,
Is hid, and, wildly screaming, the stormy winds arise ;
And the clouds flee quick and faster before their sullen
    master,
And the shadows of disaster are falling from the
    skies—
Strange sights and sounds are rising—but Maurice be
    thou wise,
       Nor heed the tempting cries.

If ever mortal needed that council, surely *he* did ;
But the wile has now succeeded—he wanders from his
    path—
The cloud its lightning sendeth, and its bolt the stout
    oak rendeth,
And the arbutus back bendeth in the whirlwind, as a
    lath !
Now and then the moon looks out, but, alas ! its pale
    face hath
       A dreadful look of wrath.

In vain his strength he squanders—at each step he
    wider wanders—
Now he pauses—now he ponders where his present
    path may lead ;
And, as he round is gazing, he sees—a sight amazing!—
Beneath him, calmly grazing, a noble jet-black steed.
"Now, Heaven be praised !" cried Maurice, "for this
    succour in my need—
       From this labyrinth I'm freed !"

Upon its back he leapeth, but a shudder through him
 creepeth,
As the mighty monster sweepeth like a torrent through
 the dell;
His mane, so softly flowing, is now a meteor
 blowing,
And his burning eyes are glowing with the light of an
 inward hell—
And the red breath of his nostrils, like steam where
 the lightning fell,
   And his hoofs have a thunder knell!

What words have we for painting the momentary
 fainting
That the rider's heart is tainting, as decay doth taint
 a corse?
But who will stoop to chiding, in a fancied courage
 priding,
When we know that he is riding the fearful Phooka
 Horse?
Ah! his heart beats quick and faster than the smit-
 ings of remorse
   As he sweepeth through the wild grass
 and gorse!

As the avalanche comes crashing, 'mid the scattered
 streamlets splashing,
Thus backward wildly dashing, flew the horse through
 Céim-an-eich—
Through that glen so wild and narrow, back he darted
 like an arrow—
Round, round by Gougane Barra, and the fountains
 of the Lee,
O'er the Giant's Grave he leapeth, and he seems to
 own in fee
   The mountains and the rivers and the
 sea!

From his flashing hoofs who *shall* lock the eagle homes of Malloc,*
When he bounds, as bounds the Miallucn† in its wild and murmuring tide?
But as winter leadeth Flora, or the night leads on Aurora,
Or as shines green Glashenglora‡ along the black hill's side—
Thus, beside that demon monster, white and gentle as a bride,
      A tender fawn is seen to glide.

It is the fawn that fled him, and that late to Alice led him—
But now it does not dread him, as it feigned to do before,
When down the mountain gliding, in that sheltered meadow hiding—
It left his heart abiding by wild Glengariff's shore—
For it was a gentle Fairy who the fawn's light form wore,
      And who watched sweet Alice o'er.

But the steed is backward prancing where late it was advancing,
And his flashing eyes are glancing, like the sun upon Loch Foyle—
The hardest granite crushing, through the thickest brambles brushing—
Now like a shadow rushing up the sides of Slieve-na-goil!§
And the fawn beside him gliding o'er the rough and broken soil,
      Without fear and without toil.

---

* "Wildly from Malloc the eagles are screaming."—*Callanan's Gougane Barra.*

† Mialloch, "the murmuring river" at Glengariff.—*Smith's Cork.*

‡ Glashenglora, a mountain torrent, which finds its way into the Atlantic Ocean through Glengariff, in the west of the county of Cork. The name, literally translated, signifies the "the noisy green water."—*Barry's Songs of Ireland,* p. 173.

§ The most remarkable and beautiful mountain at Glengariff is the noble conical one, whose ancient name is *Sliabh-na-goil* ("the mountain of the wild people"). The common-place epithet of "Sugar Loaf" has here, as elsewhere, unworthily usurped the fine old musical names which our ancestors gave to their hills.

Through woods, the sweet birds' leaf home, he rusheth
   to the sea foam—
Long, long the fairies' chief home, when the summer
   nights are cool,
And the blue sea like a Syren, with its waves the
   steed environ,
Which hiss like furnace iron when plunged within a
   pool,
Then along among the islands where the water-
   nymphs bear rule,
      Through the bay to Adragool.

Now he rises o'er Bearhaven, where he hangeth like a
   raven—
Ah! Maurice, though no craven, how terrible for thee?
To see the misty shading of the mighty mountains
   fading,
And thy winged fire-steed wading through the clouds
   as through a sea!
Now he feels the earth beneath him—he is loosen'd—
   he is free,
      And asleep in Céim-an-eich.

Away the wild steed leapeth, while his rider calmly
   sleepeth
Beneath a rock which keepeth the entrance to the
   glen,
Which standeth like a castle, where are dwelling lord
   and vassal,
Where within are wine and wassail, and without are
   warrior men—
But save the sleeping Maurice, this castle cliff had
   then
      No mortal denizen!*

Now Maurice is awaking, for the solid earth is shaking
And a sunny light is breaking through the slowly
   opening stone—

---

* There is a great square rock, literally resembling the description in the text, which stands near the Glengariff entrance to the pass of Céim-an eich.

And a fair page at the portal, crieth, "Welcome welcome! mortal,
Leave thy world (at best a short ill), for the pleasant world we own—
There are joys by thee untasted, there are glories yet unknown—
  Come kneel at Una's throne."

With a sullen sound of thunder, the great rock falls asunder,
He looks around in wonder, and with ravishment awhile—
For the air his sense is chaining, with as exquisite a paining,
As when summer clouds are raining o'er a flowery Indian isle—
And the faces that surround him, oh! how exquisite their smile,
  So free of mortal care and guile.

These forms, oh! they are finer—these faces are diviner
Than Phidias even thine are, with all thy magic art;
For beyond an artist's guessing, and beyond a bard's expressing,
Is the face that truth is dressing with the feelings of the heart;
Two worlds are there together—Earth and Heaven have each a part—
  And such, divinest Una, thou art!

And then the dazzling lustre of the hall in which they muster—
Where brightest diamonds cluster on the flashing walls around;
And the flying and advancing, and the sighing and the glancing,
And the music and the dancing on the flower-inwoven ground,
And the laughing and the feasting, and the quaffing and the sound,
  In which their voices all are drowned.

But the murmur now is hushing—there's a pushing
    and a rushing,
There's a crowding and a crushing, through that
    golden, fairy place,
Where a snowy veil is lifting, like the slow and silent
    shifting
Of a shining vapour drifting across the moon's pale
    face—
For there sits gentle Una, fairest queen of fairy race,
      In her beauty, and her majesty and grace.

The moon by stars attended, on her pearly throne
    ascended,
Is not more purely splendid than this fairy-girted
    queen;
And when her lips had spoken, 'mid the charmed
    silence broken,
You'd think you had awoken in some bright Elysian
    scene;
For her voice than the lark's was sweeter, that sings
    in joy between
      The heavens and the meadows green.

But her cheeks—ah! what are roses,—what are clouds
    where eve reposes,—
What are hues that dawn discloses,—to the blushes
    spreading there?
And what the sparkling motion of a star within the
    ocean,
To the crystal soft emotion that her lustrous dark eyes
    wear?
And the tresses of a moonless and a starless night are
    fair
      To the blackness of her raven hair.

"Ah! Mortal, hearts have panted for what to thee is
    granted—
To see the halls enchanted of the spirit world revealed;
And yet no glimpse assuages the feverish doubt that
    rages

In the hearts of bards and sages wherewith they may
 be healed ;
For this have pilgrims wandered—for this have vota-
 ries kneeled—
 For this, too, has blood bedewed the field.

"And now that thou beholdest, what the wisest and
 the oldest,
What the bravest and the boldest, have never yet
 descried—
Wilt thou come and share our being, be a part of what
 thou'rt seeing,
And flee as we are fleeing, through the boundless
 ether wide?
Or along the silver ocean, or down deep where pearls
 hide?
 And I, who am a queen, will be thy bride.

"As an essence thou wilt enter the world's mysterious
 centre"—
And then the fairy bent her, imploring to the youth—
"Thou'lt be free of death's cold ghastness, and, with
 a comet's fastness,
Thou canst wander through the vastness to the Para-
 dise of Truth,
Each day a new joy bringing, which will never leave,
 in sooth,
 The slightest stain of weariness and ruth."

As he listened to the speaker, his heart grew weak and
 weaker—
Ah! memory, go seek her, that maiden by the wave,
Who with terror and amazement is looking from her
 casement,
Where the billows at the basement of her nestled
 cottage rave
At the moon, which struggles onward through the
 tempest, like the brave,
 And which sinks within the clouds as in a
 grave.

All maidens will abhor us—and it's very painful for us
To tell how faithless Maurice forgot his plighted vow
He thinks not of the breaking of the heart he late was
    seeking—
He but listens to her speaking, and but gazes on her
    brow—
And his heart has all consented, and his lips are ready
    now
        With the awful, and irrevocable vow.

While the word is there abiding, lo! the crowd is now
    dividing,
And, with sweet and gentle gliding, in before him
    came a fawn;
It was the same that fled him, and that seemed so much
    to dread him,
When it down in triumph led him to Glengariff's grassy
    lawn,
When, from rock to rock descending, to sweet Alice
    he was drawn,
        As through Céim-an-eich he hunted from
        the dawn.

The magic chain is broken—no fairy vow is spoken—
From his trance he hath awoken, and once again is free;
And gone is Una's palace, and vain the wild steed's
    malice,
And again to gentle Alice down he wends through
    Céim-an-eich:
The moon is calmly shining over mountain, stream,
    and tree,
        And the yellow sea-plants glisten through
        the sea.

    *   *   *   *   *

The sun his gold is flinging, the happy birds are sing-
    ing,
And bells are gaily ringing along Glengariff's sea;
And crowds in many a galley to the happy marriage
    rally

Of the maiden of the valley and the youth of Céim-
    an-eich;
Old eyes with joy are weeping, as all ask on bended
    knee,
        A blessing, gentle Alice, upon thee!

THE FETCH.

BY JOHN BANIM.

[In Ireland, a Fetch is the supernatural *fac-simile* of some individual, who comes to insure to its original a happy longevity, or immediate dissolution. If seen in the morning, the one event is predicted; if in the evening, the other.—*Banim*.]

THE mother died when the child was born,
    And left me her baby to keep;
I rocked its cradle the night and morn,
    Or, silent, hung o'er it to weep.

'Twas a sickly child through its infancy,
    Its cheeks were so ashy pale;
Till it broke from my arms to walk in glee,
    Out in the sharp, fresh gale.

And then my little girl grew strong,
    And laughed the hours away;
Or sung me the merry lark's mountain song,
    Which he taught her at break of day.

When she wreathed her hair in thicket bowers,
    With the hedge-rose and harebell blue,
I called her my May, in her crown of flowers,
    And her smile so soft and new.

And the rose, I thought, never shamed her cheek,
    But rosy and rosier made it;
And her eye of blue did more brightly break,
    Through the bluebell that strove to shade it.

One evening I left her asleep in her smiles,
   And walked through the mountains lonely;
I was far from my darling, ah! many long miles,
   And I thought of her, and her only!

She darkened my path, like a troubled dream,
   In that solitude far and drear;
I spoke to my child! but she did not seem
   To hearken with human ear.

She only looked with a dead, dead eye,
   And a wan, wan cheek of sorrow:
I knew her Fetch!—she was called to die,
   And she died upon the morrow.

CUSHEEN LOO.

TRANSLATED FROM THE IRISH.
BY J. J. CALLANAN.

[This song is supposed to have been sung by a young bride, who was forcibly detained in one of those forts which are so common in Ireland, and to which the good people are very fond of resorting. Under pretence of hushing her child to rest, she retired to the outside margin of the fort, and addressed the burthen of her song to a young woman whom she saw at a short distance, and whom she requested to inform her husband of her condition, and to desire him to bring the steel knife to dissolve the enchantment.]

SLEEP, my child! for the rustling trees,
Stirr'd by the breath of summer breeze,
And fairy songs of sweetest note,
Around us gently float.

Sleep! for the weeping flowers have shed
Their fragrant tears upon thy head,
The voice of love hath sooth'd thy rest,
And thy pillow is a mother's breast.
                Sleep, my child!

Weary hath pass'd the time forlorn,
Since to your mansion I was borne,
Tho' bright the feast of its airy halls,
And the voice of mirth resounds from its walls.
                Sleep, my child!

Full many a maid and blooming bride
Within that splendid dome abide,—
And many a hoar and shrivell'd sage,
And many a matron bow'd with age.
     Sleep, my child!

Oh! thou who hearest this song of fear,
To the mourner's home these tidings bear.
Bid him bring the knife of the magic blade,
At whose lightning-flash the charm will fade
     Sleep, my child!

Haste! for to-morrow's sun will see
The hateful spell renewed for me;
Nor can I from that home depart,
Till life shall leave my withering heart.
     Sleep, my child!

Sleep, my child! for the rustling trees,
Stirr'd by the breath of summer breeze,
And fairy songs of sweetest note,
Around us gently float.

THE BURIAL.

BY THE REV. JAMES WILLS.

A FAINT breeze is playing with flowers on the hill,
The blue vault of summer is cloudless and still;
And the vale with the wild bloom of nature is gay,
But the far hills are breathing a sorrowful lay!

As winds on the *Clairseach's* sad chords when they stream,
As the voice of the dead on the mourner's dark dream!
Far away, far away, from grey distance it breaks,
First known to the breast by the sadness it wakes.

Now lower, now louder, and longer it mourns,—
Now faintly it falls, and now fitful returns;
Now near, and now nearer, it swells on the ear,
The wild *ululua*, the death-song is near!

With slow steps, sad burthen, and wild-uttered wail,
Maid, matron, and cotter wind up from the vale;
And loud lamentations salute the grey hill,
Where their fathers are sleeping, the silent and still!

Wild, wildly that wail ringeth back on the air,
From that lone place of tombs, as if spirits were there
O'er the silent, the still, and the cold they deplore,
They weep for the tearless, whose sorrows are o'er.

THE O'NEILL.

[Since this ballad was written, all necessary light has been thrown upon the character and exploits of AODH O'NEILL, by Mr. Mitchell in his most admirable and fearless life of that prince; and by the Rev. C. P. Meehan, in his important historical work on "*The Fate and Fortunes of O'Neill and O'Donel.*" To some of my readers, however, the original explanation given by the author of the ballad (in the *Belfast Magazine*) may be useful, and I therefore retain it with some abridgment. It is to the latter part of the tradition alluded to that this poem owes its origin. "Hugh O'Neill, representative and chief of the powerful family of that name, in the year 1587, accepted of a patent from Queen Elizabeth, creating him Earl of Tir-Owen; in the eyes of his kinsmen and followers this acceptance was an act of submission, and the title itself a degradation; The O'Neill being a royal name, and conferring on its holder kingly authority. The mark of favour bestowed by Elizabeth was held by the Earl until 1595, in the spring of which year he suddenly called an assembly of the chiefs of his country, formally renounced the act of submission, and resumed the original distinguished appellation of his forefathers—The O'Neill. The cause of this alteration in his conduct has been variously accounted for; but an old tradition, which is still current in the country where he flourished, attributes it wholly to the interference of a supernatural agent. After relating in a simple style what is stated above, it tells that for three nights previous to the calling of the assembly, the Banshee, or guardian spirit of the family, was heard in his castle of Dungannon, upbraiding him with his submission, conjuring him to throw off the odious epithet with which his enemies had branded him, rousing him to a sense of his danger by describing the sufferings of som of the neighbouring chiefs, charging him to arm, and promising him assistance."]

"CAN ought of glory or renown,
 "To thee from Saxon titles spring?
"Thy name a kingdom and a crown,
 "Tir-owen's chieftain, Ulster's King!"

These were the sounds that on thy ear,
 Tir-owen's startled Earl, arose,
That blanch'd thy altered cheek with fear,
 And from thy pillow chas'd repose.

In vain was clos'd that weary eye,
　In vain that prayer for peaceful sleep;
For still a viewless spirit nigh
　Broke forth in accents loud and deep:

"Can ought of glory or renown,
　"To thee from Saxon titles spring?
"Thy name a kingdom and a crown,
　"Tir-owen's chieftain, Ulster's king!

"Oft did thy eager youthful ear
　"Bend to the tale of Thomond's shame,*
"And, in thy pride of blood did swear
　"To hold with life thy glorious name!

"Yet thou didst leave thy native land,
　"For honours on a foreign shore,
"And for submission's purchas'd brand,
　"Barter'd the name thy fathers bore!

"Where are those fathers' glories gone?
　"The pride of ages that have been!
"While tamely bows their traitor son,
　"The vassal of a Saxon Queen:

"While still within a dungeon's walls,
　"Ardmira's fetter'd prince reclines,†
"While I'Maoile for her chieftain calls,‡
　"Who in a distant prison pines:

"While from that corse, yet reeking warm,
　"O'er his own fields the life-streams flow,

---

* In the reign of Henry the Eighth, the palace of Cluan-road, near Ennis, in the county of Clare, the magnificent mansion of the chief of the O'Briens, was burned to the ground by those of his own blood, in revenge for his having accepted of the comparatively degrading title of Earl of Thomond.

† O'Dogherty of Ardmir, who was seized and thrown into prison by the Lord Deputy Fitzwilliam.

‡ O'Toole of I'Maoile, father to the wife of O'Neill, also imprisoned by Fitzwilliam.

"Well may'st thou start! that mangled form
"Once was thy friend, MacMahon Roe.*

"Forget'st thou that a vessel came
"To Cineal's strand, in gaudy pride,
"Fraught with each store of valued name.
"That nature gave or art supplied:

"No voice to bid the youth beware,
"Of banquets by the Saxon spread;
"He tasted, and the treacherous snare
"Clos'd o'er the young O'Donnell's head.†

"Hopeless, desponding, still he lies,
"No aid his griefs to soothe or end;
"And oft in vain his languid eyes
"Turn bright'ning on his father's friend:

"Who was that friend?—a chief of power,
"The guardian of a kingdom's weal,
"Tir-owen's pride and Ulster's flower,
"A prince, a hero, THE O'NEILL!

"He, at whose war-horn's potent blast,
"Twice twenty chiefs in battle tried,
"Unsheath'd the sword in warlike haste,
"And rang'd their thousands on his side.

"But now he dreads the paths to tread,
"That lead to honours, power, and fame;
"And stands, each nobler feeling dead,
"Nameless, who own'd a monarch's name.

* Hugh Roe MacMahon, chief of Monaghan, who was tried before Fitzwilliam, by a jury of common soldiers, and butchered at his castle door.
† O'Donnell, son of the Chief of Tyrconnel, who was decoyed on board a vessel and carried prisoner to Dublin, where he was detained from his fourteenth until his twentieth year, when he made a desperate effort to escape, and succeeded.

"Shall Ardmir's prince for ever groan,
  "And I'Maoile's chief still fetter'd lie?
"None for MacMahon's blood atone?
  "Nought cheer O'Donnell's languid eye?

"To thee they turn, on thee they rest:
  "Release the chain'd, revenge the dead,
"Or soon the halls thy sires possess'd,
  "Shall echo to a stranger's tread!

"And in the sacred chair of stone, *
  "The base Ne Gaveloc† shalt thou see;
"Receive the name, the power, the throne,
  "That once was dear as life to thee!

"Arise! for on his native plains
  "His father's warriors marshall'd round,—
"O'Donnell, freed from Saxon chains,
  "Shall soon the signal trumpet sound:

"And soon, thy sacred cause to aid,
  "The brave O'Cahan,‡ at thy call,
"Shall brandish high the flaming blade,
  "That filled the grasp of Cuie-na-gall:

"Resume thy name, in arms arise,
  "Tear from thy breast the Saxon star,
"And let the coming midnight skies
  "Be crimson'd with thy fires of war!

"And bid around the echoing land
  "The war-horn raise thy vassal powers;
"And, once again, the Bloody Hand §
  "Waive on Dungannon's royal towers!"

* The chair of stone on which the chiefs of the O'Neills were solemnly invested with the power and titles of chief of Tir-owen, and paramount prince of Ulster.
† Hugh O'Nial, illegitimate son of John, formerly chief of Tir-owen, surnamed Ne Gaveloc, or the fettered, from his having been born during the captivity of his mother.
‡ O'Cahan of Cinachta, descended from the famous Cuie-na-gall, or the "Terror of the Stranger," who was celebrated for his exploits against the English.
§ The bloody hand is the crest of the name of O'Neill.

THE WAKE OF THE ABSENT.

BY GERALD GRIFFIN.

[It is a custom among the peasantry in some parts of Ireland, when any member of a family has been lost at sea (or in any other way which renders the performance of the customary funeral rite impossible), to celebrate the " wake," exactly in the same way, as if the corpse were actually present.]

THE dismal yew, and cypress tall,
    Waive o'er the churchyard lone,
Where rest our friends and fathers all,
    Beneath the funeral stone.
Unvexed in holy ground they sleep,
    Oh early lost! o'er thee
No sorrowing friend shall ever weep,
    Nor stranger bend the knee,
               mo Cuṁa! * lorn am I!
Hoarse dashing rolls the salt-sea wave,
Over our perished darling's grave—

The winds the sullen deep that tore,
    His death-song chanted loud,
The weeds that line the clifted shore
    Were all his burial shroud.
For friendly wail and holy dirge,
    And long lament of love,
Around him roared the angry surge,
    The curlew screamed above,
               mo Cuṁa! lorn am I
My grief would turn to rapture now,
Might I but touch that pallid brow.

The stream-born bubbles soonest burst
    That earliest left the source:
Buds earliest blown are faded first,
    In nature's wonted course!

* Mo Chuma –My grief, or, Woe is me!—ED.

With guarded pace her seasons creep,
  By slow decay expire;
The young above the aged weep,
  The son above the sire:

              Mo Cuṁa! lorn am I!
That death a backward course should hold,
To smite the young, and spare the old.

KATHLEEN'S FETCH.

[The Fetch is supposed to be the exact form and resemblance, as to air, stature, features, and dress, of a certain person, who is soon to depart this world. It is also supposed to appear to the particular friend of the doomed one, and to flit before him without any warning or intimation, but merely the mystery of the appearance at a place and time where and when the real being could not be or appear. It is most frequently thought to be seen when the fated object is about to die a sudden death by unforeseen means, and then it is said to be particularly disturbed and agitated in its motions. Unlike the superstition of the Banshee,* there is no accounting for the coming of this forerunner of death; there is no tracing it to any defined origin; but that it does come, a shadowy phantom of doom and terror, and often comes, is firmly believed by our peasantry, and many curious stories and circumstances are related to confirm the truth of the position.—AUTHOR'S NOTE.]

The reaper's weary task was done,
And down to repose sunk the autumn sun;
And the crimson clouds, in the rich-hued west,
Were folding like rose-leaves round his rest.
My heart was light, and I hummed a tune,
As I hied me home by the harvest moon;
And I bless'd her soft and tender ray,
That rose to lighten my lone pathway.

Then I thought on my Kathleen's winning smile,
(And I felt my heart grow sad the while,)
Of her cheek, like the fading rose-clouds glowing,
Of her hair, like the dying sun-light flowing;
And her words, like the song of a summer bird,
And her air and step, like the fawn's, when stirred
By the hunter's horn, as it boometh o'er
The woody glens of the steep Sliabh-mor.

        * Beanṡiḋe

The broad Lough Mask* beneath me lay,
Like a sheet of foam in the silver ray;
And its yellow shores were round it rolled,
As a gem enclosed by its fretted gold.
And there, where the old oaks mark the spot,
Arose my Kathleen's sheltered cot;
And I bounded on, for my hopes were high,
Though still at my heart rose the boding sigh.

The silver moon was veiled by a cloud,
And the darkness fell on my soul like a shroud;
And a figure in white was seen afar,
To flit on my path like a twinkling star.
I rushed, I ran,—'twas my Kathleen dear;
But why does she fly? has she aught to fear?
I called, but in vain—like the fleeting beam.
She melted away with the flowing stream.

I came to her father's cottage door,
But the sounds of wailing were on his floor;
And the keener's voice rose loud and wild,
And a mother bewailed her darling child.
My heart grew chill—I could not draw
The latch: I knew 'twas her Fetch I saw!
Yes, Kathleen, fair Kathleen, that sad night died,
The fond pulse of my soul, its hope, its pride.

THE DOOM OF THE MIRROR.

BY B. SIMMONS.

[The superstition, that whoever breaks a looking-glass is destined to misfortune, is widely entertained in Ireland. The little story related in these verses is not altogether imaginative.—AUTHOR'S NOTE.]

FAIR Judith Lee—a woful pair,
  Were steed and rider weary,
When, winding down from mountains bare,
  By crag and fastness dreary,

---

* A large and beautiful lake, bounded by the counties of Mayo and Galway.

I first beheld her—where the path
   Resigned its sterner traces
In a green depth of woods, like Wrath
   Subdued by Love's embraces.

By the oak-shadowed well she stood,
   Her rounded arms uplifted,
To bind the curls whose golden flood
   Had from its fillets drifted,—
Whilst stooping o'er the fount to fill
   The rustic urn beside her,
Her face to evening's beauty still
   Imparting beauty wider.

She told me of the road I missed—
   Gave me to drink—and even,
At parting, waived the hand she kissed,
   White as a star in heaven;
But never smiled—though prompt and warm
   I paid, in duteous phrases,
The tribute that so fair a form
   From minstrel ever raises.

The gladness murmured to her cheek,
   Unfolded not its roses—
That bluest morn will never break
   That in her eye reposes.
Some gentle woe, with dove-like wings,
   Had o'er her cast a shadow,
Soft as the sky of April flings
   Upon a vernal meadow.

In vain, with venial art to sound
   The springs of that affliction,
I hinted of my *craft*—renowned
   For omen and prediction:
In vain assuming mystic power,
   Her fortune to discover,
I guessed its golden items o'er,
   And closed them with—*a lover*

It failed for once—that final word—
  A maiden's brow to brighten,
The cloud within her soul unstirred,
  Refused to flash or lighten.
She felt and thanked the artifice,
  Beneath whose faint disguising
I would have prompted hope and peace,
  With accents sympathising

But no—she said (the while her face
  A summer-wave resembled,
Outsparkling from some leafy place,
  Then back to darkness trembled)—
For her was neither living hope
  Nor loving heart allotted,
Joy had but drawn her horoscope
  For Sorrow's hand to blot it.

Her words made silvery stop—for lo!
  Peals of sweet laughter ringing!
And through that wood's green solitudes
  Glad village-damsels winging!
As though that mirth some feeling jarred,
  The maiden, pensive-hearted,
Murmured farewell, and through the dell
  In loneliness departed.

With breeze-tossed locks and gleaming feet,
  And store of slender pitchers,
O'er the dim lawns, like rushing fawns,
  Come the fair Water-fetchers;
And there, while round that well's grey oak
  Cluster'd the sudden glory,
Fair Judith Lee, from guileless lips
  I heard thy simple story.

Of humble lot—the legends wild
  Believed by that condition,
Had mingled with her spirit mild
  Their haunting superstition.

Which grew to grief, when o'er her youth
    The doom descended, spoken
On those who see beneath their touch
    The fatal Mirror broken.

"NEVER IN LIFE TO PROSPER MORE."
    And so, from life sequestered,
With dim forebodings brooding o'er
    The shafted fate that festered
Deep in the white depths of her soul,
    The patient girl awaited
Ill's viewless train—her days to pain
    And duty consecrated.

At times she deemed the coming woe
    Through others' hearts would reach her,
Till every tie that twined her low,
    Upon the lap of Nature.
Her once-loved head unwatched, unknown
    Should sink in meek dejection,
Hushed as some Quiet carved in stone
    Above entombed affection.

E'en her young heart's instinctive want
    To be beloved and loving,
Inexorably vigilant,
    She checked with cold reproving.
For still she saw, should tempests frown,
    That treacherous anchor sever,
And Hope's whole priceless freight go down
    A shipwrecked thing for ever.

So pined that gracious form away,
    Her bliss-fraught life untasted;
A breeze-harp whose divinest voice
    On lonely winds is wasted.
And such the tale to me conveyed
    In laughing tones or lowly,
As still that rosy crowd was swayed
    By mirth or melancholy.

I've seen since then the churchyard nook
  Where Judith Lee lies sleeping;
The wild ash loves it, and a brook
  Through emerald mosses creeping,
For that lost maiden ever there
  A low sweet mass is singing,
While all around, like nuns at prayer,
  Pale water-flowers are springing.

Poor Girl! I've thought, as there reclined
  I drank the sunset's glory—
Thy tale to meditative mind
  Is but an allegory;
Once shatter *inborn Truth* divine,
  The soul's transparent mirror,
Where Heaven's reflection loved to shine,
  And what remains but terror?

Terror and Woe;—Faith's holy face
  No more our hearts relieving—
Fades from the past each early grace
  The future brings but grieving;
However fast life's blessings fall
  In lavish sunshine o'er us,
That Broken Glass distorts them all
  Whose fragments glare before us.

THE FAIRY NURSE.

BY EDWARD WALSH.

SWEET babe! a golden cradle holds thee,
And soft the snow-white fleece enfolds thee;
In airy bower I'll watch thy sleeping,
Where branchy trees to the breeze are sweeping.
      Shuheen, sho, lulo lo!

When mothers languish broken-hearted,
When young wives are from husbands parted,
Ah! little think the keeners lonely,
They weep some time-worn fairy only.
      Shuheen sho, lulo lo!

Within our magic halls of brightness,
Trips many a foot of snowy whiteness;
Stolen maidens, queens of fairy—
   And kings and chiefs a sluagh shee* airy.
         Shuheen sho, lulo lo!

Rest thee, babe! I love thee dearly,
And as thy mortal mother nearly;
Ours is the swiftest steed and proudest,
That moves where the tramp of the host is loudest.
         Shuheen sho, lulo lo!

Rest thee, babe! for soon thy slumbers
Shall flee at the magic koelshie's † numbers;
In airy bower I'll watch thy sleeping,
Where branchy trees to the breeze are sweeping.
         Shuheen sho, lulo lo!

EARL DESMOND AND THE BANSHEE.‡

Now cheer thee on, my gallant steed,
   There's a weary way before us—
Across the mountain swiftly speed,
   For the storm is gathering o'er us.

Away, away, the horseman rides;
   His bounding steed's dark form
Seem'd o'er the soft black moss to glide—
   A spirit of the storm!

Now, rolling in the troubled sky,
   The thunder's loudly crashing;
And through the dark clouds driving by,
   The moon's pale light is flashing.

In sheets of foam the mountain flood
   Comes roaring down the glen;
On the steep bank one moment stood
   The horse and rider then.

* Sluaġ Sıa.   † Coel Sıa.   ‡ beanṡiġe.

One desperate bound the courser gave,
  And plunged into the stream;
And snorting, stemm'd the boiling wave,
  By the lightning's quivering gleam.

The flood is pass'd—the bank is gain'd—
  Away with headlong speed;
A fleeter horse than Desmond rein'd
  Ne'er served at lover's need.

His scatter'd train, in eager haste,
  Far, far behind him ride;
Alone he's crossed the mountain waste,
  To meet his promised bride.

The clouds across the moon's dim form
  Are fast and faster sailing,
And sounds are heard on the sweeping storm
  Of wild unearthly wailing.

At first low moanings seem'd to die
  Away, and faintly languish;
Then swell into the piercing cry
  Of deep, heart-bursting anguish.

Beneath an oak, whose branches bare
  Were crashing in the storm,
With wringing hands and streaming hair,
  There sat a female form.

To pass that oak in vain he tried;
  His steed refus'd to stir,
Though furious 'gainst his panting side
  Was struck the bloody spur.

The moon, by driving clouds o'ercast,
  Withheld its fitful gleam;
And louder than the tempest blast
  Was heard the banshee's scream.

And when the moon unveiled once more,
　　And show'd her paly light,
Then nought was seen save the branches hoar
　　Of the oak-tree's blasted might.

That shrieking form had vanishéd
　　From out that lonely place ;
And, like a dreamy vision, fled,
　　Nor left one single trace.

Earl Desmond gazed—his bosom swell'd
　　With grief and sad foreboding ;
Then on his fiery way he held,
　　His courser madly goading.

For well that wailing voice he knew,
　　And onward hurrying fast,
O'er hills and dales impetuous flew,
　　And reach'd his home at last.

Beneath his wearied courser's hoof
　　The trembling drawbridge clangs,
And Desmond sees his own good roof,
　　But darkness o'er it hangs.

He pass'd beneath the gloomy gate,
　　No guiding tapers burn ;
No vassals in the court-yard wait,
　　To welcome his return.

The hearth is cold in the lonely hall,
　　No banquet decks the board ;
No page stands ready at the call,
　　To 'tend his wearied lord.

But all within is dark and drear,
　　No sights or sounds of gladness—
Nought broke the stillness on the ear
　　Save a sudden burst of sadness.

Then slowly swell'd the keener's strain
   With loud lament and weeping,
For round a corse a mournful train
   The sad death-watch were keeping.

Aghast he stood, bereft of power,
   Hope's fairy visions fled ;
His fears confirmed ; his beauteous flower—
   His fair-hair'd bride was dead !

THE BRIDAL WAKE.

BY GERALD GRIFFIN.

THE priest stood at the marriage board,
   The marriage cake was made,
With meat the marriage chest was stored,
   Decked was the marriage bed.
The old man sat beside the fire,
   The mother sat by him,
The white bride was in gay attire,
   But her dark eye was dim.
                Ululah ! Ululah !
The night falls quick, the sun is set,
Her love is on the water yet.

I saw a red cloud in the west,
   Against the morning light,
Heaven shield the youth that she loves best
   From evil chance to-night.
The door flings wide ! loud moans the gale,
   Wild fear her bosom fills,
It is, it is the Banshee's wail !
   Over the darkened hills.
                Ululah ! Ululah !
The day is past ! the night is dark !
The waves are mounting round his bark.

The guests sit round the bridal bed,
   And break the bridal cake;
But they sit by the dead man's head,
   And hold his wedding wake.
The bride is praying in her room,
   The place is silent all!
A fearful call! a sudden doom!
   Bridal and funeral.
                     Ululah! Ululah!
A youth to Kilfiehera 's* ta'en,
That never will return again.

THE KEEN.†

BY CROFTON CROKER.

MAIDENS, sing no more in gladness
   To your merry spinning-wheels,
Join the keener's voice of sadness—
   Feel for what a mother feels!

See the space within my dwelling—
   'Tis the cold, blank space of death;
'Twas the Banshee's‡ voice came swelling
   Slowly o'er the midnight heath.

Keeners, let your song not falter—
   He was as the hawthorn fair.
Lowly at the Virgin's altar
   Will his mother kneel in prayer.

Prayer is good to calm the spirit,
   When the keen‡ is sweetly sung:
Death, though mortal flesh inherit,
   Why should age lament the young?

'Twas the Banshee's lonely wailing;—
   Well I knew the voice of death,
On the night-wind slowly sailing
   O'er the bleak and gloomy heath!

* The name of a churchyard near Kilkee.
† An Caoine.   ‡ beanṛiġe

THE SAGA OF KING OLAF OF NORWAY AND HIS DOG.

A.D. 1,000.

BY THOMAS D'ARCY M'GEE.

[Olaf Tryggvesson was king over all Norway from about A.D. 995 to A.D. 1,000. His Saga, the sixth in Snorro Sturleson's Heimskringla, is very curious and suggestive. Among other incidents it contains the episode which suggested this ballad. It may be remarked that the Chronicles of the North-men, of the several nations, throw much reflected light on our own more statistical annals. All through the 9th, 10th, and 11th centuries, that restless race frown along the back-ground of our history, filling us with the same awful interest we feel in watching the advance of one thunder-cloud towards another. They certainly destroyed many native materials for our early history, but in their own accounts of their expeditions into Ireland they have left us much we may use.]

[Of the Early Reign of King Olaf, surnamed Tryggvesson.]

KING OLAFF, Harald Haarfager's heir, at last had reached the throne,
Though his mother bore him in the wilds by a mountain lakelet lone ;
Through many a land and danger to his right the king had past,
Uprearing still thro' darkest days, as pines against the blast ;
Yet now, when peace smiled on his throne, he cast his thoughts afar,
And sailed from out the Baltic Sea in search of western war—
His galley was that "Sea-Serpent" renowned in Sagas old,
His banner bore two ravens grim—his green mail gleamed with gold—
The king's ship and the king himself were glorious to behold.

[Of the Sea King's manner of Life.]

King Olaf was a rover true, his throne was in his barque,
The blue sea was his royal bath, stars gemm'd his curtains dark ·

The red Sun woke him in the morn, and sailed he e'er
    so far,
The untired courier of his way was the ancient Polar
    star.
't seemed as though the very winds, the clouds, the
    tides, and waves,
Like the sea-side smiths and vikings, were his lieges
    and his slaves.
His premier was a pilot old, of bronzed cheek and
    falcon eye,
A man, albeit who well loved life, yet nothing fear'd
    to die,
Who little knew of crowns or courts, and less to crouch
    or lie.

[How king Olaf made a descent on Antrim, and carried off the herds
    thereof.]

Where Antrim's adamantine shore defies the northern
    deep,
O'er red bay's broad and buoyant breast, how swift
    the galleys sweep.
The moon is hidden in her height, the night clouds ye
    may see
Flitting, like ocean owlets, from the cavern'd shore set
    free.
The full tide slumbers by the cliffs a-weary of its toil.
The goat-herds and their flocks repose upon the upland
    soil:—
The sea-king slowly walks the shore unto his instincts
    true,
While up and down the valley'd land climbeth his
    corsair crew,
Noiseless as morning mist ascends, or falls the evening
    dew.

[The king is addressed by a clown, having a marvellous cunning dog in
    his company.]

Now looking to land, and now to sea, the king walked
    on his way,
Until the faint face of the morn gleam'd on the dark-
    some bay :

A noble herd of captured kine rank round its ebb-
    dried beach ;
The galleys fast received them in, when lo! with eager
    speech,
A clown comes headlong from the hills, begging his
    oxen three,
And two white-footed heifers, from the Sov'ran of the
    Sea.
His hurried prayer the king allowed as soon as it he
    heard.
The wolf-hound of the dauntless herd, obedient to his
    word,
Counts out and drives apart his five from the many-
    headed herd.

[King Olaf offereth to purchase the peasant's dog, who bestows it on him with a condition.]

" By Odin, King of Men!" marvelling, the Monarch
    spoke,
" I'll give thee, peasant, for thy dog, ten steers of better
    yoke
Than thine own five." The hearty peasant said :
" King of the Ships, the dog is thine ; yet if I must
    be paid,
Vow, by your raven banner, never again to sack
Our valley in the hours of night ; we dread no day
    attack."
More wondered the fierce Pagan still to hear a clown
    so say,
And mused he for a moment, as was his kingly way,
If that he should not carry both the man and dog
    away.

[King Olaf taketh the vow, and saileth from the shore with the dog.]

The sea-king to the clown made vow, and on his finger
    placed
An olden ring, the sceptred hand of his great sires had
    graced,
And round his neck he flung a chain of gold. pure
    from the mine.

Which, ere another moon, was laid upon St. Colomb's
    shrine.
Then with his dog he left the shore: his sails swell to
    the blast;
Poor "Vig" hath howled a mournful cry to the bright
    shore as they past.
Now brighter beamed the sunrise, and wider spread
    the tide;
Away, away to the Scottish shore the Danish galleys
    hied,
There, revelling with their kindred, six days they did
    abide.

[The treason of the Jombsburg Vikings calleth home the king.]

The seventh*, news came from Norway, the Vikings
    had rebelled,
Homeward, homeward, fast as fate, the royal sails are
    swelled.
Off Heligoland, Jarl Thorer, and Raud the witch they
    meet;
But a mystic wind bears the evil one, unharmed, far
    from the fleet.
Jarl Thorer to the land retreats, the fierce King follows
    on,
Slaying the Traitor's strange compeer, who fast and
    far doth run.
After him flung King Olaf, his never-missing spear;
But Thorer (he was named Hiort,† and swifter than
    the deer,)
In the distance took it up, and answered with a jeer

[Thorer Hiort treacherously killeth the King's Dog.]

The Wolf-Dog then the Monarch loosed, the Traitor
    trembled sore,
Vig holds him on the forest's verge, the King speeds
    from the shore.
Trembled yet more the Caitiff, to think what he should
    do,

* *The Seventh*, meaning the Seventh day.
† Literally, a Deer.

He drew his glaive, and with a blow, pierced his captor
    through ;
And when the King came to the place, his noble dog
    lay dead,
His red mouth foamy white, and his white breast crim-
    son red.
" God's curse upon you, Thorer"—'twas from the heart,
    I ween,
Of the grieved King this ban burst out beside the
    forest green.
——The Traitor vanished into the woods, and never
    again was seen.

[How King Olaf and his Dog were buried nigh unto each other, by the Sea.]

Two cairns rise by Drontheim-fiord, with two grey
    stones hard by,
Sculptured with Runic characters, plain to the lore-
    read eye,
And there the King and here his Dog from all their
    toils repose,
And over their cairns the salt sea wind night and day
    it blows ;
And close to these they point you the ribs of a galley's
    wreck,
With a forked tongue in the curling crest, and half of
    a scaly neck,
And some late sailing scalds have told that along the
    shore side grey
They have often heard a kindly voice and a huge
    hound's echoing bay,
And some have seen the Traitor to the pine woods
    running away.

KINCORA.

Lamentation of Mac Liag for Kincora.—A.D. 1015.

TRANSLATED FROM THE IRISH,

BY JAMES CLARENCE MANGAN.

[This poem is ascribed to the celebrated poet MAC LIAG, the secretary of the renowned monarch Brian Boru, who, as is well known, fell at the battle of Clontarf in 1014, and the subject of it is a lamentation for the fallen condition of Kincora, the palace of that monarch, consequent on his death.

The decease of MAC LIAG is recorded, in the "Annals of the Four Masters," as having taken place in 1015. A great number of his poems are still in existence, but none of them have obtained a popularity so widely extended as his "Lament."

Of the palace of Kincora, which was situated on the banks of the Shannon, near Killaloe, the mound and moat alone remain.]

OH, where, Kincora! is Brian the Great?
  And where is the beauty that once was thine?
Oh, where are the princes and nobles that sate
  At the feast in thy halls, and drank the red wine
          Where, oh, Kincora.

Oh, where, Kincora! are thy valorous lords?
  Oh, whither, thou Hospitable! are they gone?
Oh, where are the Dalcassians of the golden swords?†
  And where are the warriors Brian led on?
          Where, oh, Kincora?

And where is Morogh, the descendant of kings;
  The defeater of a hundred—the daringly brave—
Who set but slight store by jewels and rings;
  Who swam down the torrent and laughed at its wave?
          Where, oh, Kincora?

And where is Donogh, King Brian's son?
  And where is Conaing, the beautiful chief?
And Kian and Core? Alas! they are gone;
  They have left me this night alone with my grief!
          Left me, Kincora!

* Cincora.
† (*Colg-n-or*) or the Swords *of Gold, i.e.,* of the *Goldhilted* Swords.

And where are the chiefs with whom Brian went forth,
   The never-vanquished sons of Erin the brave,
The great King of Onaght, renowned for his worth,
   And the hosts of Baskinn from the western wave?
               Where, oh, Kincora?

Oh, where is Duvlann of the Swift-footed Steeds?
   And where is Kian, who was son of Molloy?
And where is King Lonergan, the fame of whose deeds
   In the red battle-field no time can destroy?
               Where, oh, Kincora?

And where is that youth of majestic height,
   The faith-keeping Prince of the Scots? Even he,
As wide as his fame was, as great as was his might,
   Was tributary, oh Kincora, to thee!
               Thee, oh, Kincora!

They are gone, those heroes of royal birth,
   Who plundered no churches, and broke no trust;
'Tis weary for me to be living on earth
   When they, oh Kincora, be low in the dust!
               Low, oh, Kincora!

Oh, never again will Princes appear,
   To rival the Dalcassians of the Cleaving Swords;
I can never dream of meeting afar or anear,
   In the east or the west, such heroes and lords!
               Never, Kincora!

Oh, dear are the images my memory calls up
   Of Brian Boru!—how he never would miss
To give me at the banquet the first bright cup!
   Ah! why did he heap on me honour like this?
               Why, oh, Kincora?

I am Mac Liag, and my home is on the Lake:
   Thither often, to that palace whose beauty is fled,
Came Brian, to ask me, and I went for his sake,
   Oh, my grief! that I should live, and Brian be dead
               Dead, oh, Kincora!

THE DEATH OF KING MAGNUS BAREFOOT.

A.D. 1102.

BY THOMAS D'ARCY M'GEE.

[King Magnus Barefoot became joint King of Norway with Hakon Itson, in 1093. But Hakon, in chasing a ptarmigan over the Dovre-d, caught an ague, of which he died. After this, Magnus reigned ne for ten years. In this time he made many voyages into the west, iquering all he attacked, whether in the Isles or on the Scottish or glish shores. In 1102 he was slain in Ulster by an Irish force, near ! sea shore. In Miss Brooke's "Reliques of Irish Poetry" is a transion of an Irish poem on this event, "the author of which," that lady serves, "is said to have belonged to the family of the O'Neills." This :m agrees with Sturleson as to the date of the fight and its result, but fers in the details. I have followed the latter for the facts of Magis's previous life, as well as for the immediate cause of his death. Is scarcely necessary to add that at this period the Danes were ristians, in doctrine, if not in practice.]

On the eve of St. Bartholomew off Uladh's shore we
    lay"
(Thus the importuned Scald began his tale of woe),
And faintly round our fleet fell the August evening
    gray,
And sadly the sunset winds did blow.

I stood beside our Monarch then—deep care was on
    his brow—
'I hear no horn,' he sighed ' from the shore:
hy tarry still my errand-men ?—'tis time they were
    here now,
And that to some less guarded coast we bore,'

Into the vernal west our errand-men had gone—
To Muirkeartach, the ally of the King
Those daughter late was wed to Earl Sigurd, his son)
The dower of the bridegroom to bring.

" 'Twas midnight in the firmament, ten thouand stars
    were there,
  And from the darksome sea looked up other ten,
I lay beside our Monarch, he was sleepless, and the
    care
  On his brow had grown gloomier then.

" As the sun awaking bright its beaming lustre shed,
  From his couch rose the King slowly up,
' Elldiarn, what !—thou awake ! I must landward go,'
    he said,
  And with you or the saints I shall sup.'

" The while the sun arose, in his galley thro' the fleet
  Our noble Magnus went, and the earls all awoke,
And each prepared for land—the late errand-men to
    meet,
  Or to free them from the Irish yoke.

" It was a noble army ascending the green hills,
  As ever kingly master led—
The memory of their marching my mournful bosom
    thrills,
  And my ears catch the echoes of their tread.

" Two hours had passed away, and I wandered on
    the strand,
  Loud cries from afar smote my ear ;
I climb'd the seaward mountain and look'd upon the
    land,
  Where, in sooth, I saw a sight of fear.

" As winter-rocks all jagged with the leafless arms of
    pines,
  Stood the Irish host of spears on their path—
As the winter streams down dash thro' the terrible
    ravines,
  So our men sought the shore white with wrath.

'The arrow flights, at intervals, were thicker o'er the
    field,
  Than the sea-birds o'er Jura's rocks,
While the banners in the darkness were lost—shield
    on shield
  Within it clashed in thunderous shocks.

" At last one hoarse *farrah* broke thro' the battle-cloud,
  Like the roar of a billow in a cave ;
And the darkness was uplifted like a plague city's
    shroud,
  And there lifeless lay our Monarch brave.

" And dead beside the King lay Earl Erling's son,
  And Erving, and Ulf, the free ;
And loud the Irish cried to see what they had done,
  But they could cry as loud as we.

" Oh ! Norway, Norway, wilt thou ever more behold
  A King, like thy last, in worth ?
Whose heart feared not the world—whose hands were
    full of gold,
  For the numberless Scalds of the North.

" Ah ! well do I remember how he swept the western
    seas
  Like the wind in its wintry mood—
How he reared young Sigurd's throne upon the Or-
    cades,
  And the Isles of the South subdued—

'In his galley o'er Cantire, how we bore him from
    the main—
  How Mona in a week he won ;
By him, how Chester's Earl in Anglesea was slain—
  Oh ! Norway, that his course is run !"

THE BATTLE OF KNOCKTUAGH.*

A.D. 1189.

BY THE AUTHOR OF "THE MONKS OF KILCREA."

[About this time (1189) the Anglo-Norman power in Ireland received a severe check by the death of Sir Armoricus Tristram, brother-in-law, and, after the chivalrous fashion of the day, sworn comrade of Sir John De Courcey. Having gone with a strong force to Connaught on an expedition, he was attacked with a far superior army by Cathal O'Connor,† surnamed "The Red Handed," and slain, with all his followers.]

Close hemm'd by foes, in Ulster hills, within his
    castle pent,
For aid unto the west countrie Sir John De Courcey
    sent;
And, for the sake of knightly vow, and friendship old
    and tried,
He prayed that Sir Armor Tristram would to his
    rescue ride.

Then grieved full sore that noble knight, when he
    those tidings heard,
And deep a vow he made, with full many a holy
    word—
That, aid him Heaven and good St. Laurence, full
    vengeance should await
The knaves who did De Courcey wrong, and brought
    him to this strait.

And a goodly sight it was, o'er Clare-Galway's glassy
    plain,
To see the bold Sir Tristram pass, with all his gallant
    train:
For thirty knights came with him there, all kinsmen
    of his blood,
And seven score spears and ten, right valiant men
    and good.

* Cnoc-Tuaḋ, "The Hill of Axes," lies within a few miles of Galway.

† For an exquisite ballad on "Cathal O'Connor," see p. 104.

And clasping close, with sturdy arms, each horseman
    by the waist,
Behind each firm-fixed saddle there, a footman light
    was placed ;
And fast they spurred in sweeping trot, as if in utmost
    need,
Their harness ringing loudly round, and foam upon
    each steed.

They cross the stream—they reach the wood—the
    bending boughs give way,
And fling upon their waving plumes light showers of
    sparkling spray ;
But when they pass'd that leafy copse, and topp'd the
    hillock's crest,
Then jumped each footman down—each horseman
    laid his lance in rest.

For far and wide as eye could reach, a mighty host was
    seen
Of Irish kernes and gallowglass, with hobbelers
    between,
And proudly waving in the front fierce Cathal's stan
    dard flies,
With many more of Connaught's chiefs, and Desmond's
    tribes likewise.

Then to a knight Sir Tristram spake, with fearless eye
    and brow—
" Sir Hugolin, advance my flag, and do this errand
    now ;
Go, seek the leader of yon host, and greet him fair
    from me,
And ask, why thus, with armed men, he blocks my
    passage free ?"

Then stout Sir Hugolin prick'd forth, upon his gallant
    grey,
The banner in his good right hand, and thus aloud
    did say :—

"Ho! Irish chiefs! Sir Armor Tristram greets ye fair, by me,
And bids me ask, why thus in arms ye block his passage free?"

Then stept fierce Cathal to the front, his chieftains standing nigh :
"Proud stranger, take our answer back, and this our reason why :—
Our wolves are gaunt for lack of food—our eagles pine away,
And to glut them with your flesh, lo! we stop you here this day!"

'Now, gramercy for the thought!" calm Sir Hugolin replied.
And with a steadfast look and mien that wrathful chief he eyed :—
'Yet, should your wild birds covet not the dainty fare you name,
Then, by the rood, our Norman swords shall carve them better game!"

Then turned his horse, and back he rode unto the little band
That, halted on the hill, in firm and martial order stand ;
When told his tale, then divers knights began to counsel take,
How best they could their peril shun, and safe deliverance make.

"Against such odds, all human might is valueless!" they cried ;
"And better 'twere at once to turn, and thro' the thicket ride."
When, high o'er all, Sir Tristram spake, in accents bold and free :—
"Let all depart who fear to fight this battle out with me ;

"For never yet shall mortal say, I left him in his need,
Or brought him into danger's grasp—then trusted to my steed !
And, come what will, whate'er betide, let all depart who may,
I'll share my comrades' lot, and with them stand or fall this day !"

Then drooped with burning shame full many a knightly crest,
And nobler feelings answering swell'd throughout each throbbing breast ;
And stout Sir Hugolin spoke first :—" Whate'er our lot may be ;
Come weal, come woe, 'fore Heaven, we'll stand or fall this day with thee !"

Then from his horse Sir Tristram lit, and drew his shining blade,
And gazing on the noble beast, right mournfully he said :—
" Thro' many a bloody field thou hast borne me safe and well,
And never knight had truer friend than thou, fleet Roancelle !

"When wounded sore, and left for dead, on far Knockgara's plain,
No friendly aid or vassal near—yet, thou did'st still remain !
Close to thy master there thou mad'st thy rough and fearful bed,
And on thy side, that night, my steed, I laid my aching head !

" Yet now, my gallant horse, we part ! thy proud career is o'er,
And never shalt thou bound beneath an armed rider more."

He spoke, and kiss'd the blade—then pierced his
    charger's glossy side,
And madly plunging in the air, the noble courser
    died.

Then every horseman in his band, dismounting, did
    the same,
And in that company no steed alive was left, but twain;
On one there rode De Courcey's squire, who came
    from Ulster wild ;
Upon the other young Oswald sate, Sir Tristram's
    only child.

The father kiss'd his son, then spoke, while tears his
    eyelids fill :
" Good Hamo, take my boy, and spur with him to
    yonder hill ;
Go, watch from thence, till all is o'er ; then, north-
    ward haste in flight,
And say, that Tristram in his harness died, like a
    worthy knight."

Now pealed along the foeman's ranks a shrill and
    wild halloo !
While boldly back defiance loud the Norman bugles
    blew ;
And bounding up the hill, like hounds, at hunted
    quarry set,
The Irish kernes came fiercely on, and fiercely were
    they met.

Then rose the roar of battle loud—the shout—the
    cheer—the cry !
The clank of ringing steel, the gasping groans of those
    who die ;
Yet onward still the Norman band, right fearless cut
    their way,
As move the mowers o'er the sward upon a summer's
    day.

For round them there, like shorn grass the foe, in
    hundreds bleed ;
Yet, fast as e'er they fall, each side, do hundreds more
    succeed
With naked breasts, undaunted meet the spears of
    steel-clad men,
And sturdily, with axe and skein, repay their blows
    again.

Now, crushed with odds, their phalanx broke, each
    Norman fights alone,
And few are left throughout the field, and they are
    feeble grown ;
But, high o'er all, Sir Tristram's voice is like a trumpet
    heard,
And still, where'er he strikes, the foemen sink beneath
    his sword.

But once he raised his beaver up—alas ! it was to try
If Hamo and his boy yet tarried on the mountain
    nigh ;
When sharp an arrow from the foe, pierced right thro'
    his brain,
And sank the gallant knight a corpse upon the bloody
    plain.

Then failed the fight, for gathering round his lifeless
    body there,
The remnant of his gallant band fought fiercely in
    despair ;
And one by one they wounded fell—yet with their
    latest breath,
Their Norman war-cry shouted bold, then sank in silent
    death.

And thus Sir Tristram died; than whom no mortal
    knight could be
More brave in list or battle-field,—in banquet-hall
    more free ;

The flower of noble courtesy—of Norman peers the
    pride ;
Oh, not in Christendom's wide realms can be his loss
    supplied.

Sad tidings these to tell, in far Downpatrick's lofty
    towers,
And sadder news to bear to lone Ivora's silent bowers;
Yet shout ye not, ye Irish kernes—good cause have ye
    to rue ;
For a bloody fight and stern was the battle of Cnoc-
    ċuaḋ.

A VISION OF CONNAUGHT* IN THE THIRTEENTH CENTURY.

BY JAMES CLARENCE MANGAN.

"Et moi, j'ai ete aussi en Arcadie."—And I, I, too, have been a
 eamer.—*Inscription on a Painting by Poussin.*

    I WALKED entranced
        Through a land of morn ;
The sun, with wond'rous excess of light,
    Shone down and glanced
        Over seas of corn,
And lustrous gardens a-left and right.
    Even in the clime
        Of resplendent Spain
Beams no such sun upon such a land ;
    But it was the time,
        'Twas in the reign,
Of Cáhal Mór of the Wine-red Hand.†

---

* Conaċt.

† The Irish and Oriental poets both agree in attributing favourable or unfavourable weather and abundant or deficient harvests to the good or bad qualities of the reigning monarch. What the character of Cahal was will be seen below.—(MANGAN.)

Anon stood nigh
　　By my side a man
Of princely aspect and port sublime,
　　Him queried I,
　　"O, my Lord and Khan,*
What clime is this, and what golden time ?'
　　When he—" The clime
　　Is a clime to praise,
The clime is Erin's, the green and bland ;
　　And it is the time,
　　These be the days,
Of Cáhal Mór of the Wine-red Hand !"

Then I saw thrones,
　　And circling fires,
And a dome rose near me, as by a spell,
　　Whence flowed the tones
　　Of silver lyres,
And many voices in wreathéd swell ;
　　And their thrilling chime
　　Fell on mine ears
As the heavenly hymn of an angel-band—
　　"It is now the time,
　　These be the years,
Of Cáhal Mór of the Wine-red Hand !"

I sought the hall,
　　And, behold !—a change
From light to darkness, from joy to woe !
　　Kings, nobles, all,
　　Looked aghast and strange ;
The minstrel-group sate in dumbest show !
　　Had some great crime
　　Wrought this dread amaze,
This terror ? None seemed to understand !
　　'Twas then the time,
　　We were in the days,
Of Cáhal Mór of the Wine-red Hand.

* Identical with the Irish *Ceann*, Head, or Chief ; but I the rather gave him the Oriental title, as really fancying myself in one of the regions of Araby the Blest.—(MANGAN,)

I again walked forth;
  But lo! the sky
Showed fleckt with blood, and an alien sun
  Glared from the north,
  And there stood on high,
Amid his shorn beams, A SKELETON!*

It was by the stream
  Of the castled Maine,
One autumn eve, in the Teuton's land,
  That I dreamed this dream
  Of the time and reign
Of Cáhal Mór of the Wine-red Hand!

BATTLE OF CREDRAN.
A.D. 1257.
BY EDWARD WALSH.

[A brilliant battle was fought by Geoffrey O'Donnell, Lord of Tirconnell, against the Lord Justice of Ireland, Maurice Fitzgerald, and the English of Connaught, at Credran Cille, Roseede, in the territory of Carburry, north of Sligo, in defence of his principality. A fierce and terrible conflict took place, in which bodies were hacked, heroes disabled, and the strength of both sides exhausted. The men of Tirconnell maintained their ground, and completely overthrew the English forces in the engagement, and defeated them with great slaughter; but Geoffrey himself was severely wounded, having encountered in the fight Maurice Fitzgerald, in single combat, in which they mortally wounded each other.—*Annals of the Four Masters.*]

FROM the glens of his fathers O'Donnell comes forth,
With all Cinel-Conaill,† fierce septs of the North—
O'Boyle and O'Daly, O'Dugan, and they
That own, by the wild waves, O'Doherty's sway.

---

* "It was but natural that these portentous appearances should thus be exhibited on this occasion, for they were the heralds of a very great calamity that befel the Connacians in this year—namely, the death of Cathal of the Red Hand, son of Torlogh Mor of the Wine, and king of Connaught, a prince of most amiable qualities, and into whose heart GOD had infused more piety and goodness than into the hearts of any of his contemporaries."—*Annals of the Four Masters, A.D.* 1224.

† *Cinel-Conaill*—The descendants of Conall-Gulban, the son of Nial of the Nine Hostages, Monarch of Ireland in the fourth century. The principality was named Tir-Chonaile, or Tyrconnell, which included the county Donegal, and its chiefs were the O'Donnells.

Clan Connor, brave sons of the diadem'd Niall,
Has pour'd the tall clansmen from mountain and vale—
M'Sweeny's sharp axes, to battle oft bore,
Flash bright in the sun-light by high Dunamore.

Through Innis-Mac-Durin,* through Derry's dark brakes,
Glentocher of tempests, Sleibh-snacht of the lakes,
Bundoran of dark spells, Loch-Swilly's rich glen,
The red deer rush wild at the war-shout of men!

O! why through Tir-Chonaill, from Cuil-dubh's dark steep,
To Samer's† green border the fierce masses sweep,
Living torrents o'er-leaping their own river shore,
In the red sea of battle to mingle their roar?

Stretch thy vision far southward, and seek for reply
Where blaze of the hamlets glares red on the sky—
Where the shrieks of the hopeless rise high to their God,
Where the foot of the Sassanach spoiler has trod!

Sweeping on like a tempest, the Gall-Oglach‡ stern
Contends for the van with the swift-footed kern—
There's blood for that burning, and joy for that wail—
The avenger is hot on the spoiler's red trail!

The Saxon hath gather'd on Credran's far heights,
His groves of long lances, the flower of his knights—
His awful cross-bowmen, whose long iron hail
Finds, through Cota § and Sciath, the bare heart of the Gael!

The long lance is brittle—the mailèd ranks reel
Where the Gall-Oglach's axe hews the harness of steel,

---

* Districts in Donegal.
† *Samer*—The ancient name of Loch Earne.
‡ *Gall-Oglach, or Gallowglass*—The heavy-armed foot soldier. *Kern*, or *Ceithernach*—The light-armed soldier.
§ *Cota*—The saffron-dyed shirt of the kern, consisting of many yards of yellow linen thickly plaited. *Sciath*—The wicker shield, as its name imports.

And truer to its aim in the breast of a foeman,
Is the pike of a kern than the shaft of a bowman.

One prayer to St. Columb*—the battle-steel clashes—
The tide of fierce conflict tumultuously dashes ;
Surging onward, high-heaving its billow of blood,
While war-shout and death-groan swell high o'er the
    flood !

As meet the wild billows the deep-centr'd rock,
Met glorious Clan Conell the fierce Saxon's shock ;
As the wrath of the clouds flash'd the axe of Clan-
    Conell,
Till the Saxon lay strewn 'neath the might of O'Donnell!

One warrior alone holds the wide bloody field,
With barbed black charger and long lance and shield—
Grim, savage, and gory he meets their advance,
His broad shield up-lifting and crouching his lance.

Then forth to the van of that fierce rushing throng
Rode a chieftain of tall spear and battle-axe strong,
His bracca,† and geochal,‡ and cochal's§ red fold,
And war-horse's housings, were radiant in gold !

Say who is this chief spurring forth to the fray,
The wave of whose spear holds yon armed array ?
And he who stands scorning the thousands that sweep,
An army of wolves over shepherdless sheep ?

   * *St. Colum,* or *Colum-Cille, the dove of the Church*—The patron saint of Tyrconnell, descended from Conall Gulban.
   † *Bracca*—So called, from being striped with various colours, was the tight-fitting Iruis. It covered the ancles, legs, and thighs, rising as high as the loins, and fitted so tight to the limbs as to discover every muscle and motion of the parts which it covered.—*Walker on Dress of the Irish.*
   ‡ *Geochal*—The jacket made of gilded leather, and which was sometimes embroidered with silk.—*Ibid.*
   § *Cochal*—A sort of cloak with a large hanging collar of different colours. This garment reached to the middle of the thigh, and was fringed with a border like shagged hair, and being brought over the shoulders was fastened on the breast by a clasp, buckle, or brooch of silver or gold. In battle they wrapped the cochal several times round the left arm as a shield.—*Ibid.*

The shield of the nation, brave Geoffrey O'Donnell
(Clar-Fodhla's firm prop is the proud race of Conall),*
And Maurice Fitzgerald, the scorner of danger,
The scourge of the Gael, and the strength of the stranger.

The launch'd spear hath torn through target and mail—
The couch'd lance hath borne to his crupper the Gael—
The steeds driven backwards all helplessly reel;
But the lance that lies broken hath blood on its steel!

And now fierce O'Donnell thy battle-axe wield—
The broad-sword is shiver'd, and cloven the shield,
The keen steel sweeps grinding through proud crest
    and crown—
Clar-Fodla hath triumph'd—the Saxon is down!

THE BATTLE OF ARDNOCHER.

A.D. 1328.

BY THE AUTHOR OF "THE MONKS OF KILCREA."

[A.D. 1328, MacGeoghegan gave a great overthrow to the English, in which three thousand five hundred of them, together with the D'Altons, were slain.—*Annals of the Four Masters.*

This battle, in which the English forces met such tremendous defeat, was fought near Mullingar, on the day before the feast of St. Laurence—namely, the 9th August. The Irish clans were commanded by William MacGeoghegan, Lord of Kenil Feacha, in Westmeath, comprising the present baronies of Moycashel and Rathconrath. The English forces were commanded by Lord Thos. Butler, the Petits. Tuites, Nangles, Delemers, &c. The battle took place at the Hill of Ardnocher.—*Ibid*, p. 116.

On the eve of St. Laurence, at the cross of Glenfad,
Both of chieftains and bonaghts what a muster we had,
Thick as bees, round the heather, on the side of Slieve
    Bloom,
To the trysting they gather by the light of the moon.

---

* This is the translation of the first line of a poem of two hundred and forty-eight verses, written by Firgal og Mac-an-Bhaird on Dominick O'Donnell, in the year 1655. The original line is—
    "Gaibhle Fodhla fuil Chonaill."
      —*See O'Reilly's Account of Irish Writers.*

For the Butler from Ormond with a hosting he came,
And harried Moycashel with havoc and flame,
Not a hoof or a hayrick, nor corn blade to feed on,
Had he left in the wide land, right up to Dunbreedon.

Then gathered MacGeoghegan, the high prince of
  Donore,
With O'Connor from Croghan, and O'Dempsys *ga
  lore* ;*
And, my soul, how we shouted, as dash'd in with
  their men,
Bold MacCoghlan from Clara, O'Mulloy from the glen.

And not long did we loiter where the four *toghers*†
  met,
But his saddle each tightened, and his spurs closer
  set,
By the skylight that flashes all their red burnings
  back,
And by black gore and ashes fast the rievers we
  track.

'Till we came to Ardnocher, and its steep slope we gain,
And stretch'd there, beneath us, saw their host in the
  plain ;
And high shouted our leader ('twas the brave William
  Roe)—
"By the red hand of Nial, 'tis the Sassanach foe!"

"Now, low level your spears, grasp each battle-axe
  firm,
And for God and our Ladye strike ye downright and
  stern ;
For our homes and our altars charge ye steadfast and
  true,
And our watchword be vengeance, and *Lamh Dearg
  A boo* !"‡

* ᵹo Leoṅ (in abundance).   † coċaṗṙ (roads).
‡ Láṁ Ḋeaṙᵹ aḃu (the red hand for ever).

Oh, then down like a torrent with a *farrah* we swept,
And full stout was the Saxon who his saddle-tree kept;
For we dash'd thro' their horsemen till they reel'd from the stroke,
And their spears, like dry twigs, with our axes we broke.

With our plunder we found them, our fleet garrons and kine,
And each chalice and cruet they had snatch'd from God's shrine.
But a red debt we paid them, the Sassanach raiders,
As we scatter'd their spearmen, slew chieftains and leaders.

In the Pale there is weeping and watchings in vain.
De Lacy and D'Alton, can ye reckon your slain?
Where's your chieftain, fierce Nangle? Has De Netterville fled?
Ask the Molingar eagles, whom their carcasses fed?

Ho! ye riders from Ormond, will ye brag in your hall,
How your lord was struck down with his mail'd knights and all?
Swim at midnight the Shannon, beard the wolf in his den,
Ere you ride to Moycashel on a foray again!

BATTLE OF TYRRELL'S-PASS.
1597.
BY THE AUTHOR OF "THE MONKS OF KILCREA."

[In the valuable notes to the *Annals of the Four Masters*, the following account of the battle of Tyrrell's-pass is given at page 621:—"The Captain Tyrrell mentioned in the Annals was Richard Tyrrell, a gentleman of the Anglo-Norman family of the Tyrrells, Lords of Fertullagh, in Westmeath. He was one of the most valiant and celebrated commanders of the Irish in the war against Elizabeth, and during a period of twelve years had many conflicts with the English forces in various parts of Ireland; he was particularly famous for bold and hazardous exploits, and rapid expeditions. Copious accounts of him are given by Fynes Morrison, MacGeoghegan, and others. After the reduction of Ireland he retired to Spain. The battle of Tyrrell's-pass is described by MacGeoghegan, and mentioned by Leland, and other historians. It was fought in the summer of 1597, at a place afterwards called Tyrrell's-pass, now the name of a town in the barony of Fertullagh, in the county of Westmeath. When Hugh O'Neill, Earl of Tyrone, heard that the English forces were preparing to advance into Ulster, under the Lord Deputy Borrough, he detached Captain Tyrrell at the head of 400 chosen men, to act in Meath and Leinster, and by thus engaging some of the English forces, to cause a diversion, and prevent their joining the Lord Deputy, or co-operate with Sir Conyers Clifford. The Anglo-Irish of Meath, to the number of 1,000 men, assembled under the banner of Barnwell, Baron of Trimleston, intending to proceed and join the Lord Deputy. Tyrrell was encamped with his small force in Fertullagh, and was joined by young O'Conor Faily of the King's County. The Baron of Trimleston, having heard where Tyrrell was posted, formed the project of taking him by surprise, and for that purpose despatched his son at the head of the assembled troops. Tyrrell having received information of their advance, immediately put himself in a posture of defence, and making a feint of flying before them as they advanced, drew them into a defile covered with trees, which place has since been called Tyrrell's-pass, and having detached half of his men, under the command of O'Conor, they were posted in ambush, in a hollow adjoining the road. When the English were passing, O'Conor and his men sallied out from their ambuscade, and with their drums and fifes played Tyrrell's march, which was the signal agreed upon for the attack. Tyrrell then rushed out on them in front, and the English being thus hemmed in on both sides were cut to pieces, the carnage being so great that out of their entire force only one soldier escaped, and, having fled through a marsh, carried the news to Mullingar. O'Conor displayed amazing valour, and being a man of great strength and activity, hewed down many of their men with his own hand; while the heroic Tyrrell, at the head of his men, repeatedly rushed into the thick of the battle. Young Barnwell being taken prisoner, his life was spared, but he was delivered to O'Neill. A curious circumstance is mentioned by MacGeoghegan, that from the heat and excessive action of the sword-arm the hand of O'Conor became so swelled that it could not be extricated from the guard of his sabre until the handle was cut through with a file."]

The Baron bold of Trimbleston hath gone in proud array,
To drive afar from fair Westmeath the Irish kerns away,
And there is mounting brisk of steeds and donning shirts of mail,
And spurring hard to Mullingar 'mong riders of the Pale.

For, flocking round his banner there, from east to west there came,
Full many knights and gentlemen of English blood and name,

All prompt to hate the Irish race, all spoilers of the land,
And mustered soon a thousand spears that Baron in his band.

For trooping in rode Nettervilles and D'Altons not a few,
And thick as reeds pranced Nugent's spears, a fierce and godless crew;
And Nagle's pennon flutters fair, and, pricking o'er the plain,
Dashed Tuite of Sonna's mail-clad men, and Dillon's from Glen Shane.

A goodly feast the Baron gave in Nagle's ancient hall,
And to his board he summons there his chiefs and captains all;
And round the red wine circles fast, with noisy boast and brag
How they would hunt the Irish kerns like any Cratloe stag.

But 'mid their glee a horseman spurr'd all breathless to the gate,
And from the warder there he crav'd to see Lord Barnwell straight;
And when he stept the castle hall, then cried the Baron, "Ho!
You are De Petit's body-squire, why stops your master so?"

"Sir Piers De Petit ne'er held back," that wounded man replied,
"When friend or foeman called him on, or there was need to ride;
But vainly now you lack him here, for, on the bloody sod,
The noble knight lies stark and stiff—his soul is with his God.

H

"For yesterday, in passing through Fertullah's wooded glen,
Fierce Tyrrell met my master's band, and slew the good knight then;
And, wounded sore with axe and *skian*, I barely 'scaped with life,
To bear to you the dismal news, and warn you of the strife.

"MacGeoghegan's flag is on the hills! O'Reilly's up at Fore!
And all the chiefs have flown to arms, from Allen to Donore,
And as I rode by Granard's moat, right plainly might I see
O'Ferall's clans were sweeping down from distant Annalee."

Then started up young Barnwell there, all hot with Spanish wine—
"Revenge," he cries, "for Petit's death, and be that labour mine;
For, by the blessed rood I swear, when I Wat Tyrrell see,
I'll hunt to death the rebel bold, and hang him on a tree!"

Then rose a shout throughout the hall, that made the rafters ring,
And stirr'd o'er head the banners there, like aspen leaves in spring;
And vows were made, and wine-cups quaft, with proud and bitter scorn,
To hunt to death Fertullah's clans upon the coming morn.

These tidings unto Tyrrell came upon that self-same day,
Where, camped amid the hazel boughs, he at Lough Ennel lay.

"And they will hunt us so," he cried—" why, let them if they will ;
But first we'll teach them greenwood craft, to catch us, ere they kill."

And hot next morn the horsemen came, Young Barnwell at their head ;
But when they reached the calm lake banks, behold ! their prey was fled !
And loud they cursed, as wheeling round they left that tranquil shore,
And sought the wood of Garraclune, and searched it o'er and o'er.

And down the slopes, and o'er the fields, and up the steeps they strain,
And through Moylanna's trackless bog, where many steeds remain,
Till wearied all, at set of sun, they halt in sorry plight,
And on the heath, beside his steed, each horseman passed the night.

Next morn, while yet the white mists lay, all brooding on the hill,
Bold Tyrrell to his comrade spake, a friend in every ill—
"O'Conor, take ye ten score men, and speed ye to the dell,
Where winds the path to Kinnegad—you know that *togher* well.

"And couch ye close amid the heath, and blades of waving fern,
So glint of steel, or glimpse of man, no Saxon may discern,
Until ye hear my bugle blown, and up O'Conor, then,
And bid the drums strike Tyrrell's March, and charge ye with your men."

"Now, by his soul who sleeps at Cong," O'Conor proud replied,
"It grieves me sore before those dogs, to have my head to hide;
But lest, perchance, in scorn they might go brag it thro' the Pale,
I'll do my best that few shall live to carry round the tale."

The mist roll'd off, and "Gallants up!" young Barnwell loudly cries,
"By Bective's shrine, from off the hill, the rebel traitor flies;
Now mount ye all, fair gentlemen—lay bridle loose on mane,
And spur your steeds with rowels sharp—we'll catch him on the plain."

Then bounded to their saddles quick a thousand eager men,
And on they rushed in hot pursuit to Darra's wooded glen.
But gallants bold, tho' fair ye ride, here slacken speed ye may—
The chase is o'er!—the hunt is up!—the quarry stands at bay!

For halted on a gentle slope, bold Tyrrell placed his hand,
And proudly stept he to the front, his banner in his hand,
And plung'd it deep within the earth, all plainly in their view,
And waved aloft his trusty sword, and loud his bugle blew.

Saint Colman! 'twas a fearful sight, while drum and trumpet played,
To see the bound from out the brake that fierce O'Conor made,

As waving high his sword in air he smote the flaunt-
    ing crest
Of proud Sir Hugh De Geneville,* and clove him to
    the chest!

"On, comrades, on!" young Barnwell cries, "and
    spur ye to the plain,
Where we may best our lances use!" That counsel is
    in vain,
For down swept Tyrrell's gallant band, with shout
    and wild halloo,
And a hundred steeds are masterless since first his
    bugle blew!

From front to flank the Irish charge in battle order
    all,
While pent like sheep in shepherd's fold the Saxon
    riders fall;
Their lances long are little use, their numbers block
    the way,
And mad with pain their plunging steeds add terror
    to the fray!

And of the haughty host that rode that morning
    through the dell,
But one has 'scaped with life and limb his comrades'
    fate to tell;
The rest all in their harness died, amid the thickets
    there,
Yet fighting to the latest gasp, like foxes in a snare!

The Baron bold of Trimbleston has fled in sore dismay,
Like beaten hound at dead of night from Mullingar
    away,
While wild from Boyne to Brusna's banks there
    spreads a voice of wail,
Mavrone! the sky that night was red with burnings
    in the Pale!

* The De Genevilles succeeded the De Lacys as Lords of Meath

And late next day to Dublin town the dismal tidings came,
And Kevin's-Port and Watergate are lit with beacons twain,
And scouts spur out, and on the walls there stands a fearful crowd,
While high o'er all Saint Mary's bell tolls out alarums loud!

But far away beyond the Pale from Dunluce to Dunboy,
From every Irish hall and rath there bursts a shout of joy,
As eager Asklas hurry past o'er mountain, moor, and glen,
And tell in each the battle won by Tyrrell and his men,

Bold Walter sleeps in Spanish earth; long years have passed away—
Yet Tyrrell's-pass is called that spot, ay, to this very day,
And still is told as marvel strange, how from his swollen hand,
When ceased the fight the blacksmith filed O'Conor's trusty brand!

THE DEATH OF SCHOMBERG.
A.D. 1690.
BY DIGBY PILOT STARKEY, LL.D.,
Accountant-General, Court of Chancery.

["Frederick Schonberg, or Schomberg, first developed his warlike talents under the command of Henry and William II., of Orange; afterwards obtained several victories over the Spaniards; reinstated on the throne the house of Braganza; defeated in England the last hopes of the Stuarts; and finally died at the advanced age of eighty-two, at the battle of the Boyne, in 1690."]

'Twas on the day when kings did fight beside the Boyne's dark water,
And thunder roar'd from every height, and earth was red with slaughter,—

That morn an aged chieftain stood apart from mus-
    tering bands,
And, from a height that crown'd the flood, surveyed
    broad Erin's lands.

His hand upon his sword-hilt leant, his war-horse
    stood beside,
And anxiously his eyes were bent across the rolling
    tide :
He thought of what a changeful fate had borne him
    from the land
Where frown'd his father's castle-gate,* high o'er the
    Rhenish strand.

And plac'd before his opening view a realm where
    strangers bled,
Where he, a leader, scarcely knew the tongue of those
    he led!
He looked upon his chequered life, from boyhood's
    earliest time,
Through scenes of tumult and of strife, endur'd in
    every clime.

To where the snows of eighty years usurped the
    raven's stand,
And still the din was in his ears, the broadsword in
    his hand !
He turned him to futurity, beyond the battle plain,
But then a shadow from on high hung o'er the heaps
    of slain ;—

And through the darkness of the cloud, the chief's
    prophetic glance
Beheld, with winding-sheet and shroud, his fatal hour
    advance :

---

* Schonberg, or "the mount of beauty," is one of the most magnificent of the many now ruinous castles that overhang the Rhine. It had been the residence of the chiefs of a noble family of that name, which existed as far back as the time of Charlemagne, and of which the Duke of Schomberg was a member.

He quail'd not, as he felt him near th' inevitable
 stroke,
But, dashing off one rising tear, 'twas thus the old
 man spoke :

"God of my fathers ! death is nigh, my soul is not
 deceived—
My hour is come, and I would die the conqueror I
 have liv'd !
For thee, for freedom, have I stood—for both I fall to-
 day ;
Give me but victory for my blood, the price I gladly
 pay !

"Forbid the future to restore a Stuart's despot-gloom,
Or that, by freemen dreaded more, the tyranny of
 Rome !
From either curse, let Erin freed, as prosperous ages
 run,
Acknowledge what a glorious deed upon this day was
 done !"

He said : fate granted *half* his prayer. His steed he
 straight bestrode,
And fell, as on the routed rear of James's host he rode.
He sleeps in a cathedral's gloom,* amongst the mighty
 dead,
And frequent, o'er his hallow'd tomb, regardful pilgrims tread.
The other half, though fate deny, we'll strive for, one
 and all,
And William's—Schomberg's spirits nigh, we'll gain—
 or, fighting, fall !

1833.

* Christ Church, Dublin.

THE BATTLE OF THE BOYNE.

A.D. 1690.

BY COLONEL BLACKER.

It was upon a summer's morn, unclouded rose the sun,
And lightly o'er the waving corn their way the breezes won;
Sparkling beneath that orient beam, 'mid banks of verdure gay,
Its eastward course a silver stream held smilingly away.

A kingly host upon its side a monarch camp'd around,
Its southern upland far and wide their white pavilions crowned:
Not long that sky unclouded show'd, nor long beneath the ray
That gentle stream in silver flowed, to meet the newborn day.

Through yonder fairy-haunted glen, from out that dark ravine,*
Is heard the tread of marching men, the gleam of arms is seen;
And plashing forth in bright array along yon verdant banks,
All eager for the coming fray, are rang'd the martial ranks.

Peals the loud gun—its thunders boom the echoing vales along,
While curtain'd in its sulph'rous gloom moves on the gallant throng;
And foot and horse in mingled mass, regardless all of life,
With furious ardour onward pass to join the deadly strife.

* King William's Glen, near Townley Hall.

Nor strange that with such ardent flame each glowing
          heart beats high,
Their battle word was William's name, and " Death or
          Liberty !"
Then, Oldbridge, then thy peaceful bowers with sounds
          unwonted rang,
And Tredagh, 'mid thy distant towers, was heard th
          mighty clang ;

The silver stream is crimson'd wide, and clogg'd with
          many a corse,
As floating down its gentle tide come mingled man and
          horse.
Now fiercer grows the battle's rage, the guarded stream
          is cross'd,
And furious, hand to hand engage each bold contending
          host ;

He falls—the veteran hero falls,* renowned along the
          Rhine—
And *he* whose name, while Derry's walls endure, shall
          brightly shine.†
Oh ! would to heav'n that churchman bold, his arms
          with triumph blest,
The soldier spirit had controll'd that fir'd his pious
          breast.

And he, the chief of yonder brave and persecuted
          band,‡
Who foremost rush'd amid the wave, and gain'd the
          hostile strand :
He bleeds, brave Caillemote—he bleeds—'tis closed,
          his bright career,
Yet still that band to glorious deeds his dying accents
          cheer.

* Duke Schomberg.   † Walker, the gallant defender of Derry.
Caillemote, who commanded a regiment of Huguenots.

And now that well-contested strand successive columns gain,
While backward James's yielding band are borne across the plain.
In vain the sword green Erin draws, and life away doth fling—
Oh! worthy of a better cause and of a bolder king.

In vain thy bearing bold is shown upon that blood-stain'd ground;
Thy tow'ring hopes are overthrown, thy choicest fall around;
Nor, sham'd, abandon thou the fray, nor blush, though conquer'd there,
A power against thee fights to-day no mortal arm may dare.

Nay, look not to that distant height in hope of coming aid—
The dastard thence has ta'en his flight, and left his men betray'd.
Hurrah! hurrah! the victor shout is heard on high Dunore;
Down Platten's vale, in hurried rout, thy shatter'd masses pour.

But many a gallant spirit there retreats across the plain,
Who, change but kings, would gladly dare that battle-field again.*
Enough! enough! the victor cries; your fierce pursuit forbear,
Let grateful prayer to heaven arise, and vanquished freemen spare.

Hurrah! hurrah! for liberty, for her the sword we drew,
And dar'd the battle, while on high our Orange banners flew;

* This alludes to the expression attributed to Sarsfield—"Only change kings, and we will fight the battle over again."

Woe worth the hour—woe worth the state, when men
    shall cease to join
With grateful hearts to celebrate the glories of the
    Boyne!

THE RIVER BOYNE.

BY THOMAS D'ARCY M'GEE.

CHILD of Loch Ramor, gently seaward stealing,
In thy placid depths hast thou no feeling
    Of the stormy gusts of other days?
Does thy heart, oh, gentle nun-faced river,
Passing Schomberg's obelisk, not quiver,
    While the shadow on thy bosom weighs?

Thou hast heard the sounds of martial clangour,
Seen fraternal forces clash in anger,
    In thy Sabbath valley, River Boyne!
Here have ancient Ulster's hardy forces
Dressed their ranks and fed their travelled horses,
    Tara's hosting as they rode to join.

Forgettest thou that silent Summer morning,
When William's bugles sounded sudden warning,
    And James's answered, chivalrously clear!
When rank to rank gave the death-signal duly,
And volley answered volley quick and truly,
    And shouted mandates met the eager ear?

The thrush and linnet fled beyond the mountains,
The fish in Inver Colpa sought their fountains,
    The unchased deer scampered through Tredagh's*
    gates;
St. Mary's bells in their high places trembled,
And made a mournful music which resembled
    A hopeless prayer to the unpitying Fates.

    * Tredagh, now Drogheda.

Ah! well for Ireland had the battle ended
When James forsook what William well defended,
    Crown, friends, and kingly cause;
Well, if the peace thy bosom did recover
Had breathed its benediction broadly over
    Our race, and rites, and laws.

Not in thy depths, not in thy fount, Loch Ramor!
Were brewed the bitter strife and cruel clamour
    Our wisest long have mourned;
Foul Faction falsely made thy gentle current
To Christian ears a stream and name abhorrent,
    And all thy waters into poison turn'd.

But, as of old God's Prophet sweetened Mara,
Even so, blue bound of Ulster and of Tara,
    Thy waters to our Exodus give life;
Thrice holy hands thy lineal foes have wedded,
And healing olives in thy breast embedded,
    And banished far the littleness of strife.

Before thee we have made a solemn Fœdus,
And for Chief Witness called on Him who made us,
    Quenching before His eyes the brands of hate;
Our pact is made, for brotherhood and union,
For equal laws to class and to communion—
    Our wounds to staunch—our land to liberate.

Our trust is not in musket or in sabre—
Our faith is in the fruitfulness of labour,
    The soul-stirred, willing soil;
In Homes and granaries by justice guarded,
In fields from blighting winds and agents warded,
    In franchised skill and manumitted toil.

Grant us, O God, the soil, and sun, and seasons!
Avert Despair, the worst of moral treasons,
    Make vaunting words be vile.
Grant us, we pray, but wisdom, peace, and patience,
And we will yet re-lift among the nations
    Our fair and fallen but unforsaken Isle.

THE PILLAR TOWERS OF IRELAND.

BY DENIS FLORENCE MAC-CARTHY, M.R.I.A.

The pillar towers of Ireland, how wondrously they stand
By the lakes and rushing rivers through the valleys of our land;
In mystic file, through the isle, they lift their heads sublime,
These grey old pillar temples—these conquerors of time!

Beside these grey old pillars, how perishing and weak
The Roman's arch of triumph, and the temple of the Greek,
And the gold domes of Byzantium, and the pointed Gothic spires,
All are gone, one by one, but the temples of our sires!

The column, with its capital, is level with the dust,
And the proud halls of the mighty and the calm homes of the just;
For the proudest works of man, as certainly, but slower,
Pass like the grass at the sharp scythe of the mower!

But the grass grows again when in majesty and mirth,
On the wing of the Spring comes the Goddess of the Earth;
But for man in this world no spring-tide e'er returns
To the labours of his hands or the ashes of his urns!

Two favourites hath Time—the pyramids of Nile,
And the old mystic temples of our own dear isle;
As the breeze o'er the seas, where the halcyon has its nest,
Thus time o'er Egypt's tombs and the temples of the West!

The names of their founders have vanished in the
    gloom,
Like the dry branch in the fire or the body in the
    tomb;
But to-day, in the ray, their shadows still they cast—
These temples of forgotten gods—these relics of the
    past!

Around these walls have wandered the Briton and
    the Dane—
The captives of Armorica, the cavaliers of Spain—
Phœnician and Milesian, and the plundering Norman
    Peers—
And the swordsmen of brave Brian, and the chiefs of
    later years!

How many different rites have these grey old temples
    known?
To the mind what dreams are written in these
    chronicles of stone!
What terror and what error, what gleams of love and
    truth,
Have flashed from these walls since the world was in
    its youth?

Here blazed the sacred fire, and when the sun was
    gone,
As a star from afar to the traveller it shone;
And the warm blood of the victim have these grey old
    temples drunk,
And the death-song of the Druid and the matin of
    the Monk.

Here was placed the holy chalice that held the sacred
    wine,
And the gold cross from the altar, and the relics from
    the shrine,
And the mitre shining brighter with its diamonds
    than the East,
And the crozier of the Pontiff, and the vestments of
    the Priest!

Where blazed the sacred fire, rang out the vesper
    bell,—
Where the fugitive found shelter, became the hermit's
    cell ;
And hope hung out its symbol to the innocent and
    good,
For the Cross o'er the moss of the pointed summit
    stood !

There may it stand for ever, while this symbol doth
    impart
To the mind one glorious vision, or one proud throb
    to the heart ;
While the breast needeth rest may these grey old
    temples last,
Bright prophets of the future, as preachers of the past !

LAMENT OVER THE RUINS OF THE ABBEY OF TIMOLEAGUE.*

TRANSLATED FROM THE IRISH.

BY SAMUEL FERGUSON, LL.D., M.R.I.A.

LONE and weary as I wander'd by the bleak shore of
    the sea,
Meditating and reflecting on the world's hard destiny,
Forth the moon and stars 'gan glimmer, in the quiet
    tide beneath,
For on slumbering spring and blosom breathed not
    out of heaven a breath.

On I went in sad dejection, careless where my foot-
    steps bore,
Till a ruined church before me opened wide its ancient
    door,—

---

* Ceaċ Moloaġa. (*Teach Molaga.*)—" The House of St. Molaga".—
now called Timoleague, in Munster. Mangan has also translated this
poem very finely. According to him, the author was John O'Cullen a
native of Cork, who died in the year 1816 —ED.

Till I stood before the portals, where of old were wont to be,
For the blind, the halt, and leper, alms and hospitality.

Still the ancient seat was standing, built against the buttress grey,
Where the clergy used to welcome weary trav'llers on their way;
There I sat me down in sadness, 'neath my cheek I placed my hand,
Till the tears fell hot and briny down upon the grassy land.

There, I said in woful sorrow, weeping bitterly the while,
Was a time when joy and gladness reigned within this ruined pile;—
Was a time when bells were tinkling, clergy preaching peace abroad,
Psalms a-singing, music ringing praises to the mighty God.

Empty aisle, deserted chancel, tower tottering to your fall,
Many a storm since then has beaten on the grey head of your wall!
Many a bitter storm and tempest has your roof-tree turned away,
Since you first were formed a temple to the Lord of night and day.

Holy house of ivied gables, that were once the country's boast,
Houseless now in weary wandering are you scattered, saintly host;
Lone you are to-day, and dismal,—joyful psalms no more are heard,
Where, within your choir, her vesper screeches the cat-headed bird.

Ivy from your eaves is growing, nettles round your
    green hearthstone,
Winds howl where, in your corners, dropping waters
    make their moan.
Where the lark to early matins used your clergy forth
    to call,
There, alas! no tongue is stirring, save the daws upon
    the wall.

Refectory cold and empty, dormitory bleak and bare ;
Where are now your pious uses, simple bed and frugal
    fare ?
Gone your abbot, rule, and order, broken down your
    altar stones ;
Nought I see beneath your shelter, save a heap of
    clayey bones.

Oh! the hardship—oh! the hatred, tyranny, and cruel
    war,
Persecution and oppression that have left you as you
    are!
I myself once also prospered ;—mine is, too, an altered
    plight;
Trouble, care, and age have left me good for nought
    but grief to-night.

Gone, my motion and my vigour—gone, the use of eye
    and ear ;
At my feet lie friends and children, powerless and
    corrupting here;
Woe is written on my visage, in a nut my heart would
    lie—
Death's deliverance were welcome—Father, let the old
    man die.

AVONDHU.

BY J. J. CALLANAN.

[Avondhu—The Blackwater, Avunduff of Spenser. There are several rivers of this name in the counties of Cork and Kerry, but the one here mentioned is by far the most considerable. It rises in a mountain called Meenganine, in the latter county, and discharges itself into the sea at Youghal. For the length of its course, and the beauty and variety of scenery through which it flows, it is superior to any river in Munster.]

Oh, Avondhu, I wish I were
As once upon that mountain bare,
Where thy young waters laugh and shine
On the wild breast of Meenganine.
I wish I were by Cleada's* hill,
Or by Glenruachra's rushy rill;
But no! I never more shall view
Those scenes I loved by Avondhu.

Farewell, ye soft and purple streaks
Of evening on the beauteous Reeks;†
Farewell ye mists, that loved to ride
On Cahirbearna's stormy side.
Farewell, November's moaning breeze,
Wild minstrel of the dying trees:
Clara! a fond farewell to you,
No more we meet by Avondhu.

No more—but thou, O glorious hill,
Lift to the moon thy forehead still;
Flow on, flow on, thou dark swift river,
Upon thy free wild course for ever.
Exult young hearts in lifetime's spring,
And taste the joys pure love can bring;
But wanderer, go, they're not for you—
Farewell, farewell, sweet Avondhu.

* Cleada and Cahirbearna (the hill of the four gaps) form part of the chain of mountains which stretches westward from Millstreet to Killarney.
† Macgillicuddy's Reeks, in the neighbourhood of Killarney.

THE ROCK OF CASHEL.

BY THE REV. DR MURRAY.

FAIR was that eve, as if from earth away
    All trace of sin and sorrow
Passed, in the light of the eternal day,
    That knows nor night nor morrow.

The pale and shadowy mountains, in the dim
    And glowing distance piled !
A sea of light along the horizon's rim,
    Unbroken, undefiled !

Blue sky, and cloud, and grove, and hill, and glen,
    The form and face of man
Beamed with unwonted beauty, as if then
    New earth and heaven began.

Yet heavy grief was on me, and I gazed
    On thee through gushing tears,
Thou relic of a glory that once blazed
    So bright in bygone years !

Wreck of a ruin ! lovelier, holier far,
    Thy ghastly hues of death,
Than the cold forms of newer temples are—
    Shrines of a priestless faith.

In lust and rapine, treachery and blood,
    Its iron domes were built ;
Darkly they frown, where God's own altars stood,
    In hatred and in guilt.

But to make thee, of loving hearts the love,
    Was coined to living stone ;
Truth, peace, and piety together strove
    To form thee for their own.

And thou wast theirs, and they within thee met,
    And did thy presence fill;
And their sweet light, even while thine own is set,
    Hovers around thee still.

'Tis not work of mind, or hand, or eye,
    Builder's or sculptor's skill,
Thy site, thy beauty, or thy majesty—
    Not these my bosom thrill.

'Tis that a glorious monument thou art,
    Of the true faith of old,
When faith was one in all the nation's heart,
    Purer than purest gold.

A light, when darkness on the nations dwelt,
    In Erin found a home—
The mind of Greece, the warm heart of the Celt,
    The bravery of Rome.

But, O! the pearl, the gem, the glory of her youth,
    That shone upon her brow;
She clung for ever to the Chair of Truth—
    Clings to it now!

Love of my love, and temple of my God!
    How would I now clasp thee
Close to my heart, and, even as thou wast trod,
    So with thee trodden be!

O, for one hour a thousand years ago,
    Within thy precincts dim,
To hear the chant, in deep and measured flow,
    Of psalmody and hymn!

To see of priests the long and white array,
    Around thy silver shrines—
The people kneeling prostrate far away,
    In thick and chequer'd lines.

To see the Prince of Cashel o'er the rest,
    Their prelate and their king,
The sacred bread and chalice by him blest,
    Earth's holiest offering.

To hear, in piety's own Celtic tongue,
    The most heart-touching prayer
That fervent suppliants e'er was heard among,—
    O, to be then and there !

There was a time all this within thy walls
    Was felt, and heard, and seen ;
Faint image only now thy sight recals
    Of all that once hath been.

The creedless, heartless, murderous robber came,
    And never since that time
Round thy torn altars burned the sacred flame,
    Or rose the chant sublime.

Thy glory in a crimson tide went down,
    Beneath the cloven hoof—
Altar and priest, mitre, and cope, and crown,
    And choir, and arch, and roof.

O, but to see thee, when thou wilt rise again—
    For thou again wilt rise,
And with the splendours of thy second reign
    Dazzle a nation's eyes !

Children of those who made thee what thou wast,
    Shall lift thee from the tomb,
And clothe thee, for the spoiling of the past,
    In more celestial bloom.

And psalm, and hymn, and gold, and precious stones
    And gems beyond all price,
And priest, and altar, o'er the martyr's bones,
    And daily sacrifice.

And endless prayer, and crucifix, and shrine,
    And all religion's dower,
And thronging worshippers shall yet be thine—
    O, but to see that hour!

And who shall smite thee then?—and who shall see
    Thy second glory o'er?
When they who make thee free themselves are free,
    To fall no more.

LOCH INA.

A beautiful Salt-water Lake, in the County of Cork, near Baltimore.

I KNOW a lake where the cool waves break,
    And softly fall on the silver sand—
And no steps intrude on that solitude,
    And no voice, save mine, disturbs the strand.

And a mountain bold like a giant of old
    Turned to stone by some magic spell,
Uprears in might his misty height,
    And his craggy sides are wooded well.

In the midst doth smile a little Isle,
    And its verdure shames the emerald's green—
On its grassy side, in ruined pride,
    A castle of old is darkling seen.

On its lofty crest the wild crane's nest,
    In its halls the sheep good shelter find;
And the ivy shades where a hundred blades
    Were hung, when the owners in sleep reclined.

That chieftain of old could he now behold
    His lordly tower a shepherd's pen,
His corpse, long dead, from its narrow bed
    Would rise, with anger and shame again.

'Tis sweet to gaze when the sun's bright rays
   Are cooling themselves in the trembling wave —
But 'tis sweeter far when the evening star
   Shines like a smile at Friendship's grave.

There the hollow shells, through their wreathed cells,
   Make music on the silent shore,
As the summer breeze, through the distant trees,
   Murmurs in fragant breathings o'er.

And the sea-weed shines, like the hidden mines
   Of the fairy cities beneath the sea ;
And the wave-washed stones are bright as the thrones
   Of the ancient Kings of Araby.

If it were my lot in that fairy spot
   To live for ever, and dream 'twere mine,
Courts might woo, and kings pursue,
   Ere I would leave thee—Loved Loch-Ina.

THE RETURNED EXILE.

BY B. SIMMONS.

BLUE Corrin ! how softly the evening light goes,
Fading far o'er thy summit from ruby to rose,
As if loth to deprive the deep woodlands below
Of the love and the glory they drink in its glow :
Oh, home-looking Hill ! how beloved dost thou rise
Once more to my sight through the shadowy skies,
Watching still, in thy sheltering grandeur unfurled,
The landscape to me that so long was the world.
Fair evening—blest evening ! one moment delay
Till the tears of the Pilgrim are dried in thy ray—
Till he feels that through years of long absence, not one
Of his friends—the lone rock and grey ruin—is gone.
Not one :—as I wind the sheer fastnesses through,
The valley of boyhood is bright in my view !
Once again my glad spirit its fetterless flight

May wing through a sphere of unclouded delight,
O'er one maze of broad orchard, green meadow, and
    slope—
From whose tints I once pictured the pinions of hope ;
Still the hamlet gleams white—still the church yews
    are weeping,
Where the sleep of the peaceful my fathers are sleep-
    ing.
The vane tells, as usual, its fib from the mill,
But the wheel tumbles loudly and merrily still,
And the tower of the Roches stands lonely as ever,
With its grim shadow rusting the gold of the river.

My own pleasant River, bloom-skirted, behold,
Now sleeping in shade, now refulgently rolled,
Where long through the landscape it tranquilly flows,
Scarcely breaking, Glen-coorah, thy glorious repose !
By the Park's lovely pathways it lingers and shines,
Where the cushat's low call, and the murmur of pines,
And the lips of the lily seem wooing its stay
'Mid their odorous dells ;—but 'tis off and away,
Rushing out through the clustering oaks, in whose
    shade,
Like a bird in the branches, an arbour I made,
Where the blue eyes of Eve often closed o'er the book,
While I read of stout Sinbad, or voyaged with Cook.

Wild haunt of the Harper ! I stand by thy spring,
Whose waters of silver still sparkle and fling
Their wealth at my feet,—and I catch the deep glow,
As in long-vanished hours, of the lilacs that blow
By the low cottage porch—and the same crescent moon
That then ploughed, like a pinnace, the purple of June,
Is white on Glen-duff, and all blooms as unchanged
    As if years had not passed since thy greenwood I
    ranged—
As if ONE were not fled, who imparted a soul
Of divinest enchantment and grace to the whole,
Whose being was bright as that fair moon above,
And all deep and all pure as thy waters her love

Thou long-vanished Angel! whose faithfulness threw
O'er my gloomy existence one glorified hue!
Dost thou still, as of yore, when the evening grows dim,
And the blackbird by Downing is hushing its hymn,
Remember the bower by the Funcheon's blue side
Where the whispers were soft as the kiss of the tide?
Dost thou still think, with pity and peace on thy brow,
Of him who, toil-harassed and time-shaken now,
While the last light of day, like his hopes, has departed,
On the turf thou hast hallowed, sinks down weary-hearted,
And calls on thy name, and the night-breeze that sighs
Through the boughs that once blest thee is all that replies?

But thy summit, far Corrin, is fading in grey,
And the moonlight grows mellow on lonely Cloughlea;
And the laugh of the young, as they loiter about
Through the elm-shaded alleys, rings joyously out:
Happy souls! they have yet the dark chalice to taste,
And like others to wander life's desolate waste—
To hold wassail with sin, or keep vigil with woe;
But the same fount of yearning, wherever they go,
Welling up in their heart-depths, to turn at the last
(As the stag when the barb in his bosom is fast)
To their lair in the hills, on their childhood that rose
And find the sole blessing I seek for—REPOSE!

GLENFINISHK.*

BY JOSEPH O'LEARY.

GLENFINISHK! where thy waters mix with Araglen's wild tide,
'Tis sweet at hush of evening to wander by thy side!
'Tis sweet to hear the night-winds sigh along Macrona's wood,
And mingle their wild music with the murmur of thy flood!

* Glenfinishk (the glen of the fair waters), in the county of Cork.

Tis sweet, when in the deep-blue vault the morn is
    shining bright,
To watch where thy clear waters are breaking into light;
To mark the starry sparks that o'er thy smoother
    surface gleam,
As if some fairy hand were flinging diamonds on thy
    stream !

Oh ! if departed spirits e'er to this dark world return,
'Tis in some lonely, lovely spot like this they would
    sojourn ;
Whate'er their mystic rites may be, no human eye is
    here,
Save mine to mark their mystery—no human voice is
    near.

At such an hour, in such a scene, I could forget my
    birth—
I could forget I e'er have been, or am, a thing of earth ;
Shake off the fleshly bonds that hold my soul in thrall,
    and be,
Even like themselves, a spirit, as boundless and as free !

Ye shadowy race ! if we believe the tales of legends old,
Ye sometimes hold high converse with those of mortal
    mould :
Oh ! come, whilst now my soul is free, and bear me in
    your train,
Ne'er to return to misery and this dark world again !

THE MOUNTAIN FERN.

BY THE AUTHOR OF "THE MONKS OF KILCREA."

Oh, the Fern ! the Fern !—the Irish hill Fern !—
That girds our blue lakes from Lough Ine* to Lough
    Erne,
That waves on our crags, like the plume of a king,
And bends, like a nun, over clear well and spring!

---

* Lough Ine, a singularly romantic lake in the western mountains of Cork; of Lough Erne, I hope, to Irishmen it is unnecessary to speak.

The fairy's tall palm tree ! the heath-bird's fresh nest
And the couch the red deer deems the sweetest and best,
With the free winds to fan it, and dew-drops to gem,—
Oh, what can ye match with its beautiful stem ?
From the shrine of Saint Finbar, by lone Avonbuie,
To the halls of Dunluce, with its towers by the sea,
From the hill of Knockthu to the rath of Moyvore,
Like a chaplet it circles our green island o'er,—
In the bawn of the chief, by the anchorite's cell,
On the hill-top, or greenwood, by streamlet or well,
With a spell on each leaf, which no mortal can learn,*—
Oh, there never was plant like the Irish hill Fern !

Oh, the Fern ! the Fern !—the Irish hill Fern !—
That shelters the weary, or wild roe, or kern.
Thro' the glens of Kilcoe rose a shout on the gale,
As the Saxons rushed forth, in their wrath, from the
    Pale,
With bandog and blood-hound, all savage to see,
To hunt thro' Clunealla the wild Rapparee !
Hark ! a cry from yon dell on the startled ear rings,
And forth from the wood the young fugitive springs,
Thro' the copse, o'er the bog, and, oh, saints be his
    guide !
His fleet step now falters—there's blood on his side !
Yet onward he strains, climbs the cliff, fords the stream,
And sinks on the hill-top, mid brachen leaves green,
And thick o'er his brow are their fresh clusters piled,
And they cover his form, as a mother her child ;
And the Saxon is baffled !—they never discern
Where it shelters and saves him—the Irish hill Fern !

Oh, the Fern ! the Fern !—the Irish hill Fern !—
That pours a wild keen o'er the hero's grey cairn ;
Go, hear it at midnight, when stars are all out,
And the wind o'er the hill-side is moaning about,
With a rustle and stir, and a low wailing tone
That thrills thro' the heart with its whispering lone ;

---

* The fortunate discoverer of the fern seed is supposed to obtain the power of rendering himself invisible at pleasure.

And ponder its meaning, when haply you stray
Where the halls of the stranger in ruin decay.
With night owls for warders, the goshawk for guest,
And their dais* of honour by cattle-hoofs prest—
With its fosse choked with rushes, and spider-webs
    flung,
Over walls where the marchmen their red weapons
    hung,
With a curse on their name, and a sigh for the hour
That tarries so long—look ! what waves on the tower ?
With an omen and sign, and an augury stern,
'Tis the *Green Flag* of Time !—'tis the Irish hill Fern !

TO THE MEMORY OF FATHER PROUT.

BY DENIS FLORENCE MAC-CARTHY, M.R.I.A.

I.

In deep dejection, but with affection,
  I often think of those pleasant times,
In the days of Fraser,† ere I touched a razor,
  How I read and revell'd in thy racy rhymes,
When in wine and wassail, we to thee were vassal,
  Of Watergrass-hill, O renowned P.P.!
    May the bells of Shandon
    Toll blithe and bland on
The pleasant waters of thy memory !

II.

Full many a ditty, both wise and witty,
  In this social city have I heard since then—
(With the glass before me, how the dream comes o'er
    me,
  Of those Attic suppers, and those vanished men),

' The dais was an elevated portion of the great hall or dining-room, set part in feudal times for those of gentle blood, and was, in consequence, regarded with peculiar feelings of veneration and respect.
† " Fraser's Magazine " where the " Prout Papers " first appeared.

But no song hath woken, whether sung or spoken,
  Or hath left a token of such joy in me—
    As " The Bells of Shandon
    That sound so grand on
  The pleasant waters of the river Lee."

III.

The songs melodious, which—a new Harmodius—
  " Young Ireland" wreathed round its rebel sword,
With their deep vibrations and aspirations,
  Fling a glorious madness o'er the festive board;
But to me seems sweeter, with a tone completer,
  The melodious metre that we owe to thee—
    Of the Bells of Shandon
    That sound so grand on
  The pleasant waters of the river Lee.

IV.

There's a grave that rises o'er thy sward, Devizes,
  Where Moore lies sleeping from his land afar,*
And a white stone flashes over Goldsmith's ashes
  In the quiet cloisters by Temple Bar;
So where'er thou sleepest, with a love that's deepest,
  Shall thy land remember thy sweet song and thee,
    While the Bells of Shandon
    Shall sound so grand on
  The pleasant waters of the river Lee.

May 25, 1866.

* In Bromham churchyard, five miles south of Devizes. The spire of Bromham Church is seen from the front of Sloperton Cottage; and, indeed, from that point is the only building in view. Both cottage and tomb were visited by the writer of these lines on the 28th of May, 1867 Moore's birth-day. "Father Prout's" acquaintance he had the pleasure of making at Paris, in 1863

THOSE SHANDON BELLS.

BY DENIS FLORENCE MAC-CARTHY., M.R.I.A.

"The remains of the Rev. Francis Mahony have been laid in the family burial-place, in St. Anne Shandon Churchyard, the 'Bells,' which he has rendered famous, tolling the knell of the poet, who sang of their sweet chimes."

I.

Those Shandon bells! those Shandon bells!
Whose sweet sad tone now sobs, now swells—
Who comes to seek this hallowed ground,
And sleep within their sacred sound?

II.

'Tis one who heard these chimes when young,
And who in age their praises sung,
Within whose breast their music made
A dream of home where'er he strayed.

III.

And oh! if bells have power to-day,
To drive all evil things away,
Let doubt be dumb, and envy cease—
And round his grave reign holy peace.

IV.

True love doth love in turn beget,
And now these bells repay the debt;
Whene'er they sound, their music tells
Of him who sang sweet Shandon bells!

May 30, 1866.

ADARE.*

BY GERALD GRIFFIN.

Oh, sweet Adare! oh, lovely vale!
   Oh, soft retreat of sylvan splendour!
Nor summer sun, nor morning gale
   E'er hailed a scene more softly tender.
How shall I tell the thousand charms
   Within thy verdant bosom dwelling,
Where, lulled in Nature's fost'ring arms,
   Soft peace abides and joy excelling!

Ye morning airs, how sweet at dawn
   The slumbering boughs your song awaken,
Or linger o'er the silent lawn,
   With odour of the harebell taken.
Thou rising sun, how richly gleams
   Thy smile from far Knockfierna's mountain,
O'er waving woods and bounding streams,
   And many a grove and glancing fountain.

Ye clouds of noon, how freshly there,
   When summer heats the open meadows,
O'er parched hill and valley fair,
   All cooly lie your veiling shadows.
Ye rolling shades and vapours grey,
   Slow creeping o'er the golden heaven,
How soft ye seal the eye of day,
   And wreath the dusky brow of even.

In sweet Adare, the jocund spring
   His notes of odorous joy is breathing,
The wild birds in the woodland sing,
   The wild flowers in the vale are breathing

---

* This beautiful and interesting locality is about eight miles from Limerick.

There winds the Mague, as silver clear,
    Among the elms so sweetly flowing;
There, fragrant in the early year,
    Wild roses on the banks are blowing.

The wild duck seeks the sedgy bank,
    Or dives beneath the glistening billow,
Where graceful droop and clustering dank
    The osier bright and rustling willow.
The hawthorn scents the leafy dale,
    In thicket lone the stag is belling,
And sweet along the echoing vale
    The sound of vernal joy is swelling.

DEIRDRE'S FAREWELL TO ALBA.*

BY SAMUEL FERGUSON, LL.D., M.R.I.A.

FAREWELL to fair Alba, high house of the sun,
Farewell to the mountain, the cliff, and the dun;
Dun-Sweeny, adieu! for my love cannot stay,
And tarry I may not when love cries away.

Glen Vashan! Glen Vashan! where roebucks run free,
Where my love used to feast on the red deer with me;
Where, rocked on thy waters while stormy winds blew,
My love used to slumber, Glen Vashan, adieu!

Glendaro! Glendaro! where birchen boughs weep
Honey dew at high noon o'er the nightingale's sleep,
Where my love used to lead me to hear the cuckoo
'Mong the high hazel bushes, Glendaro, adieu!

Glen Urchy! Glen Urchy! where loudly and long
My love used to wake up the woods with his song,
While the son of the rock, from the depths of the dell,
Laughed sweetly in answer, Glen Urchy. farewell!

* Scotland.

Glen Etive! Glen Etive! where dappled does roam,
Where I leave the green sheeling I first called a home;
Where with me and my true-love delighted to dwell,
The sun made his mansion, Glen Etive, farewell!

Farewell to Inch Draynach, adieu to the roar
Of the blue billows bursting in light on the shore;
Dun Fiagh, farewell! for my love cannot stay,
And tarry I may not when love cries away.

A SIGH FOR KNOCKMANY.
BY WILLIAM CARLETON.

TAKE, proud ambition, take thy fill
   Of pleasures won through toil or crime;
Go, learning, climb thy rugged hill,
   And give thy name to future time:
Philosophy, be keen to see
   Whate'er is just, or false, or vain,
Take each thy meed, but, oh! give me
   To range my mountain glens again.

Pure was the breeze that fann'd my cheek,
   As o'er Knockmany's brow I went;
When every lonely dell could speak
   In airy music, vision sent:
False world, I hate thy cares and thee,
   I hate the treacherous haunts of men;
Give back my early heart to me,
   Give back to me my mountain glen.

How light my youthful visions shone,
   When spann'd by fancy's radiant form;
But now her glittering bow is gone,
   And leaves me but the cloud and storm!
With wasted form, and cheek all pale—
   With heart long scared by grief and pain;
Dunroe, I'll seek thy native gale,
   I'll tread my mountain glens again.

Thy breeze once more may fan my blood,
   Thy vallies all, are lovely still ;
And I may stand, where oft I stood,
   In lonely musings on thy hill.
But ah ! the spell is gone ;—no art
   In crowded town, or native plain,
Can teach a crush'd and breaking heart
   To pipe the song of youth again.

TIPPERARY.

Were you ever in sweet Tipperary, where the fields
   are so sunny and green,
And the heath-brown Slieve-bloom and the Galtees
   look down with so proud a mien ?
'Tis there you would see more beauty than is on all
   Irish ground—
God bless you, my sweet Tipperary, for where could
   your match be found ?

They say that your hand is fearful, that darkness is
   in your eye :
But I'll not let them dare to talk so black and bitter
   a lie.
Oh ! no, *macushla storin !* bright, bright, and warm
   are you,
With hearts as bold as the men of old, to yourselves
   and your country true.

And when there is gloom upon you, bid them think
   who has brought it there—
Sure a frown or a word of hatred was not made for
   your face so fair ;
You've a hand for the grasp of friendship—another to
   make them quake,
And they're welcome to whichsoever it pleases them
   most to take.

Shall our homes, like the huts of Connaught, be crumbled before our eyes?
Shall we fly, like a flock of wild geese, from all that we love and prize?
No! by those who were here before us, no churl shall our tyrant be;
Our land it is theirs by plunder, but, by Brigid, ourselves are free.

No! we do not forget the greatness did once to sweet Eire belong;
No treason or craven spirit was ever our race among;
And no frown or no word of hatred we give—but to pay them back,
In evil we only follow our enemies' darksome track.

Oh! come for a while among us, and give us the friendly hand,
And you'll see that old Tipperary is a loving and gladsome land;
From Upper to Lower Ormond, bright welcomes and smiles will spring—
On the plains of Tipperary the stranger is like a king.

THE WELSHMEN OF TIRAWLEY.

BY SAMUEL FERGUSON, LL.D., M.R.I.A.

[Several Welsh families, associates in the invasion of Strongbow, settled in the west of Ireland. Of these, the principal, whose names have been preserved by the Irish antiquarians, were the Walshes, Joyces, Heils (*a quibus* MacHale), Lawlesses, Tolmyns, Lynotts, and Barretts, which last draw their pedigree from Walynes, son of Guyndally, the *Ard Maor*, or High Steward of the Lordship of Camelot, and had their chief seats in the territory of the two Bacs, in the barony of Tirawley, and county of Mayo. *Clochan-na-n'all*, i.e., "The Blind Men's Steppingstones," are still pointed out on the Duvowen river, about four miles north of Crossmolina, in the townland of Garranard; and *Tubber-na-Scorney*, or "Scrags Well," in the opposite townland of Carns, in the same barony. For a curious *terrier* or applotment of the Mac William's revenue, as acquired under the circumstances stated in the legend preserved by Mac Firbis, see Dr. O'Donovan's highly-learned and interesting "Genealogies, &c. of Hy Fiachrach," in the publications of the *Irish Archæological Society*—a great monument of antiquarian and topographical erudition.]

SCORNEY BWEE, the Barretts' bailiff, lewd and lame,
To lift the Lynott's taxes when he came,
Rudely drew a young maid to him;
Then the Lynotts rose and slew him,
And in Tubber-na-Scorney threw him—
        Small your blame,
        Sons of Lynott !
Sing the vengeance of the Welshmen of Tirawley.

Then the Barretts to the Lynotts gave a choice,
Saying, "Hear, ye murderous brood, men and boys,
Choose ye now, without delay,
Will ye lose your eyesight, say,
Or your manhoods, here to-day ?"
        Sad your choice,
        Sons of Lynott !
Sing the vengeance of the Welshmen of Tirawley.

Then the little boys of the Lynotts, weeping, said,
"Only leave us our eyesight in our head."
But the bearded Lynotts then
Quickly answered back again,
"Take our eyes, but leave us men,
        Alive or dead,
        Sons of Wattin !"
Sing the vengeance of the Welshmen of Tirawley.

So the Barretts, with sewing-needles sharp and smooth.
Let the light out of the eyes of every youth,
And of every bearded man,
Of the broken Lynott clan;
Then their darkened faces wan
        Turning south
        To the river—
Sing the vengence of the Welshmen of Tirawley.

O'er the slippery stepping-stones of Clochan-na-n'all
They drove them, laughing loud at every fall,
As their wandering footsteps dark
Failed to reach the slippery mark,
And the swift stream swallowed stark,

> One and all,
> As they stumbled—
> Sing the vengeance of the Welshmen of Tirawley

Out of all the blinded Lynotts, one alone
Walked erect from stepping-stone to stone;
So back again they brought you,
And a second time they wrought you
With their needles; but never got you
> Once to groan,
> Emon Lynott,
For the vengeance of the Welshmen of Tirawley.

But with prompt-projected footsteps sure as ever,
Emon Lynott again crossed the river,
Though Duvowen was rising fast,
And the shaking stones o'ercast
By cold floods boiling past;
> Yet you never,
> Emon Lynott,
Faltered once before your foemen of Tirawley;

But, turning on Ballintubber bank, you stood,
And the Barretts thus bespoke o'er the flood—
"Oh, ye foolish sons of Wattin,
Small amends are these you've gotten,
For, while Scorney Bwee lies rotten,
> I am good
> For vengeance!"
Sing the vengeance of the Welshmen of Tirawley.

"For 'tis neither in eye nor eyesight that a man
Bears the fortunes of himself or of his clan;
But in the manly mind
And in loins with vengeance lined,
That your needles could never find,
> Though they ran
> Through my heartstrings!"
Sing the vengeance of the Welshmen of Tirawley

"But, little your women's needles do I reck ;
For the night from heaven never fell so black,
But Tirawley, and abroad
From the Moy to Cuan-an-fod,
I could walk it every sod,
      Path and track,
      Ford and togher,
Seeking vengeance on you, Barretts of Tirawley ?

"The night when Dathy O'Dowda broke your camp,
What Barrett among you was it held the lamp—
Showed the way to those two feet,
When through wintry wind and sleet,
I guided your blind retreat
      In the swamp
      Of Beäl-an-asa ?
O ye vengeance-destined ingrates of Tirawley !"

So leaving loud-shriek-echoing Garranard,
The Lynott like a red dog hunted hard,
With his wife and children seven,
'Mong the beasts and fowls of heaven
In the hollows of Glen Nephin,
      Light-debarred,
      Made his dwelling,
Planning vengeance on the Barretts of Tirawley.

And ere the bright-orb'd year its course had run,
On his brown round-knotted knee he nursed a son,
A child of light, with eyes
As clear as are the skies
In summer, when sunrise
      Has begun ;
      So the Lynott
Nursed his vengeance on the Barretts of Tirawley.

And, as ever the bright boy grew in strength and size,
Made him perfect in each manly exercise,
The salmon in the flood,
The dun deer in the wood,

The eagle in the cloud,
         To surprise,
         On Ben Nephin,
Far above the foggy fields of Tirawley.

With the yellow-knotted spear-shaft, with the bow,
With the steel, prompt to deal shot and blow,
He taught him from year to year,
And trained him, without a peer,
For a perfect cavalier,
         Hoping so—
         Far his forethought—
For vengeance on the Barretts of Tirawley.

And, when mounted on his proud-bounding steed,
Emon Oge sat a cavalier indeed;
Like the ear upon the wheat
When winds in autumn beat
On the bending stems, his seat;
         And the speed
         Of his courser
Was the wind from Barna-na-gee o'er Tirawley!

Now when fifteen sunny summers thus were spent,
(He perfected in all accomplishment)—
The Lynott said, "My child,
We are over long exiled
From mankind in this wild—
         Time we went
         O'er the mountain
To the countries lying over-against Tirawley."

So out over mountain-moors, and mosses brown,
And green stream-gathering vales, they journeyed
    down;
Till, shining like a star,
Through the dusky gleams afar,
The bailey of Castlebar,
         And the town
         Of MacWilliam
Rose bright before the wanderers of Tirawley.

"Look southward, my boy, and tell me as we go,
What see'st thou by the loch-head below."
"Oh, a stone-house strong and great,
And a horse-host at the gate,
And a captain in armour of plate—
   Grand the show!
   Great the glancing!
High the heroes of this land below Tirawley!

"And a beautiful Bantierna by his side,
Yellow gold on all her gown-sleeves wide;
And in her hand a pearl
Of a young, little, fair-haired girl——
Said the Lynott, "It is the Earl!
   Let us ride
   To his presence."
And before him came the exiles of Tirawley.

"God save thee, MacWilliam," the Lynott thus began;
"God save all here besides of this clan;
For gossips dear to me
Are all in company—
For in these four bones ye see
   A kindly man
   Of the Britons—
Emon Lynott of Garranard of Tirawley.

"And hither, as kindly gossip-law allows,
I come to claim a scion of thy house
To foster; for thy race,
Since William Conquer's* days,
Have ever been wont to place,
   With some spouse
   Of a Briton,
A MacWilliam Oge, to foster in Tirawley.

"And to show thee in what sort our youth are taught
I have hither to thy home of valour brought
This one son of my age,
For a sample and a pledge

 * William Fitz Adelm de Burgho, the conqueror of Connaught.

For the equal tutelage,
        In right thought,
        Word, and action,
Of whatever son ye give into Tirawley."

When MacWilliam beheld the brave boy ride and run,
Saw the spear-shaft from his white shoulder spun—
With a sigh, and with a smile,
He said,—"I would give the spoil
Of a county, that Tibbot Moyle,
        My own son,
        Were accomplished
Like this branch of the kindly Britons of Tirawley."

When the Lady MacWilliam she heard him speak,
And saw the ruddy roses on his cheek,
She said, "I would give a purse
Of red gold to the nurse
That would rear my Tibbot no worse;
        But I seek
        Hitherto vainly—
Heaven grant that I now have found her in Tirawley."

So they said to the Lynott, "Here, take our bird!
And as pledge for the keeping of thy word,
Let this scion here remain
Till thou comest back again:
Meanwhile the fitting train
        Of a lord
        Shall attend thee
With the lordly heir of Connaught into Tirawley."

So back to strong-throng-gathering Garranard,
Like a lord of the country with his guard,
Came the Lynott, before them all,
Once again over Clochan-na-n'all,
Steady-striding, erect, and tall,
        And his ward
        On his shoulders;
To the wonder of the Welshman of Tirawley

Then a diligent foster-father you would deem
The Lynott, teaching Tibbot, by mead and stream,
To cast the spear, to ride,
To stem the rushing tide,
With what feats of body beside,
   Might beseem
   A MacWilliam,
Fostered free among the Welshmen of Tirawley.

But the lesson of hell he taught him in heart and mind,
For to what desire soever he inclined,
Of anger, lust, or pride,
He had it gratified,
Till he ranged the circle wide
   Of a blind
   Self-indulgence,
Ere he came to youthful manhood in Tirawley.

Then, even as when a hunter slips a hound,
Lynott loosed him—God's leashes all unbound—
In the pride of power and station,
And the strength of youthful passion,
On the daughters of thy nation,
   All around,
   Wattin Barrett!
Oh! the vengeance of the Welshmen of Tirawley!

Bitter grief and burning anger, rage and shame,
Filled the houses of the Barretts where'er he came;
Till the young men of the Bac
Drew by night upon his track,
And slew him at Cornassack—
   Small your blame,
   Sons of Wattin!
Sing the vengeance of the Welshmen of Tirawley.

Said the Lynott, "The day of my vengeance is draw
 ing near,
The day for which, through many a long dark year,

I have toiled through grief and sin—
Call ye now the Brehons in,
And let the plea begin
    Over the bier
    Of MacWilliam,
For an eric upon the Barretts of Tirawley."

Then the Brehons to MacWilliam Burk decreed
An eric upon Clan Barrett for the deed;
And the Lynott's share of the fine,
As foster-father, was nine
Ploughlands and nine score kine;
    But no need
    Had the Lynott,
Neither care, for land or cattle in Tirawley.

But rising, while all sat silent on the spot,
He said, "The law says—doth it not?—
If the foster-sire elect
His portion to reject,
He may then the right exact
    To applot
    The short eric."
"'Tis the law," replied the Brehons of Tirawley.

Said the Lynott, "I once before had a choice
Proposed me, wherein law had little voice:
But now I choose, and say,
As lawfully I may,
I applot the mulct to-day;
    So rejoice
    In your ploughlands
And your cattle which I renounce throughout Tirawley

"And thus I applot the mulct: I divide
The land throughout Clan Barrett on every side
Equally, that no place
May be without the face
Of a foe of Wattin's race—
    That the pride
    Of the Barretts
May be humbled hence for ever throughout Tirawley.

"I adjudge a seat in every Barrett's hall
To MacWilliam: in every stable I give a stall
To MacWilliam: and, beside,
Whenever a Burke shall ride
Through Tirawley, I provide
   At his call
    Needful grooming,
Without charge from any Brughaidh of Tirawley

"Thus lawfully I avenge me for the throes
Ye lawlessly caused me and caused those
Unhappy shame-faced ones
Who, their mothers expected once,
Would have been the sires of sons—
   O'er whose woes
    Often weeping,
I have groaned in my exile from Tirawley.

"I demand not of you your manhoods; but I take—
For the Burks will take it—your Freedom! for the
  sake
Of which all manhood's given
And all good under heaven,
And, without which, better even
   You should make
    Yourselves barren,
Than see your children slaves throughout Tirawley!

"Neither take I your eyesight from you; as you took
Mine and ours: I would have you daily look
On one another's eyes
When the strangers tyrannize
By your hearths, and blushes arise,
   That ye brook
    Without vengeance
The insults of troops of Tibbots throughout Tirawley!

"The vengeance I designed, now is done,
And the days of me and mine nearly run—
For, for this, I have broken faith,
Teaching him who lies beneath

This pall, to merit death;
        And my son
        To his father
Stands pledged for other teaching in Tirawley."

Said MacWilliam — "Father and son, hang them
    high!"
And the Lynott they hanged speedily;
But across the salt-sea water,
To Scotland with the daughter
Of MacWilliam—well you got her!—
        Did you fly,
        Edmund Lindsay,
The gentlest of all the Welshmen of Tirawley!

'Tis thus the ancient Ollaves of Erin tell
How, through lewdness and revenge, it befel
That the sons of William Conquer
Came over the sons of Wattin,
Throughout all the bounds and borders
Of the land of Auley MacFiachra;
Till the Saxon Oliver Cromwell
And his valiant, Bible-guided,
Free heretics of Clan London
Coming in, in their succession,
Rooted out both Burk and Barrett,
And in their empty places
New stems of freedom planted,
With many a goodly sapling
Of manliness and virtue;
Which while their children cherish
Kindly Irish of the Irish,
Neither Saxons nor Italians,
May the mighty God of Freedom
        Speed them well,
        Never taking
Further vengeance on his people of Tirawley!

[*Note by the Editor*, 1869: The author of this spirited Ballad in republishing *The Welshmen of Tirawley* in his "*Lays of the Western Gael*," p. 70, has changed several lines, some of them being among the most vigorous in the poem. For the purposes of comparison, I have thought it would be more interesting to give the ballad as it originally appeared.]

THE OUTLAW OF LOCH LENE.

BY J. J. CALLANAN.

O, MANY a day have I made good ale in the glen,
That came not of stream, or malt;—like the brewing
    of men.
My bed was the ground; my roof, the greenwood above,
And the wealth that I sought one far kind glance from
    my love.

Alas! on that night when the horses I drove from the
    field,
That I was not near from terror my angel to shield.
She stretched forth her arms,—her mantle she flung to
    the wind,
And swam o'er Loch Lene, her outlawed lover to find.

O would that a freezing sleet-wing'd tempest did sweep,
And I and my love were alone, far off on the deep;
I'd ask not a ship, or a bark, or pinnace, to save,—
With her hand round my waist, I'd fear not the wind
    or the wave.

'Tis down by the lake where the wild-tree fringes its
    sides,
The maid of my heart, my fair one of Heaven resides;—
I think as at eve she wanders its mazes along,
The birds go to sleep by the sweet wild twist of her
    song.

AILEEN THE HUNTRESS.

BY EDWARD WALSH.

[The incident related in the following ballad happened about the year 1731. Aileen, or Ellen, was daughter of M'Cartie, of Clidane, an estate originally bestowed upon this respectable branch of the family of M'Cartie More, by James, the seventh Earl of Desmond, and which, passing safe through the confiscations of Elizabeth, Cromwell, and William, remained in their possession until the beginning of the present century. Aileen, who is celebrated in the traditions of the people for her love of hunting, was the wife of James O'Connor, of Cluain-Tairbh, grandson of David, the founder of the *Siol-t Da*, a well-known sept at this day in Kerry. This David was grandson to Thomas MacTeige O'Connor, of Ahalahanna, head of the second house of O'Connor Kerry, who, forfeiting in 1666, escaped destruction by taking shelter among his relations, the Nagles of Monanimy.—AUTHOR'S NOTE.]

FAIR Aileen M'Cartie, O'Connor's young bride,
Forsakes her white pillow with matronly pride,
And calls forth her maidens (their number was nine,
To the bawn of her mansion, a-milking the kine.
They came at her bidding, in kirtle and gown,
And braided hair, jetty, and golden, and brown,
And form like the palm-tree, and step like the fawn,
And bloom like the wild rose that circled the bawn.

As the Guebre's round tower o'er the fane of Ardfert—
As the white hind of Brandon by young roes begirt—
As the moon in her glory 'mid bright stars outhung—
Stood Aileen M'Cartie her maidens among.
Beneath the rich kerchief, which matrons may wear,
Stray'd ringleted tresses of beautiful hair;
They wav'd on her fair neck, as darkly as though
'Twere the raven's wing shining o'er Mangerton's snow!

A circlet of pearls o'er her white bosom lay,
Erst worn by thy proud Queen, O'Connor the gay,*
And now to the beautiful Aileen come down,
The rarest that ever shed light in the Laune.†

---

* O'Connor, surnamed "*Sugach*," or the Gay, was a celebrated chief of this race, who flourished in the fifteenth century.
† The river Laune flows from the Lakes of Killarney, and the celebrated Kerry Pearls are found in its waters.

The many-fring'd *falluinn** that floated behind,
Gave its hues to the sunlight, its folds to the wind—
The brooch that refrain'd it some forefather bold
Had torn from a sea-king in battle-field old!

Around her went bounding two wolf-dogs of speed,
So tall in their stature, so pure in their breed;
While the maidens awake to the new milk's soft fall,
A song of O'Connor in Carraig's proud hall.
As the milk came outpouring, and the song came out-
    sung,
O'er the wall 'mid the maidens a red-deer out-sprung—
Then cheer'd the fair lady—then rush'd the mad hound,
And away with the wild stag in air-lifted bound.

The gem-fasten'd *falluinn* is dash'd on the bawn—
One spring o'er the tall fence—and Aileen is gone;
But morning's rous'd echoes to the deep dells proclaim
The course of that wild stag, the dogs, and the dame!
By Cluain Tairbh's green border, o'er moorland and
    height,
The red-deer shapes downward the rush of his flight—
In sunlight his antlers all gloriously flash,
And onward the wolf-dogs and fair huntress dash!

By Sliabh-Mis now winding (rare hunting I ween!)
He gains the dark valley of Scota the queen†
Who found in its bosom a cairn-lifted grave,
When Sliabh-Mis first flow'd with the blood of the brave!
By Coill-Cuaigh's‡ green shelter, the hollow rocks ring—
Coill-Cuaigh, of the cuckoo's first song in the spring,
Coill-Cuaigh of the tall oak and gale-scenting spray—
God's curse on the tyrants that wrought thy decay!

  * "Falluinn"—The Irish mantle.
  † The first battle fought between the Milesians and the Tuatha de Danans for the empire of Ireland was at Sliabh-Mis, in Kerry, in which Scota, an Egyptian princess, and the relict of Milesius, was slain. A valley on the north side of Sliabh-Mis, called Glean Scoithin, or the vale of Scota, is said to be the place of her interment. The ancient chronicles assert that this battle was fought 1,300 years before the Christian era.
  ‡ "Coill-Cuaigh"—*The Wood of the Cuckoo*, so called from being the favourite haunt of the bird of summer, is now a bleak desolate moor. The axe of the stranger laid its honours low.

L

Now Maing's lovely border is gloriously won,
Now the towers of the island* gleam bright in the sun,
And now Ceall-an Amanach's† portals are pass'd,
Where headless the Desmond found refuge at last!
By Ard-na greach‡ mountain, and Avonmore's head,
To the Earl's proud pavilion the panting deer fled—
Where Desmond's tall clansmen spread banners of pride,
And rush'd to the battle, and gloriously died!

The huntress is coming, slow, breathless, and pale,
Her raven locks streaming all wild in the gale;
She stops—and the breezes bring balm to her brow—
But wolf-dog and wild deer, oh! where are they now?
On Réidhlán-Tigh-an-Eárla, by Avonmore's well,
His bounding heart broken, the hunted deer fell;
And o'er him the brave hounds all gallantly died,
In death still victorious—their fangs in his side!

'Tis evening—the breezes beat cold on her breast,
And Aileen must seek her far home in the west;
Yet weeping, she lingers where the mist-wreaths are chill,
O'er the red-deer and tall dogs that lie on the hill!
Whose harp at the banquet told distant and wide,
This feat of fair Aileen, O'Connor's young bride?—
O'Daly's—whose guerdon, tradition hath told,
Was a purple-crown'd wine-cup of beautiful gold!

* "Castle Island," or the "Island of Kerry"—The stronghold of the Fitzgeralds.

† It was in this churchyard that the headless remains of the unfortunate Gerald, the 16th Earl of Desmond, were privately interred. The head was carefully pickled, and sent over to the English queen, who had it fixed on London-bridge. This mighty chieftain possessed more than 570,000 acres of land, and had a train of 500 gentlemen of his own name and race. At the source of the Blackwater, where he sought refuge from his inexorable foes, is a mountain called "Reidhlan-Tigh-an-Earla," or "The Plain of the Earl's House." He was slain near Castle Island on 11th November, 1583.

‡ "Ard-na greach"—The height of the spoils or armies.

SHANE DYMAS' DAUGHTER.

It was the eve of holy St. Bride,
  The Abbey bells were ringing,
And the meek-eyed nuns at eventide
  The vesper hymns were singing.
Alone, by the well of good St. Bride,
  A novice fair was kneeling!
And there seem'd not o'er her soul to glide
  One shade of earthly feeling.

For ne'er did that clear and sainted well
  Reflect, from its crystal water,
A form more fair than the shadow that fell
  From O'Niall's lovely daughter.
Her eye was bright as the blue concave,
  And beaming with devotion;
Her bosom fair as the foam on the wave
  Of Erin's rolling ocean.

Yet O! forgive her that starting tear;
  From home and kindred riven,
Fair Kathleen, many a long, long year,
  Must be the Bride of Heaven.
Her beads were told, and the moonlight shone
  Sweetly on Callan Water,
When her path was cross'd by a holy nun;—
  "Benedicte, fair daughter!"

Fair Kathleen started—well did she know—
  O what will not love discover!
Her country's scourge, and her father's foe,—
  'Twas the voice of her Saxon lover.
"Raymond!"—"Oh hush, my Kathleen dear,
  My path's beset with danger;
But cast not, love, those looks of fear
  Upon thy dark-hair'd stranger.

"My red roan steed's in yon Culdee grove,
  My bark is out at sea, love!
My boat is moored in the ocean cove;
  Then haste away with me, love!
"My father has sworn my hand shall be
  To Sidney's daughter given;
And thine, to-morrow will offer thee
  A sacrifice to heaven.

"But away, my love, away with me!
  The breeze to the west is blowing;
And thither, across the dark-blue sea,
  Are England's bravest going.*
"To a land where the breeeze from the orange bowers
  Comes over the exile's sorrow,
Like the light-wing'd dreams of his early hours
  Or his hope of a happier morrow.

"And there, in some valley's loneliness,
  By wood and mountain shaded,
We'll live in the light of wedded bliss,
  Till the lamp of life be faded.
"Then thither with me, my Kathleen, fly!
  The storms of life we'll weather,
Till in bliss beneath the western sky,
  We live, love, die together!"—

Die, Saxon, now!"—At that fiend-like yell
  An hundred swords are gleaming:
Down the bubbling stream, from the tainted well,
  His heart's best blood is streaming.
In vain does he doff the hood so white,
  And vain his falchion flashing:
Five murderous brands through his corslet bright
  Within his heart are clashing!

His last groan echoing through the grove,
  His life blood on the water,
He dies,—thy first and thy only love,
  O'Niall's hapless daughter!

---

* Alluding to the settlement of Virgina, by Sir Walter Raleigh.

Vain, vain, was the shield of that breast of snow !
  In vain that eye would sustain him,
Through his Kathleen's heart the murderous blow
  Too deadly aimed, has slain him.

The spirit fled with the red, red blood
  Fast gushing from her bosom ;
The blast of death has blighted the bud
  Of Erin's loveliest blossom !
'Tis morn ;—in the deepest doubt and dread
  The gloomy hours are rolling ;
No sound save the requiem for the dead,
  Or knell of the death-bell tolling.

'Tis dead of night—not a sound is heard,
  Save from the night wind sighing ;
Or the mournful moan of the midnight bird,
  To yon pale planet crying.
Who names the name of his murder'd child ?
  What spears to the moon are glancing ?
'Tis the vengful cry of Shane Dymas wild,†
  His bonnacht-men advancing.

Saw ye that cloud o'er the moonlight cast,
  Fire from its blackness breaking ?
Heard ye that cry on the midnight blast,
  The voice of terror shrieking ?
'Tis the fire from Ardsaillach's* willow'd height,
  Tower and temple falling ;
'Tis the groan of death, and the cry of fright,
  From monks for mercy calling !

* For an account of this fierce but high-souled chieftain, see Stuart's Historical Memoirs of the city of Armagh.
† "The Height of Willows," the ancient name of Armagh.

THE LAST O'SULLIVAN BEARE.

BY THOMAS D'ARCY M'GEE.

[Philip O'Sullivan Beare, a brave captain, and the author of many works relating to Ireland, commanded a ship-of-war for Philip IV. of Spain. In his "Catholic History," published at Lisbon in 1609, he has preserved the sad story of his family." It is in brief thus:—In 1602 his father's castle of Dunbuidhe. being demolished by cannonade, his family—consisting of a wife, son, and two daughters—emigrated to Spain, where his youngest brother, Donald, joined him professionally, but was soon after killed in an engagement with the Turks. The old chief, at the age of one hundred, died at Corunna, and was soon followed by his long-wedded wife. One daughter entered a convent and took the veil; the other, returning to Ireland, was lost at sea. In this version the real names have been preserved.]

All alone—all alone, where the gladsome vi᾿ ᾿ is growing—
All alone by the bank of the Tagus darkly flowing,
No morning brings a hope for him, nor any evening cheer,
To O'Sullivan Beare thro' the seasons of the year.

He is thinking—ever thinking of the hour he left Dunbuie,
His father's staff fell from his hand, his mother wild was she ;
His brave young brother hid his face, his lovely sisters twain,
How they wrung their maiden hands to see him sail away for Spain.

They were Helen bright and Norah staid, who in their father's hall,
Like sun and shadow, frolicked round the grave armorial wall ;
In Compostella's cloisters he found many a pictured saint,
But, the Spirits boyhood canonised, no human hand can paint.

All alone—all alone, where the gladsome vine is growing—
All alone by the bank of the Tagus darkly flowing—
No morning brings a hope for him, nor any evening cheer,
To O'Sullivan Beare thro' the seasons of the year.

Oh! sure he ought to take a ship and sail back to Dunbuie—
He ought to sail back, back again to that castle o'er the sea;
His father, mother, brother, his lovely sisters twain,
'Tis they would raise the roof with joy to see him back from Spain.

Hush! hush! I cannot tell it—the tale will make me wild—
He left it, that grey castle, in age almost a child;
Seven long years with Saint James's Friars he conned the page of might—
Seven long years for his father's roof was sighing every night.

Then came a caravel from the north, deep freighted, full of woe,
His houseless family it held, for their castle it lay low,
Saint James's shrine, thro' ages famed as pilgrim haunt of yore,
Saw never wanderers so wronged upon its scalloped shore.

Yet it was sweet—their first grief past—to watch those two fond girls
Sit by the sea, as mermaid might hold watch o'er hidden pearls—
To see them sit and try to sing for that sire and mother old,
O'er whose heads full five score winters their thickening snows had rolled.

To hear them sing and pray in song for *them* in deadly
    work,
Their gallant brothers battling for Spain against the
    Turk—
Corunna's port at length they reach, and seaward ever
    stare,
Wondering what belates the ship their brothers home
    should bear.

Joy! joy!—it comes—their Philip lives!—ah! Donald
    is no more;
Like half a hope one son kneels down the exiled two
    before;
They spoke no requiem for the dead, nor blessing for
    the living;
The tearless heart of parentage has broken with its
    grieving.

Two pillars of a ruined pile—two old trees of the land—
Two voyagers on a sea of grief, long suff'rers hand in
    hand.
Thus at the woful tidings told left life and all its tears,
So died the wife of many a spring, the chief of an
    hundred years.

One sister is a black-veiled nun of Saint Ursula, in
    Spain,
And one sleeps coldly far beneath the troubled
    Irish main;
'Tis Helen bright who ventured to the arms of her
    true lover,
But Cleena's* stormy waves now roll the radiant girl
    over.

All alone—all alone, where the gladsome vine is
    growing—
All alone by the banks of the Tagus darkly flowing.
No morning brings a hope for him, nor any evening
    cheer,
To O'Sullivan Beare thro' the seasons of the year.

   * The waves off the coast of Cork, so called.

THE ROBBER OF FERNEY

The robber in his rocky hold from dawn of morning lay,
And wearily and drearily the noontide passed away—
The sun went down, and darkness fell in silence on the earth;
And now from out their wild retreat the robber band came forth.

That night by many a castle old, and many a haunted glen,
MacMahon and his outlaws rode, all wild and ruthless men;
Before them Lath-an-albany in midnight beauty lay—
Ah! woe is me! from all its fields the robber swept his prey.

And thus the country far and near, MacMahon held in awe,
And through this ancient barony, the robber's word was law;
In castle hall it chilled the sound of revelry and mirth,
But it lighted up with gladness still the lonely widow's hearth.

The robber bold, within his hold, from dawn of morning lies,
And gazes on the sinking sun with weary heart and eyes;
Till through the dark and starless night, by tower and ruin grey,
And far from all his faithful band he held his lonely way.

Alone among his enemies the outlawed chieftain stood,
With haughty eye, and fearless heart, and broadsword keen and good;
But his wild career is over, the castles of the land
Henceforth will need nor watch nor ward against the outlaw's band.

And now upon his homeward track, with heavy heart he goes—
No more in wild and midnight raid to burst upon his foes ;
No more to lead his faithful band through Ferney's valleys old,
No more within his mountain lair, carousal brave to hold.

Alas ! alas ! the light that guides both horse and rider on,
From many a kindling roof-tree burst, and many a dying groan ;
And many an agonizing shriek rings through the lurid air,
Oh ! fearful is the carnage wrought within the robber's lair.

There's silence in the castle where the last Mac Mahon lies,
His heart is dull, the light of life has faded from his eyes ;
But who can tell what dreams of woe—what visions of the dead—
What fond and broken-hearted forms surround the outlaw's bed ?

Or who can tell what influence such blessed dreams impart,
Or why they still come thronging round the dying sinner's heart ?—
Whate'er they be, the simple faith is rational and good,
They come in that last hour to lead the wandering soul to God.

WAITING FOR THE MAY.

BY DENIS FLORENCE MAC-CARTHY, M.R.I.A

Ah! my heart is weary waiting,
    Waiting for the May—
Waiting for the pleasant rambles,
Where the fragrant hawthorn brambles,
    With the woodbine alternating,
      Scent the dewy way.
Ah! my heart is weary waiting,
    Waiting for the May.

Ah! my heart is sick with longing,
    Longing for the May—
Longing to escape from study,
To the young face fair and ruddy,
    And the thousand charms belonging
      To the summer's day.
Ah! my heart is sick with longing,
    Longing for the May.

Ah! my heart is sore with sighing,
    Sighing for the May—
Sighing for their sure returning,
When the summer beams are burning,
    Hopes and flowers that dead or dying
      All the winter lay.
Ah! my heart is sore with sighing,
    Sighing for the May.

Ah! my heart is pained with throbbing
    Throbbing for the May—
Throbbing for the sea-side billows,
Or the water-wooing willows;
    Where in laughing and in sobbing
      Glide the streams away.
Ah! my heart, my heart is throbbing,
    Throbbing for the May.

Waiting sad, dejected, weary,
    Waiting for the May.
Spring goes by with wasted warnings,
Moonlit evenings, sunbright mornings;
    Summer comes, yet dark and dreary
    Life still ebbs away:
Man is ever weary, weary,
    Waiting for the May!

THE VIRGIN MARY'S BANK.

BY J. J. CALLANAN.

[From the foot of Inchidony Island, an elevated tract of sand run out into the sea, and terminates in a high green bank, which forms pleasing contrast with the little desert behind it, and the black solitary rock immediately under. Tradition tells that the Virgin came one night to this hillock to pray, and was discovered kneeling there by the crew of a vessel that was coming to anchor near the place. They laughed at her piety, and made some merry and unbecoming remarks on her beauty, upon which a storm arose and destroyed the ship and her crew. Since that time no vessel has been known to anchor near it. AUTHOR'S NOTE.]

THE evening star rose beauteous above the fading day
As to the lone and silent beach the Virgin came to pray,
And hill and wave shone brightly in the moonlight's
        mellow fall;
But the bank of green where Mary knelt was brightest
        of them all.

Slow moving o'er the waters, a gallant bark appear'd,
And her joyous crew look'd from the deck as to the
        land she near'd;
To the calm and shelter'd haven she floated like a swan,
And her wings of snow o'er the waves below in pride
        and beauty shone.

The master saw our Lady as he stood upon the prow,
And mark'd the whiteness of her robe and the radiance
        of her brow;
Her arms were folded gracefully upon her stainless
        breast,
And her eyes look'd up among the stars to Him her
        soul lov'd best.

He show'd her to his sailors, and he hail'd her with a
    cheer,
And on the kneeling Virgin they gazed with laugh and
    jeer;
And madly swore, a form so fair they never saw before;
And they curs'd the faint and lagging breeze that kept
    them from the shore.

The ocean from its bosom shook off the moonlight
    sheen,
And up its wrathful billows rose to vindicate their
    Queen;
And a cloud came o'er the heavens, and a darkness
    o'er the land,
And the scoffing crew beheld no more that Lady on
    the strand.

Out burst the pealing thunder, and the light'ning
    leap'd about;
And rushing with his watery war, the tempest gave a
    shout;
And that vessel from a mountain wave came down
    with thund'ring shock;
And her timbers flew like scatter'd spray on Inchi-
    dony's rock.

Then loud from all that guilty crew one shriek rose
    wild and high;
But the angry surge swept over them, and hush'd
    their gurgling cry;
And with a hoarse exulting tone the tempest passed
    away,
And down, still chafing from their strife, th' indignant
    waters lay.

When the calm and purple morning shone out on high
    Dunmore,
Full many a mangled corpse was seen on Inchidony's
    shore;
And to this day the fisherman shows where the scoffers
    sank:
And still he calls that hillock green, "the Virgin Mary's
    bank"

OWEN BAWN.

BY SAMUEL FERGUSON, LL.D., M.R.I.A.

[In *Blackwood's Magazine*, vol. 34, there is a long and interesting story by Dr. Ferguson, entitled *The Return of Claneboy*. The events in the narrative are placed in the summer of 1333; and the hero of the tale is O'Neill, "the youngest of the Princes of Claneboy." The scene is laid, principally, in the county Antrim; and this ballad is supposed to have been sung in the tent of O'Neill, on Slemish, near Ballymena, on the first night after he had crossed the Bann, the boundary of the British Pale. The person supposed to sing is "Turlough," the Prince's harper.]

My Owen Bawn's hair is of thread of gold spun ;
Of gold in the shadow, of light in the sun ;
All curled in a coolun the bright tresses are—
They make his head radiant with beams like a star !

My Owen Bawn's mantle is long and is wide,
To wrap me up safe from the storm by his side ;
And I'd rather face snow-drift and winter wind there,
Than lie among daisies and sunshine elsewhere.

My Owen Bawn Con* is a hunter of deer,
He tracks the dun quarry with arrow and spear—
Where wild woods are waving, and deep waters flow,
Ah, there goes my love, with the dun-dappled roe.

My Owen Bawn Con is a bold fisherman,
He spears the strong salmon in midst of the Bann ;
And rock'd in the tempest on stormy Lough Neagh,
Draws up the red trout through the bursting of spray.

My Owen Bawn Con is a bard of the best,
He wakes me with singing, he sings me to rest ;
And the cruit 'neath his fingers rings up with a sound,
As though angels harped o'er us, and fays underground.

* So in the original; but printed *Quin* by the author, in "*Lays of the Western Gael*," p. 90.—ED

They tell me the stranger has given command,
That crommeal and coolun shall cease in the land,
That all our youth's tresses of yellow be shorn,
And bonnets, instead, of a new fashion, worn;

That mantles like Owen Bawn's shield us no more,
That hunting and fishing henceforth we give o'er,
That the net and the arrow aside must be laid,
For hammer and trowel, and mattock and spade;

That the echoes of music must sleep in their caves,
That the slave must forget his own tongue for a slave's,
That the sounds of our lips must be strange in our ears,
And our bleeding hands toil in the dew of our tears,

Oh sweetheart and comfort! with thee by my side,
I could love and live happy, whatever betide;
But *thou*, in such bondage, wouldst die ere a day—
Away to Tir-oën, then, Owen, away!

There are wild woods and mountains, and streams deep and clear,
There are loughs in Tir-oën as lovely as here;
There are silver harps ringing in Yellow Hugh's hall,
And a bower by the forest side, sweetest of all!

We will dwell by the sunshiny skirts of the brake,
Where the sycamore shadows grow deep in the lake;
And the snowy swan stirring the green shadows there,
Afloat on the water, seems floating in air.

Farewell, then, black Slemish, green Collon adieu,
My heart is a-breaking at thinking of you;
But tarry we dare not, when freedom hath gone—
Away to Tir-oën, then, Owen Bawn Con!*

---

* This stanza, in consequence, perhaps, of substituting Quin for Con, rejected by the author in *Lays of the Western Gael*, p. 93.—ED.

Away to Tir-oën, then Owen away!
We will leave them the dust from our feet for a prey
And our dwelling in ashes and flames for a spoil—
'Twill be long ere they quench them with streams of
   the Foyle!

AILLEEN.

BY JOHN BANIM.

'Tis not for love of gold I go,
  'Tis not for love of fame;
Tho' fortune should her smile bestow
  And I may win a name,
                Ailleen,
  And I may win a name.

And yet it is for gold I go,
  And yet it is for fame,
That they may deck another brow,
  And bless another name,
                Ailleen,
  And bless another name.

For this, but this, I go—for this
  I lose thy love awhile;
And all the soft and quiet bliss
  Of thy young, faithful smile,
                Ailleen,
  Of thy young, faithful smile.

And I go to brave a world I hate,
  And woo it o'er and o'er,
And tempt a wave, and try a fate
  Upon a stranger shore,
                Ailleen,
  Upon a stanger shore.

Oh! when the bays are all my own,
  I know a heart will care!
Oh! when the gold is wooed and won,
  I know a brow shall wear,
               Ailleen,
  I know a brow shall wear!

And when with both returned again,
  My native land to see,
I know a smile will meet me there,
  And a hand will welcome me,
               Ailleen,
  And a hand will welcome me!

EMAN-AC-KNUCK TO EVA.*

BY J. B. CLARKE.

On the white hawthorn's bloom, in purpling streak,
I see the fairy-ring of morning break,
On the green valley's brow she golden glows,
Kissing the crimson of the opening rose,—
Knits with her thousand smiles its damask dyes,
And laughs the season on our hearts and eyes—
Rise, Eva, rise! fair spirit of my breast,
In whom I live, forsake the down of rest;

Lovelier than morn, carnationed in soft hues,
Sweeter than rifled roses in the dews
Of dawn divinely weeping—and more fair
Than the coy flowers fann'd by mountain air;
More modest than the morning's blushing smile.
Rise, Eva, rise! pride of our Western Isle—
The sky's blue beauties lose their sunny grace
Before the calm, soft splendours of thy face;

Thy breath is sweeter than the apple bloom,
When spring's musk'd spirit bathes it in perfume;

* Eman-ac-Knuck, or Ned of the Hill, a celebrated minstrel freebooter, who has been made the hero of a romance by Mrs. Peck. This poem is addressed to his wife.

The rock's wild honey steeps thy rubied lip—
Rise, Eva, rise!—I long these sweets to sip.
The polish'd ringlets of thy jetty locks
Shame the black ravens on their sun-gilt rocks.
Thy neck can boast a whiter, lovelier glow,
Than the wild cygnet's silvery plume of snow.

And from thy bosom, the soft throne of bliss,
The witch of love, in all her blessedness,
Heaves all her spells, wings all her feather'd dart
And dips her arrows in adoring hearts.
Rise, Eva, rise! the sun sheds his sweet ray,
Am'rous to kiss thee—rise, my love! we'll stray
Across the mountain,—on the blossomy heath,
The heath-bloom holds for thee its odorous breath;

From the tall crag, aspiring to the skies,
I'll pick for thee the strings of strawberries;
The yellow nuts, too, from the hazel tree—
Soul of my heart!—I'll strip to give to thee:
As thy red lips the berries shall be bright,
And the sweet nuts shall be as ripe and white
And milky as the love-begotten tide
That fills thy spotless bosom, my sweet bride!

Queen of the smile of joy! shall I not kiss
Thee in the moss-grown cot, bless'd bower of bliss—
Shall not thy rapturous lover clasp thy charms,
And fold his Eva in his longing arms—
Shall Inniscather's wood again attest
Thy beauties strain'd unto this burning breast?
Absent how long! Ah! when wilt thou return?
When shall this wither'd bosom cease to mourn?

Eva! why stay so long? why leave me lone
In the deep valley, to the cold grey stone
Pouring my plaints? O come, divinest fair!
Chase from my breast the demon of despair.
The winds are witness to my deep distress,
Like the lone wanderer of the wilderness;
For thee I languish and for thee I sigh—
My Eva come, or thy poor swain shall die!

And didst thou hear my melancholy lay?
And art thou coming, love? My Eva! say?
Thou daughter of a meek-eyed dame, thy face
Is lovelier than thy mother's, in soft grace.
O yes! thou comest, Eva! to my sight
An angel minister of heavenly light :—
The sons of frozen climes can never see
Summer's bright smile so glad as I see thee :
Thy steps to me are lovelier than the ray
Of roses on night's cheek—the blush of day.

O'DONNELL AND THE FAIR FITZGERALD

BY THE HON. GAVAN DUFFY.

A fawn that flies with sudden spring,
A wild bird fluttering on the wing,
A passing gleam of April sun,
She flashed upon me and was gone!
No chance did that dear face restore,
Nor then—nor now—nor evermore.
But sure, I see her in my dreams,
With eyes where love's first dawning beams;
And tones, like Irish music, say—
"You ask to love me, and you may;"
And so I know she *will* be mine,
That rose of princely Geraldine.

A voice that thrills with modest doubt,
A tale of love can ill pour out;
But, oh! when love wore manly guise,
And warrior feats woke woman's sighs—
With Irish sword, on Irish soil,
I might have won that kingly spoil.
But then, perchance, the Desmond race
Had deemed to mate with mine disgrace;
For mine's that strain of native blood
That last the Norman lance withstood

And still when mountain war was waged,
Their *sparths* among the Normans raged,
And burst through many a serried line
Of Lacy, Burke, and Geraldine.

And yet methinks in battle press,
My love, I could not love you less;
For, oh! 'twere sweet brave deeds to do
For our old, sainted land, and you!
To sweep, a storm, through Barrensmore,
With Docwra's scattered ranks before,
Like chaff upon our northern blast;
Nor rest till Bann's broad waves are passed,
Till Inbhar sees our flashing line,
Till Darha's lordly towers are mine,
And backward borne, as seal and sign,
The fairest maid of Geraldine.

But, Holy Bride,* how sweeter still
A hunted chief on Faughart hill,
With all the raging Pale behind,
So sweet, so strange a foe to find!
Soft love to plant where terror sprung,
With honey speech of Irish tongue;
Again to dare Clan-Geralt's swords
For hope of some sweet, stolen words.
Till many a danger passed and gone,
My suit has sped, my Bride is won—
She's proud Clan-Connell's Queen and mine,
Young Geraldine, of Geraldine.

But sure that time is dead and gone
When worth alone such love had won,
For hearts are cold, and hands are bought,
And faith, and lore, and love are nought?
Ah, trust me, no! The pure and true
The genial past may still renew;

* St. Bride, or Brigid.

Still love as then ; and still no less
Strong hearts shall snatch a brave success,
And to their end right onward go,
As Erna's tide to Assaroe.*

Oh! Saints may strive for Martyr's crown,
And warriors watch by leaguered town,
But poor is all their toil to mine,
Till won's my Bride—my Geraldine!

THE COOLUN.†

TRANSLATED FROM THE IRISH.

BY SAMUEL FERGUSON, LL.D., M.R.I.A.

OH, had you seen the Coolun,
   Walking down by the cuckoo's street,‡
With the dew of the meadows shining
   On her milk-white twinkling feet.
Oh, my love she is, and my *coleen oge*,
   And she dwells in Bal'nagar ;
And she bears the palm of beauty bright
   From the fairest that in Erin are.

In Bal'nagar is the Coolun,
   Like the berry on the bough her cheek ;
Bright beauty dwells for ever
   On her fair neck and ringlets sleek :
Oh, sweeter is her mouth's soft music
   Than the lark or thrush at dawn,
Or the blackbird in the greenwood singing
   Farewell to the setting sun.

---

* A waterfall in Tyrconnell, the O'Donnell's county.

† Un Chuil-fhionn.—*The Coolun*, the Maiden of fair flowing Locks.

‡ This word is incorrectly and unintelligibly printed in the original. I am helped, I believe, to the proper word by the following passage in Mr. Ferguson's first article on Hardiman's Minstrelsy (*University Magazine*, vol. iii. 447)—"The bagpipes are drawing their last breath from a few consumptive lungs, and French-horns have been heard in ' the street of the cuckoos.'" 1845.

Rise up, my boy! make ready
  My horse, for I forth would ride,
To follow the modest damsel,
  Where she walks on the green hill side:
For e'er since our youth were we plighted,
  In faith, troth, and wedlock true—
Oh, she's sweeter to me than nine times over
  Than organ or cuckoo!

Oh, ever since my childhood
  I loved the fair and darling child,
But our people came between us,
  And with lucre our pure love defiled:
Oh, my woe it is, and my bitter pain,
  And I weep it night and day,
That the *coleen bawn* of my early love
  Is torn from my heart away.

Sweet-heart and faithful treasure,
  Be constant still, and true;
Nor for want of herds and houses
  Leave one who would ne'er leave you.
I'll pledge you the blessed Bible,
  Without and eke within,
That the faithful God will provide for us,
  Without thanks to kith or kin.

Oh, love, do you remember
  When we lay all night alone,
Beneath the ash in the winter-storm,
  When the oak wood round did groan?
No shelter then from the blast had we,
  The bitter blast or sleet,
But your gown to wrap about our heads
  And my coat around our feet.

[This poem is called an "IRISH RUSTIC BALLAD," by Dr. Ferguson, in his *Lays of the Western Gael*, p. 211.—Ed.]

BRIGHIDIN BAN MO STORE.*

BY EDWARD WALSH.

[*Brigidin ban mo store* is, in English, *fair young bride*, or *Bridget my treasure*. The proper sound of this phrase is not easily found by the mere English-speaking Irish. The following is the best help I can afford them in the case :—" *Bree-dheen-bawn-mu-sthore.*" The proper name Brighit, or Bride, signifies *a fiery dart*, and was the name of the goddess of poetry in the pagan days of Ireland.—AUTHOR'S NOTE.]

I AM a wand'ring minstrel man,
   And Love my only theme,
I've stray'd beside the pleasant Bann,
   And eke the Shannon's stream ;
I've pip'd and play'd to wife and maid
   By Barrow, Suir, and Nore,
But never met a maiden yet
   Like bṛiġoin ban mo stoṛ.

My girl hath ringlets rich and rare,
   By Nature's fingers wove—
Loch-Carra's swan is not so fair
   As is her breast of love ;
And when she moves, in Sunday sheen,
   Beyond our cottage door,
I'd scorn the high-born Saxon queen
   For bṛiġoin ban mo stoṛ

It is not that thy smile is sweet,
   And soft thy voice of song—
It is not that thou fleest to meet
   My comings lone and long !
But that doth rest beneath thy breast,
   A heart of purest core,
Whose pulse is known to me alone,
   mo bṛiġin ban aṛtoṛ.

* bṛiġoin ban me stoṛ.

THE LAMENTATION OF FELIX M'CARTHY.

TRANSLATED FROM THE IRISH.

BY J. J. CALLANAN.

[From the inquiries we have made (says the author) concerning the tragical circumstance that gave rise to the following effusion, we learn that Felix M'Carthy had been compelled, during a period of disturbance and persecution, to fly for safety to a mountainous region, in the western part of this county (Cork). He was accompanied in his flight by a wife and four children, and found an asylum in a lone and secluded glen, where he constructed a rude kind of habitation as a temporary residence. One night, during the absence of himself and his wife, this ill-contrived structure suddenly gave way, and buried the four children, who were asleep at the time, in its ruins. What the feelings of the father were will be best learned from the following lamentation—AUTHOR'S NOTE.]

I'LL sing my children's death-song, tho'
My voice is faint and low;
Mine is the heart that's desolate—
'Tis I will mourn their fate.

I'll sing their death-song, tho' the dart
Is rankling in my heart:
No friend is here my pangs to soothe,
In this deep solitude.

Weep not the widow's grief to see,
When wild with agony!
Nor mourn to hear the bridegroom rave,
Above his partner's grave.

But weep for one whose bitter wail,
Is poured upon the gale,
Like the shrill bird that flutters nigh
The nest, where its crushed offspring lie.

Yes! I will sing this song of woe,
Till life's last spark shall glow,
Like the swan floating on the surge,
That murmurs its unwilling dirge.

Thou Callaghan, devoid of sin—
And Charles of the silken skin,
Mary and Anne, my peerless flower,
Entombed within an hour.

My four sweet children fair and brave,
Laid in one grave—
Wound of my soul, that I should say
Your death-song in one day!

Vain was the blood of Eiver's race,
And every opening grace,
And youth undarkened by a cloud—
Against an early shroud!

Mute are the tongues that sung for me,
In joyful harmony:—
Cold are the lips whose welcome kiss
To me was heavenly bliss.

Oh! but for him whose head was bow'd
'Mid Calvary's mocking crowd—
Soon would I fly the painful day,
And follow in their way.

Yet mourned not He in voiceless gloom,
O'er Lazarus in the tomb—
Rushed not the flood from his dimm'd eyes?
Heav'd not his breast with sighs?

Yes, for *his kindred* from the day,
That earthward darkling lay,—
Then do not chide that I should mourn
For them that *won't return*.

And mourned not the pure Virgin, when
Her Son, transfixed by men,
Writh'd in the throes of his dark agony?
Then blame not me.

At midnight's hour of silence deep,
Seal'd in their balmy sleep,
Oh! crushing grief,—oh! scathing blow,
My lov'd ones were laid low.

Methought, when bow'd this head with time,
Around me they would twine,
Nor reck'd that I should mourn their lot
A thing of nought.

'Twas meet to him, affection they should prove
Who gave them all his love,
And to old age the right concede,
Their path to lead.

Beauty and strength have left my brow,
Nor care nor wisdom have I now;
Little the blow of death I dread
Since all my hopes have fled.

No more—no more shall music's voice
My heart rejoice—
Like a brain-stricken fool, whose ear
Is clos'd 'gainst earthly cheer.

When wailing at the dead of night,
They cross my aching sight—
They come, and beck'ning me away,
They chide my long delay.

At midnight hour—at morn—at eve,
My sight they do not leave;
Within—abroad—their looks of love,
Around me move.

Oh! in their visits no affection's lost!
I love the pathways by their shadows cross'd
Soon, by the will of heaven's King,
To their embrace I'll spring.

I pity her who never more will know
Contentment here below:
Who fed them at the fountain of her breast,
And hush'd their infant rest.

Her faded eyes, her anguish speak—
And her clasp'd hands, so weak!
'Tis she, alas! of Erin's daughters
Hath seen* the *ruin of slaughters*.†

PASTHEEN FION.‡

IRISH RUSTIC SONG.

BY SAMUEL FERGUSON, LL.D., M.R.I.A.

[In Hardiman's "Irish Minstrelsy," vol. i., p. 330, there is a note upon the original of *Paistheen Fion*. The name may be translated either fair youth or fair maiden, and the writer supposes it to have a political meaning, and to refer to the son of James II.—ED.

Oh, my fair Pastheen is my heart's delight;
Her gay heart laughs in her blue eye bright;
Like the apple blossom her bosom white,
And her neck like the swan's on a March morn bright!
    Then, Oro, come with me! come with me! come
        with me!
    Oro, come with me! brown girl, sweet!
    And, oh! I would go through snow and sleet
    If you would come with me, brown girl, sweet!

Love of my heart, my fair Pastheen!
Her cheeks are as red as the rose's sheen,
But my lips have tasted no more, I ween,
Than the glass I drank to the health of my queen!

---

* This last expression may appear strange to the English reader, but it is a literal translation of the original.—AUTHOR'S NOTE.

† This poem is taken from *Bolster's Quarterly Magazine*, vol. i., Cork, 1826. It is not included in the collection of Callanan's Poems, published in 1829, in London.—"Cusheen Loo," p. 78, is also taken from the same magazine, and it is likewise omitted from that collection.

‡ FION is printed FINN in *The Lays of the Western Gale*, p. 204.

    Then, Oro, come with me ! come with me ! come
        with me !
    Oro, come* with me ! brown girl, sweet !
    And, oh ! I would go through snow and sleet
    If you would come with me, brown girl, sweet !

Were I in the town, where's mirth and glee,
Or 'twixt two barrels of barley bree,
With my fair Pastheen upon my knee,
'Tis I would drink to her pleasantly !
    Then, Oro, come with me ! come with me ! come
        with me !
    Oro, come with me ! brown girl, sweet !
    And, oh ! I would go through snow and sleet
    If you would come with me, brown girl, sweet !

Nine nights I lay in longing and pain,
Betwixt two bushes, beneath the rain,
Thinking to see you, love, once again ;
But whistle and call were all in vain !
    Then, Oro, come with me ! come with me ! come
        with me !
    Oro, come with me ! brown girl, sweet !
    And, oh ! I would go through snow and sleet
    If you would come with me, brown girl sweet !

I'll leave my people, both friend and foe ;
From all the girls in the world I'll go ;
But from you, sweetheart, oh, never ! oh, no !
Till I lie in the coffin, stretched, cold and low !
    Then, Oro, come with me ! come with me ! come
        with me !
    Oro, come with me ! brown girl, sweet !
    And, oh ! I would go through snow and sleet
    If you would come with me, brown girl, sweet !

* The emphasis is on "Come," *Author's Note*—See *Lays of the Western Gael*, p. 204.

THE PATRIOT'S BRIDE.
BY THE HON. GAVAN DUFFY.

Oh! give me back that royal dream
    My fancy wrought,
When I have seen your sunny eyes
    Grow moist with thought;
And fondly hop'd, dear Love, your heart from mine
    Its spell had caught;
And laid me down to dream that dream divine,
    But true methought,
Of how *my* life's long task would be, to make *yours*
    blessed as it ought.

To learn to love sweet Nature more
    For your sweet sake,
To watch with you—dear friend, with you!—
    Its wonders break;
The sparkling Spring in that bright face to see
    Its mirror make—
On summer morns to hear the sweet birds sing
    By linn and lake;
And know your voice, your magic voice, could still a
    grander music wake!

On some old shell-strewn rock to sit
    In Autumn eves,
Where grey Killiney cools the torrid air
    Hot autumn weaves;
Or by that Holy Well in mountain lone,
    Where Faith believes
(Fain would I b'lieve) its secret, darling, wish
    The heart achieves.
Yet, oh, its Saint was not more pure than she to whom
    My fond heart cleaves.

To see the dank mid-winter night
    Pass like a noon,
Sultry with thought from minds that teemed,
    And glowed like June:

Whereto would pass in sculp'd and pictured train
            Art's magic boon;
And Music thrill with many a haughty strain,
            And dear old tune,
Till hearts grew sad to hear the destined hour to part
      had come so soon.

To wake the old weird world that sleeps
            In Irish lore;
The strains sweet foreign Spenser sung
            By Mulla's shore;
Dear Curran's airy thoughts, like purple birds
            That shine and soar;
Tone's fiery hopes, and all the deathless words
            That Grattan swore;
The songs that once our own dear Davis sung; ah,
      me! to sing no more.

To search with mother-love the gifts
            Our land can boast—
Soft Erna's isles, Neagh's wooded slopes,
            Clare's iron coast;
Kildare, whose legends grey our bosoms stir
            With fay and ghost;
Grey Mourne, green Antrim, purple Glenmalur—
            Lene's fairy host;
With raids to many a foreign land to learn to love
      dear Ireland most.

And all those proud old victor-fields
            We thrill to name;
Whose mem'ries are the stars that light
            Long nights of shame;
The Cairn, the Dun, the Rath, the Tower, the Keep,
            That still proclaim
In chronicles of clay and stone, how true, how deep,
            Was Eire's fame,
Oh! we shall see them all, with her, that dear, dear
      friend we two have loved the same.

Yet ah! how truer, tend'rer still
        Methought did seem
That scene of tranquil joy, that happy home,
        By Dodder's stream;
The morning smile, that grew a fixéd star
        With love-lit beam,
The ringing laugh, locked hands, and all the far
        And shining stream
Of daily love, that made our daily life diviner than a
    dream.

For still to me dear Friend, dear Love,
        Or both—dear Wife,
Your image comes with serious thoughts,
        But tender, rife;
No idle plaything to caress or chide
        In sport or strife;
But my best chosen friend, companion, guide,
        To walk through life
Link'd hand in hand—two equal, loving friends, true
    husband and true wife.

THE COULIN FORBIDDEN.

BY CARROLL MALONE.

[In the twenty-eighth year of the reign of Henry VIII. an act was made respecting the habits and dress in general of the Irish, whereby all persons were restrained from being shorn or shaven above the ears, or from wearing glibbes, or Coulins (long locks) on their heads, or hair on their upper lip, called Crommeal. On this occasion a song was written by one of our bards, in which an Irish virgin is made to give the preference to her dear Coulin (or the youth with the flowing locks), to all strangers (by which the English were meant), or those who wore their habits. Of this song the air alone has reached us, and is universally admired.—*Walker, as quoted in Moore's Melodies.*

It so happens, however, on turning to the above statute, that no mention is to be found therein of the Coulin. But in the year 1295, a Parliament was held in Dublin; and then an act was passed which more than expressly names the Coulin, and minutely describes it for its more effectual prohibition. This, the only statute made in Ireland that names the Coulin, was passed two hundred and forty-two years before the act cited by Mr. Moore; and, in consequence of it, some of the Irish chieftains who lived near the seat of English government, or wished to keep up intercourse with the English districts, did, in or soon after that year, 1295, cut off their Coulins, and a distinct memorial of the event was made in writing by the Officers of the Crown. It was on this occasion that the bard, ever adhesive to national habits, endeavoured to tire the patriotism of a conforming cheiftain; and, in the character of some favourite virgin, declares her preference for her lover with the Coulin, before him who complaisantly assumed the adornments of foreign fashion.—*Dublin Penny Journal.*]

THE last time she looked in the face of her dear,
She breathed not a sigh, and she shed not a tear;
But she took up his harp, and she kissed his cold cheek—
"'Tis the first, and the last, for thy Norah to seek."

For beauty and bravery Cathan was known,
And the long flowing coulin he wore in Tyrone;
The sweetest of singers and harpers was he,
All over the North, from the Bann to the sea.

O'er the marshes of Dublin he often would rove,
To the glens of O'Toole, where he met with his love;
And at parting they pledged that, next midsummer's day,
He would come for the last time, and bear her away.

The king had forbidden the men of O'Neal,
With the coulin adorned, to come o'er the pale;
But Norah was Irish, and said, in her pride,
"If he wear not his coulin, I'll ne'er be his bride."

The bride has grown pale as the robe that she wears,
For the Lammas is come, and no bridegroom appears;
And she harkens and gazes when all are at rest,
For the sound of his harp, and the sheen of his vest.

Her palfrey is pillioned, and she has gone forth
On the long rugged road that leads down to the North;—
Where Eblana's strong castle frowns darkly and drear,
Is the head of her Cathan upraised on a spear.

The Lords of the Castle had murdered him there,
And all for the wearing that poor lock of hair:
For the word she had spoken in mirth or in pride,
Her lover, too fond and too faithful, had died

'Twas then that she looked on the face of her dear,
She breathed not a sigh, and she dropped not a tear
She took up his harp, and she kissed his cold cheek
" Farewell ! 'tis the first for thy Norah to seek."

And afterward, oft would the wilderness ring,
As, at night, in sad strains, to that harp she would sing
Her heartbreaking tones,—we remember them well—
But the words of her wailing, no mortal can tell.

THE IRISH EMIGRANT'S MOTHER.
BY DENIS FLORENCE MAC-CARTHY, M.R.I.A.

" OH ! come, my mother, come away, across the sea-
    green water ;
Oh ! come with me, and come with him, the husband
    of thy daughter ;
Oh! come with us, and come with them, the sister and
    the brother,
Who, prattling, climb thine aged knees, and call thy
    daughter—mother.

" Oh ! come, and leave this land of death—this isle of
    desolation—
This speck upon the sun-bright face of God's sublime
    creation,
Since now o'er all our fatal stars the most malign
    hath risen,
When Labour seeks the Poorhouse, and Innocence
    the Prison.

" 'Tis true, o'er all the sun-brown fields the husky
    wheat is bending ;
'Tis true, God's blessed hand at last a better time is
    sending ;
'Tis true, the island's agêd face looks happier and
    younger,
But in the best of days we've known the sickness and
    the hunger.

"When health breathed out in every breeze, too oft we've known the fever—
Too oft, my mother, have we felt the hand of the bereaver;
Too well remember many a time the mournful task that brought him,
When freshness fanned the Summer air, and cooled the glow of Autumn.

" But then the trial, though severe, still testified our patience,
We bowed with mingled hope and fear to God's wise dispensations;
We felt the gloomiest time was both a promise and a warning,
Just as the darkest hour of night is herald of the morning.

" But now through all the black expanse no hopeful morning breaketh—
No bird of promise in our hearts, the gladsome song awaketh;
No far-off gleams of good light up the hills of expectation—
Nought but the gloom that might precede the world's annihilation.

" So, mother, turn thine aged feet, and let our children lead 'em
Down to the ship that wafts us soon to plenty and to freedom;
Forgetting nought of all the past, yet all the past forgiving;
Come, let us leave the dying land, and fly unto the living.

" They tell us, they who read and think of Ireland's ancient story,
How once its Emerald Flag flung out a Sunburst's fleeting glory

Oh! if that sun will pierce no more the dark clouds
    that efface it,
Fly where the rising Stars of Heaven commingle to
    replace it.

"So, come, my mother, come away, across the sea-
    green water;
Oh! come with us, and come with him, the husband
    of thy daughter;
Oh! come with us, and come with them, the sister
    and the brother,
Who, prattling, climb thine aged knees, and call thy
    daughter—mother."

"Ah! go, my children, go away—obey this inspiration;
Go, with the mantling hopes of health and youthful
    expectation;
Go, clear the forests, climb the hills, and plough the
    expectant prairies;
Go, in the sacred name of God, and the Blessed
    Virgin Mary's.

"But though I feel how sharp the pang from thee
    and thine to sever,
To look upon these darling ones the last time and for
    ever;
Yet in this sad and dark old land, by desolation
    haunted,
My heart has struck its roots too deep ever to be
    transplanted.

"A thousand fibres still have life, although the trunk
    is dying—
They twine around the yet green grave where thy
    father's bones are lying;
Ah! from that sad and sweet embrace no soil on earth
    can loose 'em,
Though golden harvests gleam on its breast, and
    golden sands in its bosom.

"Others are twined around the stone, where ivy
    blossoms smother
The crumbling lines that trace thy names, my father
    and my mother;
God's blessing be upon their souls—God grant, my
    old heart prayeth,
Their names be written in the Book whose writing
    ne'er decayeth.

"Alas! my prayers would never warm within those
    great cold buildings,
Those grand cathedral churches with their marbles
    and their gildings;
For fitter than the proudest dome that would hang in
    splendour o'er me,
Is the simple chapel's white-washed wall, where my
    people knelt before me.

"No doubt it is a glorious land to which you now are
    going,
Like that which God bestowed of old, with milk and
    honey flowing;
But where are the blessed saints of God, whose lives
    of his law remind me,
Like Patrick, Brigid, and Columbkille, in the land
    I'd leave behind me?

"So leave me here, my children, with my old ways
    and old notions;
Leave me here in peace, with my memories and
    devotions;
Leave me in sight of your father's grave, and as the
    heavens allied us,
Let not, since we were joined in life, even the grave
    divide us.

"There's not a week but I can hear how you prosper
    better and better,
For the mighty fireships o'er the sea will bring the
    expected letter:

And if I need aught for my simple wants, my food or
    my winter firing,
Thou'lt gladly spare from thy growing store a little
    for my requiring.

"Remember with a pitying love the hapless land that
    bore you;
At every festal season be its gentle form before you;
When the Christmas candle is lighted, and the holly
    and ivy glisten,
Let your eye look back for a vanished face—for a
    voice that is silent, listen!

"So go, my children, go away—obey this inspiration;
Go, with the mantling hopes of health and youthful
    expectation;
Go, clear the forests, climb, the hills, and plough the
    expectant prairies;
Go, in the sacred name of God, and the Blessed
    Virgin Mary's."

THE MUSTER OF THE NORTH.
A.D. 1641.
BY THE HON. GAVAN DUFFY.

[We deny, and have always denied, the alleged massacre of 1641. But that the people rose under their Chiefs, seized the English towns, and expelled the English settlers, and in doing so committed many excesses, is undeniable—as is equally the desperate provocation. The ballad here printed is not meant as an apology for these excesses, which we condemn and lament, but as a true representation of the feelings of the insurgents in the first madness of success.]

Joy! joy! the day is come at last, the day of hope and
    pride,
And see! our crackling bonfires light old Banra's joy-
    ful tide,
And gladsome bell, and bugle horn, from Inbhar's*
    captured Towers,
Hark! how they tell the Saxon swine, this land is ours,
    IS OURS!

        * Newry.

Glory to God! my eyes have seen the ransomed fields
    of Down,
My ears have drunk the joyful news, "Stout Feidhlim*
    hath his own."
Oh! may they see and hear no more, oh! may they
    rot to clay,
When they forget to triumph in the conquest of to-day.

Now, now we'll teach the shameless Scot to purge his
    thievish maw,
Now, now the courts may fall to pray, for justice is the
    law,
Now shall the Undertaker† square for once his loose
    accounts,
We'll strike, brave boys, a fair result, from all his false
    amounts.

Come, trample down their robber rule, and smite its
    venal spawn,
Their foreign laws, their foreign church, their ermine
    and their lawn,
With all the specious fry of fraud that robb'd us of our
    own;
And plant our ancient laws again, beneath our lineal
    throne.

Our standard flies o'er fifty towers, o'er twice ten thou-
    sand men;
Down have we pluck'd the pirate Red, never to rise
    again;
The Green alone shall stream above our native field
    and flood—
The spotless Green, save where its folds are gemmed
    with Saxon blood!

---

* Phelim.
† The Scotch and English adventurers planted in Ulster by James I.
were called Undertakers.

Pity !* no, no ; you dare not, Priest—not you, our
    Father, dare
Preach to us now that Godless creed—the murderer's
    blood to spare ;
To spare his blood, while tombless still our slaughtered
    kin implore
" Graves and revenge" from Gobbin-Cliffs and Car-
    rick's bloody shore !†

Pity—could we "forget—forgive," if we were clods of
    clay,
Our martyr'd priests, our banished chiefs, our race in
    dark decay,
And worse than all— you know it, Priest—the daughters
    of our land,
With wrongs we blushed to name until the sword was
    in our hand !

Pity ! well, if you needs must whine, let pity have its
    way,
Pity for all our comrades true, far from our side to-
    day ;
The prison-bound who rot in chains, the faithful dead
    who poured
Their blood 'neath Temple's lawless axe or Parson's
    ruffian sword.

They smote us with the swearer's oath, and with the
    murderer's knife,
We in the open field will fight, fairly for land and life ;
But, by the Dead and all their wrongs, and by our
    hopes to-day,
One of us twain shall fight their last, or be it we or
    they—

  * Leland, the Protestant Historian, states that the Catholic Priests
"*laboured zealously to moderate the excesses of war ;*" and frequently
protected the English by concealing them in their places of worship, and
even under their altars.
  † The scene of the dreadful massacre of the unoffending inhabitants of
Island Magee by the garrison of Carrickfergus.

They banned our faith, they banned our lives, they
    trod us into earth,
Until our very patience stirred their bitter hearts to
    mirth ;
Even this great flame that wraps them now, not *we*
    but *they* have bred;
Yes, this is their own work, and now, their work be on
    their head.

Nay, Father, tell us not of help from Leinster's Nor-
    man Peers,
If that we shape our holy cause to match their selfish
    fears—
Helpless and hopeless be their cause, who brook a vain
    delay,
Our ship is launched, our flag's afloat, whether they
    come or stay.

Let silken Howth and savage Slane still kiss their
    tyrant's rod,
And pale Dunsany still prefer his Master to his God ;
Little we heed their father's sons the Marchmen of the
    Pale,
If Irish hearts and Irish hands have Spanish blades
    and mail?

Then, let them stay to bow and fawn, or fight with
    cunning words ;
I fear me more their courtly arts than England's hire-
    ling swords ;
Natheless their creed they hate us still, as the De-
    spoiler hates,
Could they love us and love their prey—our kinsmen's
    lost estates !

Our rude array's a jagged rock to smash the spoiler's
    power,
Or need we aid, His aid we have who doomed this
    gracious hour;

Of yore He led his Hebrew host to peace through
    strife and pain,
And us He leads the self-same path, the self-same goal
    to gain.
Down from the sacred hills whereon a SAINT* com-
    muned with God,
Up from the vale where Bagnell's blood manured the
    reeking sod,
Out from the stately woods of Triuch,† M'Kenna's
    plundered home,
Like Malin's waves, as fierce and fast, our faithful
    clansmen come.
Then, brethren, *on!*—O'Neill's dear shade would frown
    to see you pause—
Our banished Hugh, our martyred Hugh, he's watch-
    ing o'er your cause—
His gen'rous error lost the land—he deem'd the
    Norman true,
Oh, forward! friends, it must not lose the land again
    in you!

DRIMIN DHU.

A JACOBITE RELIC—TRANSLATED FROM THE IRISH.

BY SAMUEL FERGUSON, LL.D., M.R.I.A.

AH, Drimin Dhu deelish, ah pride of the flow,‡
Ah, where are your folks, are they living or no?
They're down in the ground, 'neath the sod lying low,
Expecting King James with the crown on his brow.

But if I could get sight of the crown on his brow,
By night and day travelling to London I'd go;
Over mountains of mist and soft mosses below,
Till I'd beat on the kettle-drums, Drimin Dhubh, O.

Welcome home, welcome home, Drimin Dhubh, O!
Good was your sweet milk for drinking, I trow;
With your face like a rose, and your dew-lap of snow,
I'll part from you never, ah, Drimin Dhubh, O!

* St. Patrick, whose favourite retreat was Leath Chathail (Leceal Cathal's half), in the county Down.
  † Improperly written Truagh.   ‡ The soft grassy part of the bog.

DARK ROSALEEN.

TRANSLATED FROM THE IRISH.

BY JAMES CLARENCE MANGAN.

[This impassioned ballad, entitled in the original *Roisin Duh* (or The Black Little Rose), was written in the reign of Elizabeth by one of the poets of the celebrated Tirconnellian chieftain, Hugh the Red O'Donnell. It purports to be an allegorical address from Hugh to Ireland on the subject of his love and struggles for her, and his resolve to raise her again to the glorious position she held as a nation before the irruption of the Saxon and Norman spoilers. The true character and meaning of the figurative allusions with which it abounds, and to two only of which I need refer here—viz., the "Roman wine" and "Spanish ale" mentioned in the first stanza—the intelligent reader will, of course, find no difficulty in understanding.]

O MY Dark Rosaleen,
  Do not sigh, do not weep!
The priests are on the ocean green,
  They march along the deep.
There's wine . . . . from the royal Pope,
  Upon the ocean green;
And Spanish ale shall give you hope,
  My Dark Rosaleen!
  My own Rosaleen!
Shall glad your heart, shall give you hope,
Shall give you health, and help, and hope,
  My Dark Rosaleen!

Over hills, and through dales,
  Have I roamed for your sake;
All yesterday I sailed with sails
  On river and on lake.
The Erne, ... at its highest flood,
  I dashed across unseen,
For there was lightning in my blood,
  My Dark Rosaleen!
  My own Rosaleen!
Oh! there was lightning in my blood,
Red lightning lightened through my blood,
  My Dark Rosaleen!

All day long, in unrest,
   To and fro, do I move,
The very soul within my breast
   Is wasted for you, love!
The heart . . . . in my bosom faints
   To think of you, my queen,
My life of life, my saint of saints,
   My Dark Rosaleen!
   My own Rosaleen!
To hear your sweet and sad complaints,
My life, my love, my saint of saints,
   My Dark Rosaleen!

Woe and pain, pain and woe,
   Are my lot, night and noon,
To see your bright face clouded so,
   Like to the mournful moon.
But yet . . . . will I rear your throne
   Again in golden sheen;
'Tis you shall reign, shall reign alone,
   My Dark Rosaleen!
   My own Rosaleen!
'Tis you shall have the golden throne
'Tis you shall reign, and reign alone,
   My Dark Rosaleen!

Over dews, over sands,
   Will I fly for your weal:
Your holy delicate white hands
   Shall girdle me with steel.
At home . . . . in your emerald bowers,
   From morning's dawn till e'en,
You'll pray for me, my flower of flowers,
   My Dark Rosaleen!
   My fond Rosaleen!
You'll think of me through daylight's hours,
My virgin flower, my flower of flowers,
   My Dark Rosaleen!

I could scale the blue air,
　I could plough the high hills,
Oh, I could kneel all night in prayer,
　To heal your many ills !
And one . . . . beamy smile from you
　Would float like light between
My toils and me, my own, my true,
　My Dark Rosaleen !
　My fond Rosaleen !
Would give me life and soul anew,
A second life, a soul anew,
　My Dark Rosaleen !

O ! the Erne shall run red
　With redundance of blood,
The earth shall rock beneath our tread.
　And flames wrap hill and wood,
And gun-peal, and slogan cry,
　Wake many a glen serene,
Ere you shall fade, ere you shall die.
　My Dark Rosaleen !
　My own Rosaleen !
The Judgment Hour must first be nigh,
Ere you can fade, ere you can die,
　My Dark Rosaleen !

SHANE BWEE; OR, THE CAPTIVITY OF THE GAEL.

GEIBIONN NA-N-GAOIDEIL.*

BY JAMES CLARENCE MANGAN.

[A Translation of the Jacobite song called "Géibionn na-n-Gaoideil,' written by Owen Roe O'Sullivan, a Kerry poet, who flourished about the middle of the last century.†]

'Twas by sunset I walked and wandered
  Over hill sides and over moors,
    With a many sighs and tears
Sunk in sadness, I darkly pondered
  All the wrongs our lost land endures
    In these latter night-black years.
" How," I mused, " has her worth departed!
  What a ruin her fame is now!
    We, once freest of the Free,
We are trampled and broken-hearted,
  Yea, even our Princes themselves must bow
    Low before the vile Shane Bwee!"‡

Nigh a stream, in a grassy hollow,
  Tired, at length, I lay down to rest;
    There the birds and balmy air
Bade new reveries and cheerier follow,
  Waking newly within my breast
    Thoughts that cheated my despair.
Was I waking or was I dreaming?
  I glanced up, and behold! there shone
    Such a vision over me!
A young girl, bright as Erin's beaming
  Guardian spirit—now sad and lone,
    Through the Spoiling of Shane Bwee!

* Ӡeıbıonn na-n-Ӡaoıoeıl.

† His death, it has been stated by the late Mr. Edward Walshe, occurred in the year 1784. We may, therefore, suppose this song to have been written by the author in his youth—perhaps about the year 1740.

‡ *Seagan Buidhe*, Yellow John, a name applied first to the Prince of Orange, and afterwards to his adherents generally.

O, for pencil to paint the golden
　　Locks that waved in luxuriant sheen
　　　　To her feet of stilly light!
(Not the Fleece that in ages olden
　　Jason bore o'er the ocean green
　　　　Into Hellas, gleamed so bright.)
And the eyebrows thin-arch'd over
　　Her mild eyes, and more, even more
　　　　Beautiful, methought, to see
Than those rainbows that wont to hover
　　O'er our blue island-lakes of yore.
　　　　Ere the Spoiling by Shane Bwee!

" Bard!" she spake, " deem not this unreal.
　　I was niece of a Pair whose peers
　　　　None shall see on Earth again—
ÆONGUS CON, and the Dark O'NIALL,*
　　Rulers over Ierne in years
　　　　When her sons as yet were Men.
Times have darkened; and now our holy
　　Altars crumble and castles fall;
　　　　Our groans ring through Christendee.
Still, despond not! HE comes, though slowly,
　　He, the Man, who shall disenthral
　　　　The PROUD CAPTIVE of Shane Bwee!"

Here she vanished; and I, in sorrow
　　Blent with joy, rose and went my way
　　　　Homeward over moor and hill.
O, Great God! Thou from whom we borrow
　　Life and strength, unto Thee I pray!
　　　　Thou, who swayest at Thy will
Hearts and councils, thralls, tyrants, freemen,
　　Wake through Europe the ancient soul,
　　　　And on every shore and sea,
From the Blackwater to the Dniemen,
　　Freedom's Bell will ere long time toll
　　　　The deep death-knell of Shane Bwee!

* Niall Dubh.

THE VOICE OF LABOUR.
A CHANT OF THE CITY MEETINGS.
A.D. 1843.

BY THE HON. GAVAN DUFFY.

YE who despoil the sons of toil, saw ye this sight to-day,
When stalwart trade in long brigade, beyond a king's array,
Marched in the blessed light of heaven, beneath the open sky,
Strong in the might of sacred RIGHT, that none dare ask them why?
These are the slaves, the needy knaves, ye spit upon with scorn—
The spawn of earth, of nameless birth, and basely bred as born;
Yet know, ye soft and silken lords, were we the thing ye say,
Your broad domains, your coffered gains, your lives were ours to-day!

Measure that rank, from flank to flank; 'tis fifty thousand strong;
And mark you here, in front and rear, brigades as deep and long;
And know that never blade of foe, or Arran's deadly breeze,
Tried by assay of storm or fray, more dauntless hearts than these;
The sinewy smith, little he recks of his own child— the sword;
The men of gear, think you they fear *their* handiwork —a Lord?
And undismayed, yon sons of trade might see the battle's front,
Who bravely bore, nor bowed before, the deadlier face of want.

What lack we here of show and form that lure you
    slaves, to death?
Not serried bands, nor sinewy hands, nor music's
    martial breath;
And if we broke the slavish yoke our suppliant race
    endure,
No robbers we—but chivalry—the Army of the Poor.
Shame on ye now, ye Lordly crew, that do your bet-
    ters wrong—
We are no base and braggart mob, but merciful and
    strong.
Your henchmen vain, your vassal train, would fly our
    first defiance;
In us—in our strong, tranquil breasts—abides your
    sole reliance.

Ay! keep them all, castle and hall, coffers and costly
    jewels—
Keep your vile gain, and in its train the passions that
    it fuels.
We envy not your lordly lot—its bloom or its decay-
    ance;
But ye *have* that we claim as ours—our right in long
    abeyance:
Leisure to live, leisure to love, leisure to taste our
    freedom—
Oh! suff'ring poor, oh! patient poor, how bitterly you
    need them!
"Ever to moil, ever to toil," that is your social charter,
And city slave or peasant serf, the TOILER is its martyr.

Where Frank and Tuscan shed their sweat the goodly
    crop is theirs—
If Norway's toil make rich the soil, she eats the fruit
    she rears—
O'er Maine's green sward there rules no lord, saving
    the Lord on high;
But we are serfs in our own land—proud masters, tell
    us why?

The German burgher and his men, brother with brothers live,
While toil must wait without *your* gate what gracious crusts you give.
Long in your sight, for our own right, we've bent and still we bend ;—
Why did we bow? why do we now?—Proud masters this must end.

Perish the past—a generous land is this fair land of ours,
And enmity may no man see between its Towns and Towers.
Come, join our bands—here take our hands—now shame on him that lingers.
Merchant or Peer, you have no fear from labour's blistered fingers.
Come, join at last—perish the past—its traitors, its seceders—
Proud names and old, frank hearts and bold, come join and be our Leaders.
But know, ye lords, that be your swords with us or with our Wronger,
Heaven be our guide, we Toilers bide this lot of shame no longer.

THE WEXFORD INSURGENT.

TRANSLATED FROM THE IRISH.

The heroes of Wexford have burst through their chains,
And the voice of the freeman is loud o'er her plains—
The Sassanachs are broken, their horsemen have fled,
And the pride of their host on the mountain lie dead.

For roused is the blood of the bold *Shilmaleer*,
The pride of the conflict when foemen are near—
And the heroes of Bargy and Bantry are there,
In the shock ever foremost, in flight in the rear.

Oh ! soon will the hearths of the traitors be lone,
And their halls but re-echo the shriek and the groan,
And the red flame shall burst thro' their roof to the sky,
For the hour of our freedom and vengeance is nigh.

The men of the mountain are down in the vale,
And the flags of Shelburny are loose to the gale—
And tho' gentle the Forth, yet her sons never slight,
For the mildest in peace are oft boldest in fight.

The cold-blooded Sassanach is low on the hill,
Like the red rock he presses, as lone and as chill—
There, pulseless and cold, the pale beams of the moon
Show the deep-riven breast of the fallen dragoon.

And low lies his charger, his bosom all torn,
And from the dark helmet the horse-hair is shorn,
And the hearts of the great, and the brave, and the proud,
Have been trampled in death when the battle was loud.

Oh ! long in fair England each maiden may mourn—
The pride of her bosom will never return ;
His heart's blood is scattered—his last prayer is said—
And the dark raven flaps his wild wing o'er the dead.

Yes, long she may call him from battle in vain—
The sight of her lover she ne'er shall regain :
All cold is his bosom, and crimson his brow,
And the night wind is sighing its dirge o'er him now

THE DREAM OF JOHN MACDONNELL.
TRANSLATED FROM THE IRISH.
BY JAMES CLARENCE MANGAN.

[John MacDonnell, usually called MacDonnell *Claragh*, from his family residence, was a native of the county of Cork, and may be classed among the first of the purely Irish poets of the last century. He was born in 1691, and died in 1754. His poems are remarkable for their energy, their piety of tone, and the patriotic spirit they everywhere manifest. The following is one of them, and deserves to be regarded as a very curious topographical "Jacobite relic."]

I LAY in unrest—old thoughts of pain,
   That I struggled in vain to smother,
Like midnight spectres haunted my brain—
   Dark fantasies chased each other ;
When, lo ! a figure—who might it be ?
   A tall fair figure stood near me !
Who might it be ? An unreal Banshee ?
   Or an angel sent to cheer me ?

Though years have rolled since then, yet now
   My memory thrillingly lingers
On her awful charms, her waxen brow,
   Her pale translucent fingers ;—
Her eyes that mirrored a wonder world,
   Her mien of unearthly mildness,
And her waving raven tresses that curled
   To the ground in beautiful wildness.

"Whence comest thou, Spirit ?" I asked, methought
   "Thou art not one of the Banished ?"
Alas, for me ! she answered nought,
   But rose aloft and vanished ;
And a radiance, like to a glory, beamed
   In the light she left behind her ;
Long time I wept, and at last me-dreamed
   I left my shieling to find her.

And first I turned to the thund'rous North
   To Gruagach's mansion kingly ;
Untouching the earth, I then sped forth
   To Inver-lough, and the shingly

And shining strand of the fishful Erne,
    And thence to Croghan the golden,
Of whose resplendent palace ye learn
    So many a marvel olden!

I saw the Mourna's billows flow—
    I passed the walls of Shenady,
And stood in the hero-thronged Ardroe,
    Embossed amid greenwoods shady;
And visited that proud pile that stands
    Above the Boyne's broad waters,
Where Ængus dwells with his warrior bands
    And the fairest of Ulster's daughters.

To the halls of Mac-Lir, to Creevroe's height,
    To Tara, the glory of Erin,
To the fairy palace that glances bright
    On the peak of the blue Cnocfeerin,
I vainly hied. I went west and east—
    I travelled seaward and shoreward—
But thus was I greeted in field and at feast
    "Thy way lies onward and forward!"

At last I reached, I wist not how,
    The royal towers of Ival,
Which, under the cliff's gigantic brow,
    Still rise without a rival;
And here were Thomond's chieftains all,
    With armour, and swords, and lances;
And here sweet music filled the hall,
    And damsels charmed with dances.

And here, at length, on a silvery throne,
    Half seated, half reclining,
With forehead white as the marble stone,
    And garments so starrily shining,
And features beyond the poet's pen—
    The sweetest, saddest features—
Appeared before me once again,
    That fairest of Living Creatures!

"Draw near, O mortal!" she said, with a sigh,
  "And hear my mournful story!
The guardian Spirit of ERIN am I,
  But dimmed is mine ancient glory.
My priests are banished, my warriors wear
  No longer Victory's garland;
And my Child,* my Son, my beloved Heir,
  Is an exile in a far land!"

I heard no more—I saw no more—
  The bands of slumber were broken;
And palace and hero, and river and shore,
  Had vanished, and left no token.
Dissolved was the spell that had bound my will,
  And my fancy thus for a season:
But a sorrow therefore hangs over me still,
  Despite of the teachings of Reason!

THE ORANGEMAN'S WIFE.

BY CARROLL MALONE.

I WANDER by the limpid shore,
  When fields and flowr'ets bloom,
But, oh! my heart is sad and sore—
  My soul is sunk in gloom—
All day I cry ohone! ohone!
  I weep from night till morn—
I wish that I were dead and gone,
  Or never had been born.

My father dwelt beside Tyrone,
  And with him children five;
But I to Charlemont had gone,
  At service there to live.
O brothers fond! O sister dear!
  How ill I paid your love!
O father! father! how I fear
  To meet thy soul above!

* Charles Stuart.

My mother left us long ago;
   A lovely corpse was she,—
But we had longer days of woe
   In this sad world to be.
My weary days will soon be done—
   I pine in grief forlorn;
I wish that I were dead and gone,
   Or never had been born.

It was the year of ninety-eight;
   The wreckers came about;
They burned my father's stack of wheat,
   And drove my brothers out;
They forced my sister to their lust—
   God grant my father rest!
For the captain of the wreckers thrust
   A bayonet through his breast.

It was a dreadful, dreadful year;
   And I was blindly led,
In love, and loneliness, and fear,
   A loyal man to wed;
And still my heart is his alone,
   It breaks, but cannot turn:
I wish that I were dead and gone,
   Or never had been born.

Next year we lived in quiet love,
   And kissed our infant boy;
And peace had spread her wings above
   Our dwelling at the Moy.
And then my wayworn brothers came
   To share our peace and rest;
And poor lost Rose, to hide her shame
   And sorrow in my breast.

They came, but soon they turned and fled—
   Preserve my soul, O God!
It was my husband's hand, they said,
   That shed my father's blood.

All day I cry ohone! ohone!
I weep from night till morn;
And oh, that I were dead and gone,
Or never had been born!

THE IRISH CHIEFS.

BY THE HON. GAVAN DUFFY.

Oh! to have lived like an IRISH CHIEF, when hearts were fresh and true,
And a manly thought, like a pealing bell, would quicken them through and through;
And the seed of a gen'rous hope right soon to a fiery action grew,
And men would have scorned to talk, and talk, and never a deed to do.
    Oh! the iron grasp,
    And the kindly clasp,
  And the laugh so fond and gay;
    And the roaring board,
    And the ready sword,
  Were the types of that vanished day.

Oh! to have lived as Brian lived, and to die as Brian died;
His land to win with the sword, and smile,* as a warrior wins his bride.
To knit its force in a kingly host, and rule it with kingly pride,
And still in the girt of its guardian swords over victor fields to ride;
    And when age was past,
    And when death came fast,
  To look with a softened eye
    On a happy race
    Who had loved his face,
  And to die as a king should die.

* Our great Brian is called an usurper, inasmuch as he combined, by force and policy, the scattered and jealous powers of the island into one sovereignty, and ruled it himself by the D e right of being the fittest ruler

Oh! to have lived dear Owen's life—to live for a
  solemn end,
To strive for the ruling strength and skill God's saints
  to the Chosen send ;
And to come at length, with that holy strength, the
  bondage of fraud to rend,
And pour the light of God's freedom in where
  Tyrants and Slaves were denned ;
    And to bear the brand
    With an equal hand,
   Like a-soldier of Truth and Right,
    And, oh ! Saints to die,
    While our flag flew high,
   Nor to look on its fall or flight.

Oh ! to have lived as Grattan lived, in the glow of his
  manly years,
To thunder again those iron words that thrill like the
  clash of spears ;
Once more to blend for a holy end, our peasants, and
  priests, and peers,
Till England raged, like a baffled fiend, at the tramp
  of our Volunteers.
    And, oh ! best of all,
    Far rather to fall
   (With a blesseder fate than he),
    On a conqu'ring field,
    Than one right to yield,
   Of the Island so proud and free !

Yet, scorn to cry on the days of old, when hearts were
  fresh and true,
If hearts be weak, oh ! chiefly *then* the Missioned their
  work must do ;
Nor wants our day its own fit way, the want is in *you*
  and *you* ;
For these eyes have seen as kingly a King as ever dear
  Erin knew.

And with Brian's will,
And with Owen's skill,
And with glorious Grattan's love,
He had freed us soon—
But death darkened his noon,
And he sits with the saints above.

Oh! could you live as Davis lived—kind Heaven be his bed!
With an eye to guide, and a hand to rule. and a calm and kingly head,
And a heart from whence, like a Holy Well, the soul of his land was fed—
No need to cry on the days of old that your holiest hope be sped.
Then scorn to pray
For a by-past day—
The whine of the sightless dumb!
To the true and wise
Let a king arise,
And a holier day is come!

DARRYNANE.

BY DENIS FLORENCE MAC-CARTHY, M.R.I.A.

[Written in 1844, after a visit to Darrynane Abbey.]

I.

Where foams the white torrent, and rushes the rill,
Down the murmuring slopes of the echoing hill—
Where the eagle looks out from his cloud-crested crags,
And the caverns resound with the panting of stags—
Where the brow of the mountain is purple with heath,
And the mighty Atlantic rolls proudly beneath,
With the foam of its waves like the snowy *fenane**—
Oh! that is the region of wild Darrynane!

---

* *Fenane.*—" In the mountains of Slievelougher, and other parts of this county, the country people, towards the end of June, cut the coarse mountain grass, called by them *fenane*; towards August this grass grows white."—*Smith's Kerry.*

II.

Oh! fair are the islets of tranquil Glengariff,
And wild are the sacred recesses of Scariff—
And beauty, and wildness, and grandeur, commingle
By Bantry's broad bosom, and wave-wasted Dingle;
But wild as the wildest, and fair as the fairest,
And lit by a lustre that thou alone wearest—
And dear to the eye and the free heart of man
Are the mountains and valleys of wild Darrynane!

III.

And who is the Chief of this lordly domain?
Does a slave hold the land where a monarch might reign?
Oh! no, by St. Finbar,* nor cowards, nor slaves,
Could live in the sound of these free, dashing, waves!
A Chieftain, the greatest the world has e'er known—
Laurel his coronet—true hearts his throne—
Knowledge his sceptre—a Nation his clan—
O'Connell, the Chieftain of proud Darrynane!

IV.

A thousand bright streams on the mountains awake,
Whose waters unite in O'Donoghue's Lake—
Streams of Glanflesk and the dark Gishadine
Filling the heart of that valley divine!
Then rushing in one mighty artery down
To the limitless ocean by murmuring Lowne!†
Thus Nature unfolds in her mystical plan
A type of the Chieftain of wild Darrynane!

V.

In him every pulse of our bosoms unite—
Our hatred of wrong and our worship of right—
The hopes that we cherish, the ills we deplore,
All centre within his heart's innermost core,

---

* The abbey on the grounds of Darrynane was founded in the seventh century by the monks of St. Finbar.
† The river Lowne is the only outlet by which all the streams that form the Lakes of Killarney discharge themselves into the sea—*Lan*, or *Lowne*, in the old Irish signifying full.

Which, gathered in one mighty current, are flung
To the ends of the earth from his thunder-toned
    tongue!
Till the Indian looks up, and the valiant Affghân
Draws his sword at the echo from far Darrynane!

VI.

But here he is only the friend and the father,
Who from children's sweet lips truest wisdom can
    gather,
And seeks from the large heart of Nature to borrow
Rest for the present and strength for the morrow!
Oh! who that e'er saw him with children about him,
And heard his soft tones of affection, could doubt him?
My life on the truth of the heart of that man
That throbs like the Chieftain's of wild Darrynane!

VII.

Oh! wild Darrynane, on thy ocean-washed shore,
Shall the glad song of mariners echo once more?
Shall the merchants, and minstrels, and maidens of
    Spain,
Once again in their swift ships come over the main?
Shall the soft lute be heard, and the gay youths of
    France
Lead our blue-eyed young maidens again to the dance?
Graceful and shy as thy fawns, Killenane,*
Are the mind-moulded maidens of far Darrynane!

VIII.

Dear land of the South, as my mind wandered o'er
All the joys I have felt by thy magical shore,
From those lakes of enchantment by oak-clad Glená
To the mountainous passes of bold Iveragh!

---

* "Killenane lies to the east of Cahir. It has many mountains towards the sea. These mountains are frequented by herds of fallow deer, that range about in perfect security."—*Smith's Kerry.*

Like birds which are lured to a haven of rest,
By those rocks far away on the ocean's bright breast*—
Thus my thoughts loved to linger, as memory ran
O'er the mountains and valleys of wild Darrynane!

1844.

DEIRDRA'S LAMENT FOR THE SONS OF USNACH.

BY SAMUEL FERGUSON, LL.D., M.R.I.A.

["Then was there no man in the host of Ulster that could be found who would put the sons of Usnach to death, so loved were they of the people and nobles. But in the house of Conor was one called Maini, Rough Hand, son of the King of Lochlin, and Naisi had slain his father and two brothers, and he undertook to be their executioner. So the sons of Usnach were there slain, and the men of Ulster, when they beheld their death, sent forth their heavy shouts of sorrow and lamentation. Then Deirdra fell down beside their bodies, wailing and weeping, and she tore her hair and garments, and bestowed kisses on their lifeless lips, and bitterly bemoaned them. And a grave was opened for them, and Deirdra, standing by it, with her hair dishevelled, and shedding tears abundantly, chanted their funeral song."†]

THE lions of the hill are gone,
And I am left alone—alone—
Dig the grave both wide and deep,
For I am sick, and fain would sleep!

The falcons of the wood are flown,
And I am left alone—alone—
Dig the grave both deep and wide,
And let us slumber side by side.

The dragons of the rock are sleeping,
Sleep that wakes not for our weeping—
Dig the grave, and make it ready,
Lay me on my true-love's body.

* The Skellig Rocks. In describing one of them, Keating says "That there is a certain attractive virtue in the soil which draws down all the birds which attempt to fly over it, and obliges them to light upon the rock."

† Hibernian Nights' Entertainments, University Magazine, vol. iv p. 686.

Lay their spears and bucklers bright
By the warriors' sides aright;
Many a day the three before me
On their linked bucklers bore me.

Lay upon the low grave floor,
'Neath each head, the blue claymore;
Many a time the noble three
Reddened these blue blades for me.

Lay the collars, as is meet,
Of their greyhounds at their feet;
Many a time for me have they
Brought the tall red deer to bay.

In the falcon's jesses throw,
Hook and arrow, line and bow;
Never again, by stream or plain,
Shall the gentle woodsmen go.

Sweet companions, ye were ever—
Harsh to me, your sister, never;
Woods and wilds, and misty valleys,
Were with you as good's a palace.

Oh, to hear my true-love singing,
Sweet as sound of trumpets ringing;
Like the sway of ocean swelling
Rolled his deep voice round our dwelling.

Oh! to hear the echoes pealing
Round our green and fairy sheeling,
When the three, with soaring chorus,
Passed the silent skylark o'er us.

Echo now, sleep, morn and even—
Lark alone enchant the heaven!
Ardan's lips are scant of breath,
Neesa's tongue is cold in death.

Stag, exult on glen and mountain !
Salmon, leap from loch to fountain !
Heron, in the free air warm ye !
Usnach's sons no more will harm ye !

Erin's stay no more you are,
Rulers of the ridge of war !
Never more 'twill be your fate
To keep the beam of battle straight !

Woe is me ! by fraud and wrong,
Traitors false and tyrants strong,
Fell clan Usnach bought and sold,
For Barach's feast and Conor's gold !

Woe to Eman, roof and wall !
Woe to Red Branch, hearth and hall !
Tenfold woe and black dishonour
To the foul and false clan Conor !

Dig the grave both wide and deep,
Sick I am, and fain would sleep !
Dig the grave and make it ready,
Lay me on my true-love's body !

THE PENAL DAYS.

[" In Scotland what a work have the four-and-twenty letters to show for themselves ! The natural enemies of vice, and folly, and slavery ; the great sowers, but the still greater weeders of the human soil."—*John Philpot Curran.*]

In that dark time of cruel wrong, when on our country's breast,
A dreary load, a ruthless code, with wasting terrors press'd—
Our gentry stripp'd of land and clan, sent exiles o'er the main,
To turn the scales on foreign fields for foreign monarchs' gain ;

Our people trod like vermin down, all fenceless flung
  to sate
Extortion, lust, and brutal whim, and rancorous bigot
  hate—
Our priesthood tracked from cave to hut, like felons
  chased and lashed,
And from their ministering hands the lifted chalice
  dashed—
In that black time of law-wrought crime, of stifling
  woe and thrall,
There stood supreme one foul device, one engine worse
  than all:
Him whom they wished to keep a slave, they sought
  to make a brute—
They banned the light of heaven—they bade instruc
  tion's voice be mute.

God's second priest—the Teacher—sent to feed men's
  mind with lore—
They marked a price upon his head, as on the priest's
  before.
Well—well they knew that never, face to face beneath
  the sky,
Could tyranny and knowledge meet, but one of them
  should die:
That lettered slaves will link their might until their
  murmurs grow
To that imperious thunder-peal which despots quail
  to know;
That men who learn will learn their strength—the
  weakness of their lords—
Till all the bonds that gird them round are snapt like
  Sampson's cords.
This well they knew, and called the power of igno-
  rance to aid:
So might, they deemed, an abject race of soulless serfs
  be made—
When Irish memories, hopes, and thoughts, were
  withered, branch and stem—
A race of abject, soulless serfs, to hew and draw for them.

Ah, God is good and nature strong—they let not thus
    decay
The seeds that deep in Irish breasts of Irish feeling
    lay :
Still sun and rain made emerald green the loveliest
    fields on earth,
And gave the type of deathless hope, the little sham-
    rock, birth ;
Still faithful to their Holy Church, her direst straits
    among,
To one another faithful still, the priests and people
    clung,
And Christ was worshipped, and received with trem-
    bling haste and fear,
In field and shed, with posted scouts to warn of blood-
    hounds near ;
Still, crouching 'neath the sheltering hedge, or stretched
    on mountain fern,
The teacher and his pupils met, feloniously—to learn ;
Still round the peasant's heart of hearts his darling
    music twined,
A fount of Irish sobs or smiles in every note enshrined.
And still beside the smouldering turf were fond tradi-
    tions told
Of heavenly saints and princely chiefs—the power and
    faith of old.

Deep lay the seeds, yet rankest weeds sprang mingled
    —could they fail ?
For what were freedom's blessed worth, if slavery
    wrought not bale ?
As thrall, and want and ignorance, still deep and
    deeper grew,
What marvel weakness, gloom, and strife fell dark
    amongst us too ;
And servile thoughts, that measure not the inborn
    wealth of man—
And servile cringe, and subterfuge to scape our master's
    ban ;

And drunkeness—our sense of woe a little while to steep—
And aimless feud, and murderous plot—oh, one could pause and weep !
Mid all the darkness, faith in Heaven still shone a saving ray,
And Heaven o'er our redemption watched, and chose its own good day.
Two men were sent us—one for years, with Titan strength of soul,
To beard our foes, to peal our wrongs, to band us and control.
The other at a later time, on gentler mision came,
To make our noblest glory spring from out our saddest shame !
On all our wondrous, upward course hath Heaven its finger set,
And we—but, oh, my countrymen, there's much before us yet !

How sorrowful the useless powers our glorious Island yields—
Our countless havens desolate, our waste of barren fields ;
The all unused mechanic might our rushing streams afford,
The buried treasures of our mines, our sea's unvalued hoard !
But, oh, there is one piteous waste, whence all the rest have grown—
One worst neglect, the mind of man left desert and unsown.
Send KNOWLEDGE forth to scatter wide, and deep to cast its seeds,
The nurse of energy and hope, of manly thoughts and deeds.
Let it go forth : right soon will spring those forces in its train
That vanquish Nature's stubborn strength, that rifle earth and main—

Itself a nobler harvest far than Autumn tints with
    gold,
A higher wealth, a surer gain than wave and mine
    enfold.
Let it go forth unstained, and purged from Pride's
    unholy leaven,
With fearless forehead raised to Man, but humbly
    bent to Heaven;

Deep let it sink in Irish hearts the story of their isle,
And waken thoughts of tenderest love, and burning
    wrath the while;
And press upon us, one by one, the fruits of English
    sway,
And blend the wrongs of bygone times with this our
    fight to day;
And show our Father's constancy by truest instinct led,
To loathe and battle with the power that on their sub-
    stance fed;
And let it place beside our own the world's vast page,
    to tell
That never lived the nation yet could rule another
    well.
Thus, thus our cause shall gather strength; no feeling
    vague and blind,
But stamped by passion on the heart, by reason on the
    mind.
Let it go forth—a mightier foe to England's power
    than all
The rifles of America—the armaments of Gaul!
It *shall* go forth, and woe to them that bar or thwart
    its way—
'Tis God's own light—all Heavenly bright—we care
    not who says nay

O——.

CAROLAN AND BRIDGET CRUISE.

BY SAMUEL LOVER.

[It is related of Carolan, the Irish bard, that when deprived of sight, and after the lapse of twenty years, he recognized his first love by the touch of her hand. The Lady's name was Bridget Cruise; and though not a pretty name, it deserves to be recorded, as belonging to the woman who could inspire such a passion.—AUTHOR'S NOTE.]

"TRUE love can ne'er forget;
Fondly as when we met,
Dearest, I love thee yet,
    My darling one!"
Thus sung a minstrel gay
His sweet impassion'd lay,
Down by the ocean's spray,
    At set of sun;
But wither'd was the minstrel's sight,
Morn to him was dark as night;
Yet his heart was full of light
    As he thus his lay begun.

"True love can ne'er forget;
Fondly as when we met,
Dearest, I love thee yet,
    My darling one!
Long years are past and o'er,
Since from this fatal shore,
Cold hearts and cold winds bore
    My love from me."
Scarcely the minstrel spoke,
When quick, with flashing stroke,
A boat's light oar the silence broke
    O'er the sea.

Soon upon her native strand
Doth a lovely lady land,
While the minstrel's love-taught hand
    Did o'er his wild harp run:

"True love can ne'er forget;
Fondly as when we met,
Dearest, I love thee yet,
　　My darling one!"
Where the minstrel sat alone,
There, that lady fair hath gone,
Within his hand she placed her own;
　　The bard dropp'd on his knee.

From his lips soft blessings came,
He kiss'd her hand with truest flame,
In trembling tones he named—*her* name,
　　Though he could not see;
But oh! the touch the bard could tell
Of that dear hand, remember'd well.
Ah! by many a secret spell
　　Can true love find her own!
For true love can ne'er forget;
Fondly as when they met;
He loved his lady yet,
　　His darling one.

THE STREAMS.

BY MRS. DOWNING.

[This poem is taken from a volume entitled *Scraps from the Mountains* by Christabel, published in Dublin in 1840. It contains many beautiful pieces, in which Mrs. Downing has succeeded in uniting much of the grace and harmony of Mrs. Hemans, to the tenderness and passion of L. E. L. What is still better, they are thoroughly Irish in sent'ment and expression.]

The streams, the dancing streams,
　　How they roll and shine,
Like youth's fairest dreams,
　　When youth is most divine!
Clearness where their bed is
　　'Mid pebbles in glossy ranks,
Brightness on their eddies,
　　Blossoms on their banks.

Look within the valley,
   Many a charm is there—
The winding, shaded alley,
   The woodbine glist'ning fair;
The berries' crimson flush,
   The wild birds' cadence low,
But, chief of all, the gush
   Of the streamlet's singing flow.

Stand beneath the mountains,
   And down each craggy side,
From their secret fountains,
   See lines of silver glide—
Mark how the ripples fling
   Their sparkles round, and say
If there is anything
   More beautiful than they.

List in night's deep hushing,
   The season time of dreams,
What are these come rushing?
   The troubled, sleepless streams!
Now their waters flashing,
   Like starry-spangled hairs—
Rolling, bounding, dashing—
   What music like to theirs?

Oh! in the sheltered glen,
   Or on the hill-side fair,
When spring flowers bloom, or when
   The summer birds are there
In all that we may see,
   'Neath morn's or evening's beams,
Can aught in nature be
   More lovely than the streams?

IRISH MARY.

BY JOHN BANIM.

Far away from Erin's strand,
   And valleys wide and sounding waters,
Still she is, in every land,
   One of Erin's real daughters:
Oh! to meet her here is like
   A dream of home and natal mountains.
On our hearts their voices strike—
   We hear the gushing of their fountains!
Yes! our Irish Mary dear!
   Our own, our real Irish Mary!
A flower of home, fresh blooming come,
   Art thou to us, our Irish Mary!

Round about us here we see
   Bright eyes like hers, and sunny faces,
Charming all! if all were free
   Of foreign airs, of borrowed graces.
Mary's eye it flashes truth!
   And Mary's spirit, Mary's nature,
"Irish Lady," fresh in youth,
   Have beamed o'er every look and feature!
Yes! our Irish Mary dear!
   When *La Tournure* doth make us weary,
We have you, to turn unto
   For native grace, our Irish Mary.

Sighs of home!—her Erin's songs
   O'er all their songs we love to listen;
Tears of home!—her Erin's wrongs
   Subdue our kindred eyes to glisten!
Oh! should woe to gloom consign
   The clear fire-side of love and honour,

You will see a holier sign
  Of Irish Mary bright upon her !
Yes ! our Irish Mary dear
  Will light that home, though e'er so dreary—
Shining still o'er clouds of ill,
  Sweet star of life, our Irish Mary !

THE LAST FRIENDS.

BY FRANCES BROWN.

[One of the United Irishmen, who lately returned to his country, after many years of exile, being asked what had induced him to revisit Ireland when all his friends were gone, he answered, " I came back to see the mountains."]

I CAME to my country, but not with the hope
  That brightened my youth like the cloud-lighting bow
For the region of soul that seemed mighty to cope
  With time and with fortune, had fled from me now ;
And love, that illumined my wanderings of yore,
  Hath perished, and left but a weary regret
For the star that can rise on my midnight no more—
  But the hills of my country they welcome me yet !

The hue of their verdure was fresh with me still,
  When my path was afar by the Tanais' lone track ;
From the wide-spreading deserts and ruins that fill
  The land of old story, they summoned me back ;
They rose on my dreams through the shades of the west,
  They breathed upon sands which the dew never wet,
For the echoes were hushed in the home I loved best—
  But I knew that the mountains would welcome me yet !

The dust of my kindred is scattered afar,
  They lie in the desert, the wild, and the wave ;
For serving the strangers through wandering and war,
  The isle of their memory could grant them no grave,

And I, I return with the memory of years,
   Whose hope rose so high though its sorrow is set ;
They have left on my soul but the trace of their tears—
   But our mountains remember their promises yet !

Oh ! where are the brave hearts that bounded of old,
   And where are the faces my childhood hath seen ?
For fair brows are furrowed, and hearts have grown cold,
   But our streams are still bright, and our hills are still green ;
Ay, green as they rose to the eyes of my youth,
   When brothers in heart in their shadows we met ;
And the hills have no memory of sorrow or death,
   For their summits are sacred to liberty yet !

Like ocean retiring, the morning mists now
   Roll back from the mountains that girdle our land;
And sunlight encircles each heath-covered brow
   For which time had no furrow and tyrants no brand !
Oh, thus let it be with the hearts of the isle,
   Efface the dark seal that oppression hath set ;
Give back the lost glory again to the soil,
   For the hills of my country remember it yet.

THE IRISH EXILES.

A CHRISTMAS CAROL.

BY MARTIN MAC DERMOTT.

When round the festive Christmas board, or by the Christmas hearth,
   That glorious mingled draught is pour'd—wine, melody, and mirth !
When friends long absent tell, low-toned, their joys and sorrows o'er,

And hand grasps hand, and eyelids fill, and lips meet
    lips once more—
Oh! in that hour 'twere kindly done, some woman's
    voice would say—
"Forget not those who're sad to-night—poor exiles,
    far away!"

Alas! for them this morning's sun saw many a moist
    eye pour
Its gushing love, with longings vain, the waste Atlantic
    o'er;
And when he turned his lion-eye this ev'ning from the
    West,
The Indian shores were lined with those who watched
    his couchêd crest;
But not to share his glory, then, or gladden in his ray,
They bent their gaze upon his path—those exiles, far
    away!

It was—oh! how the heart will cheat!—because they
    thought, beyond
His glowing couch lay that Green Isle of which their
    hearts were fond;
And fancy brought old scenes of home into each
    welling eye,
And through each breast poured many a thought that
    filled it like a sigh!
'Twas then—'twas then, all warm with love, they knelt
    them down to pray
For Irish homes and kith and kin—poor exiles, fa-
    away!

And then the mother blest her son, the lover blest the
    maid,
And then the soldier was a child, and wept the whilst
    he prayed,
And then the student's pallid cheek flushed red as
    summer rose,
And patriot souls forgot their grief to weep for Erin's
    woes;

And, oh! but then warm vows were breathed, that come what might or may,
They'd right the suffering isle they loved—those exiles, far away!

And some there were around the board, like loving brothers met,
The few and fond and joyous hearts that never can forget;
They pledged—"The girls we left at home, God bless them!" and they gave,
"The memory of our absent friends, the tender and the brave!"
Then up, erect, with nine times nine—hip, hip, hip—hurrah!
Drank—"Erin *slantha gal go-bragh!*"* those exiles, far away.

Then, oh! to hear the sweet old strains of Irish music rise,
Like gushing memories of home, beneath far foreign skies—
Beneath the spreading calabash, beneath the trellised vine,
The bright Italian myrtle bower, or dark Canadian pine—
Oh! don't these old familiar tones—now sad, and now so gay—
Speak out your very, very hearts—poor exiles, far away.

But, Heavens! how many sleep afar, all heedless of these strains—
Tired wanderers! who sought repose through Europe battle plains—
In strong, fierce, headlong fight they fell—as ships go down in storms—
They fell—and *human* whirlwinds swept across their shattered forms!

* erin slancha gal go brag.

No shroud, but glory, wrapt them round; nor pray'r nor tear had they—
Save the wandering winds and the heavy clouds—poor exiles, far away!

And might the singer claim a sigh, he, too, could tell how, tost
Upon the stranger's dreary shore, his heart's best hopes were lost—
How he, too, pined to hear the tones of friendship greet his ear,
And pined to walk the river side, to youthful musing dear,
And pined, with yearning silent love, amongst *his own* to stay—
Alas! it is so sad to be an exile far away!

Then, oh! when round the Christmas board, or by the Christmas hearth,
That glorious mingled draught is poured—wine, melody, and mirth!
When friends long absent tell, low-toned, their joys and sorrows o'er,
And hand grasps hand, and eye-lids fill, and lips meet lips once more—
In that bright hour, perhaps—perhaps, some woman's voice would say—
"Think—think on those who weep to-night, poor exiles, far away!

A SHAMROCK FROM THE IRISH SHORE.

(On receiving a Shamrock in a Letter from Ireland.)

BY DENIS FLORENCE MAC-CARTHY, M.R.I.A.

I.

O, POSTMAN! speed thy tardy gait—
   Go quicker round from door to door;
For thee I watch, for thee I wait,
   Like many a weary wanderer more.
Thou bringest news of bale and bliss—
   Some life begun, some life well o'er.
He stops—he rings!—O Heaven! what's this?
   A Shamrock from the Irish shore!

II.

Dear emblem of my native land,
   By fresh fond words kept fresh and green;
The pressure of an unfelt hand—
   The kisses of a lip unseen;
A throb from my dead mother's heart—
   My father's smile revived once more—
Oh, youth! oh, love! oh, hope thou art,
   Sweet Shamrock from the Irish shore!

III.

Enchanter, with thy wand of power,
   Thou mak'st the past be present still:
The emerald lawn—the lime-leaved bower—
   The circling shore—the sunlit hill;
The grass, in winter's wintriest hours,
   By dewy daisies dimpled o'er,
Half hiding, 'neath their trembling flowers,
   The Shamrock of the Irish shore!

IV.

And thus, where'er my footsteps strayed,
   By queenly Florence, kingly Rome—
By Padua's long and lone arcade—
   By Ischia's fires and Adria's foam—
By Spezzia's fatal waves that kissed
   My Poet sailing calmly o'er ;
By all, by each, I mourned and missed
   The Shamrock of the Irish shore !

V.

I saw the palm-tree stand aloof,
   Irresolute 'twixt the sand and sea ;
I saw upon the trellised root
   Outspread the wine that was to be :
A giant-flowered and glorious tree
   I saw the tall magnolia soar :
But there, even there, I longed for thee,
   Poor Shamrock of the Irish shore !

VI.

Now on the ramparts of Boulogne,
   As lately by the lonely Rance,
At evening as I watch the sun,
   I look ! I dream ! Can this be France ?
Not Albion's cliffs, how near they be,
   He seems to love to linger o'er ;
But gilds, by a remoter sea,
   The Shamrock on the Irish shore !

VII.

I'm with him in that wholesome clime—
   That fruitful soil, that verdurous sod—
Where hearts unstained by vulgar crime
   Have still a simple faith in God.
Hearts that in pleasure and in pain,
   The more they're trod rebound the more,
Like thee, when wet with Heaven's own rain,
   O, Shamrock of the Irish shore !

VIII.

Memorial of my native land,
  True emblem of my land and race—
Thy small and tender leaves expand
  But only in thy native place.
Thou needest for thyself and seed
  Soft dews around, kind sunshine o'er;
Transplanted, thou'rt the merest weed,
  O Shamrock of the Irish shore!

IX.

Here on the tawny fields of France,
  Or in the rank, red English clay,
Thou showest a stronger form, perchance;
  A bolder front thou may'st display,
More able to resist the scythe
  That cut so keen, so sharp before;
But then thou art no more the blithe
  Bright Shamrock of the Irish shore!

X.

Ah, me! to think thy scorns, thy slights,
  Thy trampled tears, thy nameless grave
On Fredericksburg's ensanguined heights,
  Or by Potómac's purple wave!
Ah, me! to think that power malign
  Thus turns thy sweet green sap to gore,
And what calm rapture might be thine,
  Sweet Shamrock of the Irish shore!

XI.

Struggling, and yet for strife unmeet,
  True type of trustful love thou art;
Thou liest the whole year at my feet,
  To live but one day at my heart.
One day of festal pride to lie
  Upon the loved one's heart—what more?
Upon the loved one's heart to die,
  O Shamrock of the Irish shore!

XII.

And shall I not return thy love?
  And shalt thou not, as thou shouldst, be
Placed on thy son's proud heart above
  The red rose or the fleur-de-lis?
Yes, from these heights the waters beat,
  I vow to press thy cheek once more,
And lie for ever at thy feet,
  O Shamrock of the Irish shore!

Boulogne-sur-Mer, March 17, 1865.

SPRING FLOWERS FROM IRELAND.

BY DENIS FLORENCE MAC-CARTHY, M.R.I.A.

On receiving an early crocus and some violets in a second letter from Ireland.

WITHIN the letter's rustling fold
  I find once more, a glad surprise—
A little tiny cup of gold—
  Two little lovely violet eyes;
A cup of gold with emeralds set,
  Once filled with wine from happier spheres;
Two little eyes so lately wet
  With spring's delicious dewy tears.

Oh! little eyes that wept and laughed,
  Now bright with smiles, with tears now dim—
Oh! little cup that once was quaffed
  By fay-queens fluttering round thy rim.
I press each silken fringe's fold—
  Sweet little eyes once more ye shine—
I kiss thy lip, oh! cup of gold,
  And find thee full of memory's wine.

Within their violet depths I gaze,
  And see as in the camera's gloom,
The Island with its belt of bays,
  Its chieftained heights all capped with broom—
Which as the living lens it fills,
  Now seems a giant charmed to sleep—
Now a broad shield embossed with hills
  Upon the bosom of the deep.

When will the slumbering giant wake?
  When will the shield defend and guard?
Ah, me! prophetic gleams forsake
  The once wrapt eyes of seer or bard.
Enough, if shunning Samson's fate,
  It doth not all its vigour yield;
Enough, if plenteous peace, though late,
  May rest beneath the sheltering shield.

I see the long and lone defiles
  Of Keimaneigh's bold rocks uphurled,
I see the golden fruited isles
  That gem the queen-lakes of the world;
I see—a gladder sight to me—
  By soft Shangânagh's silver strand,
The breaking of a sapphire sea
  Upon the golden-fretted sand.

Swiftly the tunnel's rock-hewn pass,*
  Swiftly the fiery train runs through—
Oh! what a glittering sheet of glass!
  Oh! what enchantment meets my view!
With eyes insatiate I pursue,
  Till Bray's bright headland bounds the scene—
'Tis Baiæ, by a softer blue!
  Gäeta, by a gladder green!

* The Railway Tunnel at Dalkey.

By tasselled groves, o'er meadows fair,
    I'm carried in my blissful dream,
To where—a monarch in the air—
    The pointed mountain reigns supreme ;
There in a spot remote and wild,
    I see once more the rustic seat,
Where Carrigoona, like a child,
    Sits at the mightier mountain's feet.

There by the gentler mountain's slope,
    That happiest year of many a year,
That first swift year of love and hope,
    With her then dear and ever dear.
I sat upon the rustic seat—
    The seat an aged bay-tree crowns,
And saw outspreading from our feet
    The golden glory of the Downs.

The furze-crowned heights, the glorious glen,
    The white-walled chapel glistening near,
The house of God, the homes of men,
    The fragrant hay, the ripening ear ;
There where there seemed nor sin, nor crime,
    There in God's sweet and wholesome air—
Strange book to read at such a time—
    We read of Vanity's false Fair.

We read the painful pages through—
    Perceived the skill, admired the art,
Felt them if true, not wholly true—
    A truer truth was in our heart.
Save fear and love of ONE, hath proved
    The sage, how vain is all below ;
And one was there who feared and loved,
    And one who loved that she was so.

The vision spreads, the memories grow,
    Fair phantoms crowd the more I gaze.
Oh ! cup of gold, with wine o'erflow,
    I'll drink to those departed days :

And when I drain the golden cup
  To them, to those I ne'er can see,
With wine of hope I'll fill it up,
  And drink to days that yet may be.

I've drank the future and the past,
  Now for a draught of warmer wine—
One draught the sweetest and the last—
  Lady, I'll drink to thee and thine.
These flowers that to my breast I fold,
  Into my very heart have grown—
To thee I drain the cup of gold,
  And think the violet eyes thine own.

Boulogne, March, 1865.

WINGS FOR HOME.

BY DENIS FLORENCE MAC-CARTHY, M.R.I.A.

My heart hath taken wings for home;
  Away! away! it cannot stay.
My heart hath taken wings for home,
Nor all that's best of Greece or Rome
  Can stop its way.
My heart hath taken wings for home,
  Away!

My heart hath taken wings for home,
  O Swallow, Swallow, lead the way!
O little bird! fly north with me,
I have a home beside the sea
  Where thou canst sing and play.
My heart hath taken wings for home,
  Away!

My heart hath taken wings for home,
  But thou, O little bird ! wilt stay ;
Thou hast thy young ones with thee here,
  Thy mate floats with thee through the clear
    Italian depths of day.
My heart hath taken wings for home,
    Away !

My heart hath taken wings for home,
  Away ! away ! it cannot stay.
One spring from Brunelleschi's dome,
To Venice by the Adrian foam,
  Then westward be my way.
My heart hath taken wings for home,
    Away !

Florence, June, 1862.

ITALIAN MYRTLES.

(AS TYPICAL OF IDEAL IRISH MAIDENHOOD.)

BY DENIS FLORENCE MAC-CARTHY, M.R.I.A.

[Suggested by seeing, for the first time, fire-flies in the myrtle-hedges at Spezzia.]

I.

By many a soft Ligurian bay
  The myrtles glisten green and bright,
Gleam with their flowers of snow by day,
  And glow with fire-flies through the night,
And yet, despite the cold and heat,
Are ever fresh, and pure, and sweet.

II.

There is an Island in the West,
  Where living myrtles bloom and blow,
Hearts where the fire-fly Love may rest
  Within a Paradise of snow—
Which yet, despite the cold and heat,
Are ever fresh, and pure, and sweet.

III.

Deep in that gentle breast of thine—
    Like fire and snow within the pearl—
Let purity and love combine,
    O warm, pure-hearted Irish girl!
And in the cold and in the heat
Be ever fresh, and pure, and sweet.

IV.

Thy bosom bears as pure a snow
    As e'er Italia's bowers can boast,
And though no fire-fly lends its glow—
    As on the soft Ligurian coast—
'Tis warmed by an internal heat
Which ever keeps it pure and sweet.

V.

The fire-flies fade on misty eves—
    The inner fires alone endure;
Like to the rain that wets the leaves,
    Thy very sorrows keep thee pure—
They temper a too ardent heat—
And keeps thee ever pure and sweet.

La Spezia, 1862.

"NOT KNOWN."

BY DENIS FLORENCE MAC-CARTHY, M.R.I.A.

On receiving through the Post-Office a Returned Letter from an old residence, marked on the envelope "Not Known."

A beauteous summer-home had I
    As e'er a bard set eyes on,—
A glorious sweep of sea and sky
    Near hills and far horizon.

Like Naples was the lovely bay,
  The lovely hill like Rio—
And there I lived for many a day
  In Campo de Estío.

It seemed as if the magic scene
  No human skill had planted;
The trees remained for ever green,
  As if they were enchanted:
And so I said to Sweetest-eyes,
  My dear, I think that *we* owe
To fairy hands this paradise
  Of Campo de Estío.

How swiftly flew the hours away!
  I read and rhymed and revelled;
In interchange of work and play,
  I built, and drained, and levelled;
"The Pope" so "happy," days gone by
  (Unlike our ninth Pope Pio),
Was far less happy then than I
  In Campo de Estío.

For children grew in that sweet place,
  As in the grape wine gathers—
Their mother's eyes in each bright face—
  In each light heart, their father's:
Their father, who by some was thought
  A literary *leo*,
Ne'er dreamed he'd be so soon forgot
  In Campo de Estío.

But so it was:—Of hope bereft,
  A year had scarce gone over,
Since he that sweetest place had left,
  And gone—we'll say—to Dover,
When letters came where he had flown,
  Returned him from the "P. O.,"
On which was writ, O Heavens! "NOT KNOWN
  IN CAMPO DE ESTIO"!

"Not known" where he had lived so long,
  And which his love created,
Where scarce a shrub that now is strong
  But had its place debated;
Where scarce a flower that now is shown,
  But shows *his* care : O Dio !
And now to be described, "Not known
  In Campo de Estío !"

That pillar from the Causeway brought—
  This fern from Connemara—
That pine so long and widely sought—
  This Cedrus deodara—
That bust (if Shakespeare's doth survive,
  And busts had brains and *brio*),
Might keep his name at least alive
  In Campo de Estío.

When Homer went from place to place,
  The glorious siege reciting
(Of course I pre-suppose the case
  Of reading and of writing),
I've little doubt the Bard divine
  His letters got from Scio,
Inscribed "Not known," Ah ! me, like mine
  From Campo de Estío.

The poet, howsoe'er inspired,
  Must brave neglect and danger;
When Philip Massinger expired
  The death-list said "a stranger !"
A stranger ! yes on earth, but let
  The poet sing *laus Deo !*—
Heaven's glorious summer waits him yet—
  God's "Campo de Estío."

1866.

THE PASCHAL FIRE OF ST. PATRICK *

BY DENIS FLORENCE MAC-CARTHY, M.R.I.A.

On Tara's hill the daylight dies—
 On Tara's plain 'tis dead :
" 'Till Baal's unkindled fires shall rise,
 No fire must flame instead."
'Tis thus the king commanding speaks,
 Commands and speaks in vain—
For lo ! a fire defiant breaks,
 From out the woods of Slane.

For there in prayer is Patrick bent,
 With Christ his soul is knit,
And there before his simple tent
 The Paschal fire is lit.
" What means this flame that through the night
 Illumines all the vale ?
What rebel hand a fire dare light
 Before the fires of Baal ?"

O king ! when Baal's dark reign is o'er,
 When thou thyself art gone;
This fire will light the Irish shore,
 And lead its people on :
Will lead them on full many a night
 Through which they're doomed to go
Like that which led the Israelite
 From bondage and from woe.

This fire, this sacred fire of God,
 Young hearts shall bear afar
To lands no human foot hath trod,
 Beneath the western star.

* See Lanigan's *Ecclesiastical History of Ireland*, t. I., p. 224.

To lands where Faith's bright flag, unfurled
  By those who here have knelt,
Shall give unto a newer world
  The sceptre of the Celt.

And thus 'twill be, that there and here,
  In hovel or in hall,
One night in each revolving year
  This memory shall recall.
One hour of brightness in their night,
  Where'ér the Gael may roam,
When love this festal fire shall light
  For Patrick and for Home !

St. Patrick's Day, 1867.

OVER THE SEA.

BY DENIS FLORENCE MAC-CARTHY, M.R.I.A.

SAD eyes ! why are ye steadfastly gazing
      Over the Sea ?
Is it the flock of the Ocean-Shepherd grazing
      Like lambs on the lea ?
Is it the dawn on the orient billows blazing
      Allureth ye ?

Sad heart ! why art thou tremblingly beating—
      What troubleth thee ?
There where the waves from the fathomless water
    comes greeting,
      Wild with their glee !
Or rush from the rocks, like a routed battalion retreat-
    ing,
      Over the sea !

Sad feet ! why are ye constantly straying
    Down by the sea ?
There, where the winds in the sandy harbour are playing
    Child-like and free—
What is the charm, whose potent enchantment obeying,
    There charmeth ye ?

Oh ! sweet is the dawn, and bright are the colours it glows in !
    Yet not to me !
To the beauty of God's bright creation my bosom is frozen,
    Nought can I see !
Since *She* has departed—the dear one, the loved one, the chosen,
    Over the Sea !

Pleasant it was when the billows did struggle and wrestle,
    Pleasant to see !
Pleasant to climb the tall cliffs where the sea-birds nestle,
    When near to thee !
Nought can I now behold but the track of thy vessel
    Over the Sea !

Long as a Lapland winter, which no pleasant sunlight cheereth,
    The summer shall be ;
Vainly shall autumn be gay, in the rich robes it weareth,
    Vainly for me !
No joy can I feel till the prow of thy vessel appeareth
    Over the Sea !

Sweeter than Summer, which tenderly, motherly
    bringeth
        Flowers to the bee!
Sweeter than autumn, which bounteously, lovingly
    flingeth
        Fruits on the tree!
Shall be winter, when homeward returning thy swift
    vessel wingeth
        Over the Sea!

THE CONVICT AND THE CROSS.

I.

"Oh! let me wear the little cross, the little cross that
    once I wore,
When oft, a happy boy, I roamed along the Lee's
    lamenting shore;
And as I heard the stream glide by, that sobbed to
    leave so sweet a land,
A more lamenting human tide swept onward to the
    distant strand;
Even then I vowed, come weal, come woe, if faintest
    hope should ever gleam
That life and verdure here at home might spring from
    that now wasted stream,
That I would take my humble part—that I the
    glorious risk would share,
And what the patriot heart inspired the patriot hand
    would do and dare.
But ah! I faint, mine eyes grow dim in thinking of
    the days of yore—
Oh! let me wear the little cross that once a happy
    child I wore!

II.

" 'Twill tell me of a mother's love ; forgive me, O thou
    sacred sign !
'Twill tell me more than mother's love—'twill tell me
    of a love divine ;
'Twill tell me of a captive bound, a captive bound by
    ruthless hands—
The thorny crown, the draught of gall, the ruffian
    jeers of ribald bands—
The shame, the agony, the death ! ah, me ! the years
    have rolled and rolled,
And still in this most awful type, unselfish love
    thy fate behold !
These it will tell, and oh ! perchance, a softer thought
    'twill whisper too—
Father, forgive, forgive even *them*, for ah ! they know
    not what they do.
But ah ! I faint, mine eyes grow dim, my lease of life
    is well nigh o'er—
Oh ! let me wear the little cross, that once a happy
    child I wore !"

III.

The cross was sent ; some kindly heart, that heard
    the captive's dying prayer,
Left at the gate the little cross smooth-folded round
    with loving care ;
Coarse hands, and cold the sacred fold with scorn
    and careless languor broke,
And found, enshrined in snowy fleece, a little cross of
    Irish oak.
" Ho ! ho !" they cried, "what emblem's this ? what
    popish charm is this we see ?
Some talisman, perchance, it is to set the Irish rebel
    free !"

And so it is, although ye mock, beyond your bolts,
    beyond your bars,
"Twill lead his soul enfranchished forth, above the
    sun, above the stars;
For though ye kept it from his hands, within his
    faithful heart he bore
The little cross, the saving cross. that once a happy
    child he wore.

IV.

A curse be on such heartless rules, and shame to them
    who such could shape,
Could bring to life such monstrous forms, such
    worms of twaddle and of tape—
Scourge, if ye will, the honest backs of those who
    scorn your lash, and ye—
But torture not the soul with thongs, and leave the
    immortal spirit free.
From Tobolsk's mines, from Ethiop's plains, from
    Abyssinian tyrants learn
That men are not machines, nor move by springs,
    that *you* alone discern—
Imprison, exile, hang all those your ruthless laws
    have foemen made;
But let the soul, in going forth, be strengthened by
    Religion's aid.
Not yours to judge the priceless worth, not yours to
    scan the countless store
Of grace and hope the cross can give, the cross a
    Christian child once wore.

M.

1806.

THE CELTIC TONGUE.

BY REV. MICHAEL MULLIN.

[Born in the Parish of Kilmore, co. Galway, 1833. Died at Chicago, Mich., April 23, 1869.]

'Tis fading, oh, 'tis fading! like leaves upon the trees!
In murmuring tone 'tis dying, like the wail upon the breeze!
'Tis swiftly disappearing, as footprints on the shore
Where the Barrow, and the Erne, and Loch Swilly's waters roar—
Where the parting sunbeam kisses Loch Corrib in the West,
And Ocean, like a mother, clasps the Shannon to her breast!
The language of old Erin, of her history and name—
Of her monarchs and her heroes—her glory and her fame—
The sacred shrine where rested, thro' sunshine and thro' gloom,
The spirit of her martyrs, as their bodies in the tomb.
The time-wrought shell, where murmur'd, 'mid centuries of wrong,
The secret voice of Freedom in annal and in song—
Is slowly, surely sinking, into silent death at last,
To live but in the memories of those who love the Past.

The olden tongue is sinking like a patriarch to rest,
Whose youth beheld the Tyrian* on our Irish coasts a guest;
Ere the Roman or the Saxon, the Norman or the Dane,
Had first set foot in Britain, o'er trampled heaps of slain;

---

* An old Irish tradition says that during the commerce of the Tyrians with Ireland, one of the Princes of Tyre was invited over by the Monarch of Ireland, and got married to one of the Irish princesses during his sojourn there.

Whose manhood saw the Druid rite at forest-tree and rock,
And savage tribes of Britain round the Shrines of Zernebock ;*
And for generations witnessed all the glories of the Gael,
Since our Celtic sires sung war-songs round the sacred fires of Baal ;
The tongues that saw its infancy are ranked among the dead,
And from their graves have risen those now spoken in their stead.
The glories of old Erin, with their liberty have gone,
Yet their halo linger'd round her, while the Gaelic speech liv'd on ;
For 'mid the desert of her woe, a monument more vast
Than all her pillar-towers, it stood—that old Tongue of the Past !

'Tis leaving, and for ever, the soil that gave it birth,
Soon,—very soon, its moving tones shall ne'er be heard on earth,
O'er the island dimly fading, as a circle o'er the wave,
Receding, as its people lisp the language of the slave,†
And with it too seem fading as sunset into night
The scattered rays of liberty that lingered in its light,
For ah ! tho' long, with filial love, it clung to motherland,
And Irishmen were Irish still, in language, heart and hand ;
T'instal its Saxon Rival,‡ proscribed it soon became,
And Irishmen are Irish now in nothing but in name ;

---

* Zernebrock and Odin were two of the gods of the early Britons.
† Tacitus says,—" The language of the conqueror in the mouth of the conquered is ever the language of the slave."—*Germania.*
‡ Acts of Parliament were enacted to destroy the Irish, and to encourage the growth of the English language.

The Saxon chain our rights and tongues alike doth hold in thrall,
Save where amid the Connaught wilds and hills of Donegal—
And by the shores of Munster, like the broad Atlantic blast,
The olden language lingers yet, and binds us to the Past.

Thro' cold neglect 'tis dying now; a stranger on our shore!
No Tara's hall re-echoes to its music as of yore—
No Lawrence* fires the Celtic clans round leaguered Athaclee†—
No Shannon wafts from Limerick's towers their war song to the sea.
Ah! magic Tongue, that round us wove its spells so soft and dear!
Ah! pleasant Tongue, whose murmurs were as music to the ear.
Ah! glorious Tongue, whose accents could each Celtic heart enthral!
Ah! rushing Tongue, that sounded like the swollen torrent's fall!
The tongue that in the Senate was lightning flashing bright—
Whose echo in the battle was the thunder in its might!
That Tongue, which once in chieftain's hall poured loud the minstrel lay,
As chieftain, serf, or minstrel old is silent there to-day!
That Tongue whose shout dismayed the foe at Kong and Mullaghmast,‡
Like those who nobly perished there is numbered with the Past!

---

* St. Lawrence O'Toole, Archbishop of Dublin, succeeded in organizing the Irish chieftains under Roderick O'Connor, King of Connaught, against the first band of adventurers under Strongbow.

† Athaclee, *Athacleith*, the Irish name of Dublin. *Baile-ath-Cliath*, literally means the *Town of the ford of hurdles*.

‡ "Nothing so affrighted the enemy at the raid of Mullaghmast, as the unintelligible password in the Irish tongue, with which the Irish troops burst upon the foe."—*Green Book*.

The Celtic Tongue is passing, and we stand coldly
    by,
Without a pang within the heart, a tear within the
    eye—
Without one pulse for Freedom stirred, one effort
    made to save
The Language of our Fathers from dark oblivion's
    grave!
Oh, Erin! vain your efforts—your prayers for Free
    dom's crown,
Whilst offered in the language of the foe that clove it
    down;
Be sure that tyrants ever with an art from darkness
    sprung,
Would make the conquered nation slaves alike in
    limb and tongue;
Russia's great Czar ne'er stood secure o'er Poland's
    shatter'd frame,
Until he trampled from her heart the tongue that bore
    her name.
Oh, Irishmen, be Irish still! stand for the dear old
    tongue
Which, as ivy to a ruin, to your native land has clung!
Oh, snatch this relic from the wreck! the only and
    the last,
And cherish in your heart of hearts the language of
    the Past!

THE END.

James Duffy & Co.'s Catalogue

OF

STANDARD WORKS

OF

HISTORY, AMUSEMENT AND INSTRUCTION,

SUITABLE FOR PRIZES.

☞ Books marked with an Asterisk * are "Author's."

At 1d.

DUFFY'S TALES FOR THE YOUNG, &c.
Royal 32mo, fancy wrapper.

1. Anger; or Alice Mordaunt.
2. Beatrice Alfieri; or, the Festival of the Rosary.
3. Eulalia St. Aubert.
4. Hugh Morton; or, the Broken Vow.
5. Lady of the Lake. People's Edition. Sewed.
6. Moore's Irish Melodies. People's Edition. Sewed.
7. The Little Culprit; or, the Golden Necklace.
8. Walter and Emily; or, the Fatal Effects of Disobedience.

At 1½d.

DUFFY'S JUVENILE LIBRARY (Paper Covers). 18mo.

1. Busy Peter.
2. Cathleen.
3. Fidelity Rewarded.
4. Little Alice.
5. Michael and his Dog.
6. Simple Sarah.
7. The Two Friends.
8. The Young Musicians
9. The Little Adventurer
10. The Little Drummer.
11. The Two Boys.
12. White Lies.

At 2d.

BROTHER JAMES'S TALES. Illustrated. Ptd. Wrapper.

1. Catherine Hall; or, the Deserted Child.
2. Clara Costello; a True Story.
3. City Man (The), and the Cousin in the Third Degree.
4. Eva O'Beirne; or, the Little Lace Maker.
5. Gerald O'Reilly; or, the Triumph of Principle.
6. Little Mary; or, the Child of Providence.
7. Little St. Agnes, and Frost Land.
8. Miles O'Donnell; or, the Story of a Life.
9. O'Hara Blake; or, the Lost Heir.
10. Rody O'Leary; or, the Outlaw.
11. Rosary of Pearl (The); or, the Ordeal by Touch.
12. The Two Friends; or, the Reward of Industry.
13. True to the Last, and other Tales.
14. The Bequest; or, All is not Gold that Glitters.
15. The Rose and the Lily; or, the Twin Sisters.
16. The Cousins; or, the Test of Friendship.

At 6d.

1. Altar at Woodbank; a Tale of Holy Eucharist. By Mrs. Agnew. Royal 16mo, cloth, limp.
2. Art MacMurrogh, Memoir and Life. 18mo, wpr.
3. Art Maguire; or, the Broken Pledge. ,,
4. Captive Mother; a Tale of Confirmation. By Mrs. Agnew. Ryl. 16mo, cloth, limp.
5. Davis's Literary and Historical Essays. 18mo, wpr.
6. Eve of St. Michael; a Tale of Penance. By Mrs. Agnew. Royal 16mo, cloth, limp.
7. Emily Sunderland; a Tale of Matrimony. Ryl. 16mo, cloth, limp.

At 6d. Each—*continued.*

Faversham Grange; or, the Daughter of the Piscatori. Post 8vo, cloth.

From Sunrise to Sunrise; or, Christmas in the Olden Time. Post 8vo, cloth.

Fun—Humour—Laughter—to while away an hour on a Journey.

Gerald Griffin. His Life and Poems. By John Power.

Heir of Rochdale; a Tale of Baptism. By Mrs. Agnew. Royal 16mo, cloth, limp.

Historical Notes on the Services of the Irish Officers in the French Army.

History of the Irish Volunteers, 1782. 18mo, wpr.

History of the "Protestant" Reformation. By Cobbett. Post 8vo, wrapper.

Hail Mary; or, the Beauties of the Angelical Salutation. 16mo, cloth, gilt.

Into the Sunlight. Post 8vo, cloth.

Irish Franciscans (Memoir of). By J. F. O'Donnell. 18mo, wrapper.

Knight of Clyffe Abbey; a Tale of Extreme Unction. By Mrs. Agnew.

Lalla Rookh. By Thomas Moore. 18mo, cloth, gilt edges.

Lady of the Lake. By Sir Walter Scott. Royal 32mo, cloth, gilt edges.

Life of O'Connell. By Canon O'Rourke. 18mo, wrapper.

Life and Times of Hugh O'Neill. By John Mitchel. 18mo, wrapper.

Life of the Venerable Joan of Arc. Imp. 32mo, cloth, limp.

May Eve; or, the Lost Sheep restored to the Fold. 16mo, cloth, gilt.

At 6d. Each—*continued.*

26. Mary Anne O'Halloran. 16mo, cloth, gilt edges
27. Mangan's Essays, in Prose and Verse. 18mo, wpr.
28.   „   German Anthology. 2 vols., wrapper, each 6d.
29. Memoir of Cardinal M'Cabe, Archbishop of Dublin.
30. Moore's Irish Melodies. Royal 32mo, gilt edges.
31. National Ballads, Songs, and Poems. By Thomas Davis. 18mo, wrapper.
32. O'Connell's Memoir on Ireland, Native and Saxon.
33. On the Snow Clad Heights. Post 8vo, cloth.
34.*Paddy Blake's Sojourn among the Soupers. Wpr.
35. Paddy Go Easy and His Wife Nancy. 18mo, wpr.
36. Penalty of a Crime. Post 8vo, cloth.
37. Priest of Northumbria; a Tale of Holy Orders. By Mrs. Agnew.
38. Rody the Rover. 18mo, wrapper.
39. Redmond Count O'Hanlon. 18mo, wrapper.

SCHMID (Canon), Works by—(*Post 8vo, cloth*):—

40. —— The Inundation of the Rhine, and Clara.
41. —— Lewis, the Little Emigrant.
42. —— The Easter Eggs, and Forget-me-not.
43. —— The Cakes, and the Old Castle.
44. —— The Hop Blossoms.
45. —— Christmas Eve.
46. —— The Carrier Pigeon, the Bird's Nest, etc.
47. —— Jewels and the Redbreast.
48. —— The Copper Coins and Gold Coins, etc.
49. —— The Cray-Fish, the Melon, the Nightingale.
50. —— The Fire, and the Best Inheritance.
51. —— Henry of Eichenfels; or, the Kidnapped Boy
52. —— Godfrey, the Little Hermit.

At 6d. Each—*continued*.

SCHMID (Canon), Works by—*continued*.

53. —— The Water Pitcher, and the Wooden Cross.
54. —— The Rose Bush, and the Forest Chapel.
55. —— The Lamb.
56. —— The Madonna; the Cherries; and Anselmo.
57. —— The Canary Bird; the Firefly; the Chapel of Wolfsbuhl; and Titus and his Family.

GERALD GRIFFIN, Works by—(16mo, *cloth, gilt edges*):

58. —— The Kelp Gatherer; a Tale.
59. —— The Day of Trial.
60. —— The Voluptuary Cured.
61. —— The Young Milesian.
62. —— The Beautiful Queen of Leix.
63. —— The Story of Psyche.

64. Thomasine's Poems. 18mo, wrapper.
65. The White Hen; an Irish Fairy Tale. 16mo, cloth, gilt edges.
66. The Queen of Italy.   16mo, cloth, gilt edges.
67. The Golden Pheasant.   ,,
68. The Dying Woodcutter.   ,,
69. The Danger of Ignorance.   ,,
70. The Poor Scholar; and other Tales. By William Carleton. 18mo, wrapper.
71. The Red Well; and other Tales. 18mo, wrapper.
72. The Book of Irish Ballads. By Denis Florence MacCarthy. 18mo, wrapper.
73. The Ballad Poetry of Ireland. By C. G. Duffy. 42nd Edition. 18mo, wrapper.
74. Traits and Stories of the Irish Peasantry. By W. Carleton. 18mo, wrapper.

At 6d. Each—*continued.*

75. The Songs of Ireland. By Michael J. Barry. 18mo, wrapper.
76. The Spirit of the Nation. New and Revised Edition. 18mo, wrapper.
77. Valentine Redmond; or, the Cross of the Forest. 16mo, cloth.
78. Voyage Autour de ma Chambre. By Count X. de Maestre. 18mo, wrapper.
79. Wonderful Doctor (The). An Easter Tale. Post 8vo, cloth.

At 1s.

1. A Memoir on Ireland. By the late Daniel O'Connell, M.P. 18mo, cloth.
2. Adventures of Mr. Moses Finegan, an Irish Pervert. 18mo, cloth.
3. Antonio; or, the Orphan of Florence. Cloth, gilt edges.
4. All for Prince Charlie. By E. M. Stewart. Sq. 16mo, cloth, gilt edges.
5. Art MacMurrogh. By Thomas D'Arcy M'Gee. 18mo, cloth.
6. Ballad Poetry of Ireland. By Sir Charles Gavan Duffy. 18mo, cloth.
7. Book of Irish Ballads. By Denis F. M'Carthy, M.R.I.A. 18mo, cloth.
8. Bird's Eye View of Irish History. By Sir Charles G. Duffy. Wrapper.

CARLETON, Works by—(18*mo, cloth*):—

9. —— Paddy Go Easy and his Wife Nancy.
10. —— Redmond Count O'Hanlon.
11. —— Art Maguire; or, the Broken Pledge.

At 1s. Each—*continued.*

CARLETON, Works by—*continued.*

12. —— Rody the Rover; or, the Ribbonman.
13. —— The Poor Scholar; and other Tales.
14. —— The Red Well. Party Fight.
15. —— Traits and Stories of the Irish Peasantry.

16. Cobbett's History of the "Protestant" Reformation. Post 8vo, cloth.
17. Daughter of Tyrconnell (The). By Mrs. Sadlier. Sq. 16mo, cloth, gilt edges.
18. Dillon's Historical Notes. 18mo, cloth.
19. Essay on the Antiquity and Constitution of Parliaments in Ireland. By H. J. Monck Mason. 18mo, cloth.
20. Extraordinary Adventures of a Watch. Square 16mo, cloth.
21. Franciscan Monasteries. By Rev. C. P. Meehan. Printed Cover.
22. Fate of Father Sheehy (The). Cap. 8vo, cloth.
23. Frederic; or, the Hermit of Mount Atlas. Cloth, gilt edges.
24. Fridolin and Dietrich. By Canon Schmid. Cap. 8vo, cloth.
25. Florestine; or, Unexpected Joy.
26. Ferdinand; or, the Triumph of Filial Love. By Father Charles. Sq. 16mo, cloth.
27. Genevieve of Brabant. By Christopher Von Schmid. Gilt, cloth.
28. Geraldines (The). By Rev. C. P. Meehan. 18mo, cl.
29. Gerald Marsdale; or, the Out-Quarters of St. Andrew. 8vo, cloth.
30 to 39. Griffin (Gerald). Life and Works. 10 vols., pictorial cover, as in 2s. series (11 to 20).
40. Golden Pheasant, and other Tales. Sq. 16mo, cloth, gilt.

At 1s. Each—*continued.*

41. Great Day (The); or, Means of Perseverance after first Communion. By Mrs. J. Sadlier. Cap. 8vo, cloth.
42. History of Ireland. By J. O'Neill Daunt, Esq. 18mo, cloth.
43. Ireland Since the Union. By J. O'Neill Daunt. 18mo, cloth.
44. Irish Songs (Ten), Set to Music by Professor Glover. 4to, wrapper.
45. Kelp Gatherer, Day of Trial, Voluptuary Cured. Cloth, gilt edges.
46. *Life and Scenery in Missouri. By a Missionary Priest. 18mo, cloth.
47. Life of John Mitchel. By P. A. S. 18mo, cloth.
48. Life and Letters of John Martin. By the Author of Life of John Mitchel. 18mo, cloth.
49. Life of Thomas Moore. By James Burke, Esq. 18mo, cloth.
50. Life of Hugh O'Neill. By John Mitchel. 18mo, cl.
51. Life of our Lord Jesus Christ. By Saint Bonaventure. Royal 32mo, cloth.
52. Lost Genevieve. By Cecilia Mary Caddell. Sq. 16mo, cloth.
53. Leo; or, the Choice of a Friend. Sq. 16mo, cloth, gilt edges.
54. Literary and Historical Essays. By Thomas Davis. 18mo, cloth.
55. Little Wanderers. By Miss E. M. Stewart. Post 8vo, cloth, limp.
56. Moore's Irish Melodies and National Airs. 18mo, cl.
57. MacNevin—The History of the Irish Volunteers of 1782. 18mo, cloth.
58. Madden (Dr.), Literary Remains of the United Irishmen, 1798. 18mo, cloth.
59. Martha; or, the Hospital Sister. Cl., gilt edges.

At 1s. Each—*continued*.

60. Memories of the Irish Franciscans. By J. F. O'Donnell. 18mo, cloth.
61. Mary Anne O'Halloran, White Hen, etc. Cloth, gilt edges. Sq. 16mo.
62. Mangan (J. C.) German Anthology. 2 vols., 1s. each. 18mo, cloth.
63. Mangan (J. C.) Essays in Prose and Verse. 1 vol. 18mo, cloth.
64. National Ballads. By Thomas Davis, M.R.I.A. 18mo, cloth.
65. Nettlethorpe; or, the London Miser. By Brother James. Cloth.
66. Old Marquise (An). By Vin. Vincent. 18mo, cl.
67. Rise and Fall of the Irish Nation. By Sir Jonah Barrington. 8vo, boards.
68. Rory of the Hills, a Tale of Irish Life. Post 8vo, boards.
69. Songs of Ireland. By Michael J. Barry, Esq. B.L. 18mo, cloth.
70. Spirit of the Nation. New and Revised Edition. 18mo, cloth.
71. Speeches of The Rt. Hon. Edmund Burke. ⎫
72.   ,,   ,,   John P. Curran.   ⎪
73.   ,,   ,,   Henry Grattan.   ⎬ Printed cover.
74.   ,,   Daniel O'Connell, 2 vols.   ⎪
75.   ,,   The Rt. Hon. Lord Plunket.   ⎪
76.   ,,   ,,   Richard Lalor Sheil. ⎭
77 to 95. Schmid (Canon)—Tales. 19 vols. Cap. 8vo, cloth, gilt edges. (See List in 6d. Series).
96. School and Home Song Book, Tonic Sol-fa Ed. By P. Goodman. Cloth.
97. "Thomasine's" Poems—Wild Flowers from the Wayside. With an Introduction By Sir Charles Gavan Duffy. 18mo, cloth.

At 1s. Each—*continued.*

98. The Life of O'Connell. By V. R. John Canon O'Rourke. 18mo, cloth.
99. The False Friend. By Br. James. Sq. 16mo, gilt edges.
100. The Hamiltons; or, Sunshine and Storm. Sq. 16mo, cloth.
101. The Orange Girl. By Lady C. Thynne. Sq. 16mo, cloth.
102. The Partners; or, Fair and Easy goes Far in the Day. By Brother James. Cloth.
103. The Shipwreck; or, the Deserted Island. Cloth.
104. The Young Crusader; a Catholic Tale. Cloth.
105. The Solitary of Mount Carmel. Cl., gilt edges.
106. Valentine Redmond, and other Tales. Sq. 16mo, cloth, gilt edges.
107. Watch and Hope. By Miss O'Neill Daunt. Sq. 16mo, cloth, gilt edges.
108. Willy Reilly and his Dear Colleen Bawn. Paper wrapper.
109. Young Milesian, Beautiful Queen of Leix, and Story of Psyche. Square 16mo, cl., gilt edges.

Foolscap 8vo Series. Cloth.

1. Coaina, the Rose of the Algonquins. Cloth. By Mrs. Anna H. Dorsey.
2. Father Rowland, a North American Tale. Cloth.
3. Flower Basket. By Canon Schmid.
4. Geoffrey of Killingworth; or, the Grey Friar's Legacy.
5. Life of St. Columba, or Columbkille. By Saint Adamnan. Cloth.
6. Old Grey Rosary. The Refuge of Sinners. By Mrs. A. H. Dorsey. Cloth.

At 1s. Each.

FOOLSCAP 8VO SERIES. CLOTH.—*continued.*

7. Oriental Pearl; or, the Catholic Emigrants.
8. Pearl among the Virtues (The); or, Words of Advice to Christian Youth.
9. Rosary (The) of Pearl, and Six other Tales. By Miss E. M. Stewart.
10. Simon Kerrigan; or, Confessions of an Apostate.

At 1s. 6d.

1. All for Prince Charlie. By E. M. Stewart. 16mo, Cloth, gilt.
2. Bird's Eye View of Irish History. By Sir C. G. Duffy. Square 16mo, cloth.
3. Carleton's, The Evil Eye. Post 8vo. Illustrated, fancy cover.
4. Caddell's (Miss) Blind Agnese. Fancy cl., gilt.
5.   "   Flowers and Fruit.   "
6.   "   Miner's Daughter.   "
7.   "   The Virgin Mother and the Child Divine. Fancy cloth, gilt.
8. Duffy's Juvenile Library. 18mo. Fancy cloth, gilt edges.
9. Exiled from Erin; a Story of Irish Peasant Life. By M. E. T. Crown 8vo, cloth.
10. Franciscan Monasteries (The Irish). By Rev. C. P. Meehan. Cloth.
11. Fridolin and Dietrich. By Canon Schmid. Cap. 8vo, cloth, gilt edges.
12. Holly and Ivy for Christmas Holidays. By Anthony Evergreen. Cloth.
13. Juvenile Library (The). By Brother James. 16mo, cloth, gilt.

At 1s. 6d. Each—*continued*.

14. King and the Cloister. By E. M. Stewart. 16mo, cloth, gilt.
15. Loretto; or, the Choice. By George H. Miles, Esq. 16mo, cloth, gilt.
16. Legends of the Cloister. By Miss E. M. Stewart. Post 8vo, cloth.
17. Life of O'Connell. By Canon O'Rourke. Cloth extra, gilt edges.
18. Light and Shade. By Rev. T. J. Potter. Cap. 8vo, cloth, gilt.
19. Lights and Leaders of Irish Life. 8vo, boards.
20. Popular Tales; or, Deeds of Genius. By J. M. Percy. 16mo, cloth, gilt.
21. Recreative Reading. By the Rambler from Clare. Sewed.
22. Rose of Tannenbourg. A Moral Tale. Cap. 8vo, cl.
23. Rosary of Pearl (The); and Six other Tales. By E. M. Stewart. Gilt.
24. The Two Victories; a Catholic Tale. By Rev. T. J. Potter. Sq. 16mo, cloth.
25. Victims of the Penal Laws. By E. M. Stewart. 18mo, cloth, gilt.
26. Willie Burke; or, the Orphan in America. By Mrs. J. S. Sadlier.
27. Williams (Richard D'Alton), Complete Poetical Works of. Edited by P.A.S. 18mo, cloth.

At 2s.

1. Banim's, The Peep o' Day, or John Doe; and Crohoore of the Bill-hook. Paper boards.
2. Banim's, The Croppy; a Tale of the Irish Rebellion 1798. Paper boards.

STANDARD WORKS, HISTORY, AMUSEMENT, ETC. 13

At 2s. Each—*continued.*

CARLETON, Works by—(*Post 8vo, fancy cover*):—

3. —— Valentine M'Clutchy, the Irish Agent.
4. —— Willy Reilly and his Dear Colleen Bawn.
5. —— Black Baronet.
6. —— The Evil Eye. Cloth, plain.

---

7. Confederation of Kilkenny. By Rev. C. P. Meehan. Imp. 32mo, cloth.
8. Cross and Shamrock (The). By a Missionary Priest. Post 8vo.
9. D'Altons of Crag (The). By Dean O'Brien. Cap. 8vo, cloth.
10. Gerald Marsdale; or, the Out-Quarters of Saint Andrew's Priory. By Mrs. Stanley Carey. Cloth, gilt edges.

GRIFFIN (GERALD), Works by—(*Cap. 8vo, cloth*):—

11. —— The Collegians.
12. —— Card Drawing, etc.
13. —— Hollandtide.
14. —— The Rivals; and Tracy's Ambition.
15. —— Tales of the Juryroom.
16. —— The Duke of Monmouth.
17. —— Poetical Works.
18. —— Life of. By his Brother.
19. —— Tales of the Five Senses, etc.
20. —— The Invasion.

---

21. German Anthology. By James C. Mangan. 2 vols., cloth.
22. Holly and Ivy for Christmas Holidays. Cl., gilt.

At 2s. Each—*continued.*

23. *Hugh Roach, the Ribbonman. By James Murphy. Boards.
24. *Ireland Before the Union, including Lord Chief Justice Clonmell's unpublished Diary. By W. J. Fitzpatrick, LL.D. Sixth Edition, with Illustrations. Crown 8vo, fancy cover.
25. Jack Hazlitt. By Dean O'Brien. Post 8vo, cloth.
26. Life and Death of the Most Rev. Francis Kirwan, Bishop of Killala. By Rev. C. P. Meehan. 8vo, fancy cloth.
27. Little Wanderers. By Miss E. M. Stewart. Post 8vo, cloth, gilt.
28. People's Martyr (The). By Miss E. M. Stewart. Post 8vo, cloth, gilt.
29. Prophet of the Ruined Abbey (The). Post 8vo, cl.
30. Robber Chieftain (The). An Historical Tale of Dublin Castle. Boards.
31. Recreative Readings. By the Rambler from Clare. Cloth.
32. Rise and Fall of the Irish Nation, with Black List. 8vo, cloth.
33. Rory of the Hills, a Tale of Irish Life. Post 8vo, cl.
34. Shemus Dhu; or, the Black Pedlar of Galway. By the late Rev. M. Kavanagh, P.P.
35. Speeches of The Rt. Hon. Philpot Curran. ⎫
36.   "   The Rt. Hon. Henry Grattan.   ⎪
37.   "   D. O'Connell, M.P. (Select.) 2 vols. ⎬ Cr. 8vo, cloth.
38.   "   The Rt. Hon. Lord Plunket.   ⎪
39.   "   "   Richard Lalor Sheil. ⎪
40.   "   "   Edmund Burke.   ⎭
41.   "   Daniel O'Connell. Centenary Edition. 2 vols., paper boards.

At 2s. 6d.

1. Ailey Moore. By R. P. O'Brien, D.D. 3rd Ed. Cap. 8vo, cloth.
2. Banim's, The Peep o' Day, or John Doe; and Crohoore of the Bill-hook. Cloth, plain.
3. Banim's, The Croppy; a Tale of the Irish Rebellion 1798. Cloth, plain.
4. Banim's, Peter of the Castle; and the Fetches. Cloth, plain.
5. Black Baronet. By William Carleton. Cl., plain.
6. Evil Eye. By William Carleton. Cl., gilt edges.
7. Father Charles's Flowers from Foreign Fields. 2 vols. (each).
8. Gift of Friendship. By Brother James. Sq. 16mo, fancy cloth, gilt edges.
9. Grey Friar's Legacy, and other Tales. Cap. 8vo, art linen, gilt top.
10. *Jabez Murdock, Poetaster and "Adjint." By Banna Borka. Post 8vo, cloth.
11. Life of Blessed Margaret Mary Alacoque of the Sacred Heart. By Rev. Albert Barry. Cap. 8vo, cloth.
12. O'Connell's Speeches. Centenary Edition. 2 vols Crown 8vo, fancy cover.
13. On the Snow Clad Heights, and other Tales. Cap. 8vo, art linen, gilt top.
14. Rector's Daughter (The). By Rev. T. J. Potter. New Edition. Cap. 8vo, cloth.
15. Ursuline Catholic Offering (The). Cap. 8vo, cloth.
16. Valentine M'Clutchy. Cloth, plain. By William Carleton.
17. Willy Reilly. Cloth, plain.
18. *What will the World Say? By Rhoda E. White. Boards.

At 3s.

1. Ballad Poetry of Ireland. By Sir Charles Gavan Duffy. Cloth, gilt edges.
2. Banim's, The Peep o' Day, or John Doe; and Crohoore of the Bill-hook. Cloth, gilt.
3. Banim's, The Croppy; a Tale of the Irish Rebellion 1798. Cloth, gilt.
4. Blakes and Flanagans (The). By Mrs. J. Sadlier. Cloth.
5. Brother James' Tales. 12 Illustrations. Sq. 16mo, cloth, gilt.
6. Catholic Souvenir (The); or, Tales Explanatory of the Sacraments. By Mrs. Agnew. Sq. 8vo, cloth, bevelled, gilt edges.
7. Carleton's Black Baronet; or, the Chronicles of Ballytrain. Cloth, gilt.
8. Carleton's Valentine M'Clutchy, the Irish Agent. Post 8vo, new edition, cloth, gilt.
9. Carleton's Willy Reilly, and his dear Colleen Bawn. Forty-first edition. Post 8vo, cloth, gilt.
10. D'Altons of Crag (The). By Dean O'Brien. Cap. 8vo, cloth, gilt edges.
11 to 20. Griffin's (Gerald) Works, per Two Shilling List. Cloth, gilt edges. 10 vols.
21. Jack Hazlitt. By Dean O'Brien. Cl., gilt edges.
22. Keating's History of Ireland. By Dermod O'Connor. Crown 8vo, cloth.
23. Knocknagow; or, the Homes of Tipperary. By C. J. Kickham. Cloth.
24. *Reminiscences of Rome. By Rev. E. M'Cartan, P.P. 8vo, cloth.
25. Sister Mary's Annual. Cloth, gilt edges.
26. Trial and Trust. By Canon Schmid. Post 8vo, art linen, gilt top.

At 3s. Each—*continued.*

27. Two Roads of Life. By Canon Schmid. Post 8vo, art linen, gilt top.
28. The Poets and Poetry of Munster, with Original Music. By the late James Clarence Mangan. Sq. 16mo, fancy cloth.
29. Trust in God. By Canon Schmid. Cloth.

At 3s. 6d.

1. Ailey Moore. Cap. 8vo, fancy cloth, bevelled, gilt edges.
2. *Beauties of Nature (The), and other Lectures, etc. By J. J. O'Dea, B.A. Post 8vo, cloth.
3. Centenary Edition—O'Connell's Select Speeches. 2 vols. in one, cloth.
4. Haverty's History of Ireland. Abridged. New Edition. 12mo, half bound.
5. Mangan—The Poets and Poetry of Munster, with Original Music. By James Clarence Mangan. Cloth, extra gilt.
6. St. Martha's Home. By Miss Emily Bowes. Gilt.
7. Ursuline Catholic Offering (The). Cloth.
8. *What will the World Say? By Rhoda White. Fancy cloth.

At 4s.

1. Catholic Keepsake. Canon Schmid. Cloth, extra gilt. Post 8vo.
2. Franciscan Monasteries. By Rev. C. P. Meehan. Fifth edition. Crown 8vo, cloth, extra.
3. Select Speeches of Daniel O'Connell, M.P. 2 vols. Crown 8vo, green cloth.

At 4s. 6d.

Catholic Children's Magazine; Vols. II., III., IV., V., VI., and VII. In cloth extra, gilt edges, coloured frontispiece. 4to.

At 5s.

1. *Ancient History, from the Creation to Fall of Western Empire in A.D. 476. With Maps and Plans. By A. J. B. Vuibert. Post 8vo, cloth.
2. Burke's Lingard—History of England, abridged, 40th edition. 648 pp. 12mo, embossed leather.
3. Fate and Fortunes of the Earls of Tyrone and Tyrconnell. By the late Rev. C. P. Meehan. Third edition, demy 8vo, cloth.
4. History of Ireland from the Siege of Limerick to the Present Time. By John Mitchel. 2 vols., crown 8vo, cloth.
5. *Ireland under English Rule. Translated from the French of the Rev. Father Adolphe Perraud. 8vo, cloth.
6. *O'Hanlon, The Poetical Works of "Lageniensis." Crown 8vo, cloth.

At 6s.

1. Ballads of Ireland. By Edward Hayes. 2 vols., crown 8vo, cloth.
2. Haverty's History of Ireland. New edition. Royal 8vo, cloth.
3. *History of Ballysadare and Kilvarnet. By V. R. T. O'Rorke, D.D. 8vo, cloth.

At 7s. 6d.

1. *Battle of the Faith in Ireland. By Very Rev. Canon O'Rourke, P.P.
2. *Dissertations on Irish Church History. By Rev. Matthew Kelly, S.J.
3. Ecclesiastical History of Ireland. By Rev. M. J. Brenan, O.S.F. 8vo, cloth, extra.
4. *History of the Catholic Archbishops of Dublin since the Reformation. By His Eminence Cardinal Moran. Vol. I. 8vo, cloth.
5. *Life, Times, and Correspondence of the Right Rev. Dr. Doyle (J.K.L.), Bishop of Kildare and Leighlin. By W. J. Fitzpatrick, M.R.I.A. New edition, 2 vols., crown 8vo, cloth.
6. Moore's Melodies. Edited by Professor Glover. 4to, with Music. Cloth.

At 9s.

1. Hayes' Ballads of Ireland. 2 vols., crown 8vo, cloth, gilt edges.

At 10s.

1. Griffin's (Gerald) Works. 10 vols., 1s. each.
2. O'Reilly and O'Donovan's Irish-English Dictionary. 4to.
3. Songs of our Land, the Spirit of the Nation, with Music. New edition. Cloth, gilt edges.
4. M'Hale (the Most Rev. John)—An Irish Translation of the Holy Bible. Vol. I. Genesis to Deuteronomy.
5. M'Hale's First Eight Books of Homer's Iliad translated into Irish. 8vo.
6. *History of Sligo. By Very Rev. T. O'Rorke, D.D. 2 vols., demy 8vo, cloth.
7. *Malone. — Church History of Ireland. By Sylvester Malone, P.P., M.R.I.A. Third ed., 2 vols., crown 8vo, cloth.

MISCELLANEOUS LIST.

*Irish Pedigrees; Origin and Stem of the Irish Nation. By J. O'Hart. 2 vols.	25s.
Duffy's Tales for the Young. Cloth	8d.
Fun, Humour, Laughter. Threepenny worth to while away an Hour on a Journey	6d.
*Irish Landed Gentry when Cromwell came to Ireland. By John O'Hart. Demy 8vo, cloth	12s. 6d.
Lady of the Lake. In stiff printed cover	4d.
Madden (Dr.), Easter Offerings	8d.
Moore's Irish Melodies, with Symphonies and Accompaniments, by Sir John Stevenson. Edited by Prof. Glover. Music size, morocco, extra gilt	21s.
Orators of Ireland. 7 vols. Half morocco, gilt	42s.
,, Half calf	31s. 6d.
Songs of our Land, the Spirit of the Nation. 4to. With Music. New ed., morocco	21s.
Butler's Lives of the Saints. 12 vols. Crown 8vo, cloth, 30s.; Half calf	36s.

Lives of the Saints and Religious Biography—See General Catalogue, pp. 30 to 33.

CATHOLIC ART REPOSITORY.

Rosary Beads, Crucifixes in Plastique, Nickel and Ivory; Inlaid Crosses, Brass and Nickel; Lamps, Ruby and Blue; Bead Cases, Wood, Coco, and Leather; Sodality, Communion, and Confirmation Medals; Statues, plain and decorated, all sizes and subjects; Holy Water Fonts, Lace Prints, Memorial Cards, Stations of the Cross. Altar Charts, Orationes, Breviaries, Diurnals, Rituals, Missals, Missal Stands, Registers, etc.

Quotations on Application Post Free.

www.ingramcontent.com/pod-product-compliance
Lightning Source LLC
Chambersburg PA
CBHW031946230426
43672CB00010B/2062